NOT–FOR–PROFIT ACCOUNTING, TAX, AND REPORTING REQUIREMENTS

Fourth Edition

NOT-FOR-PROFIT ACCOUNTING, TAX, AND REPORTING REQUIREMENTS

Fourth Edition

EDWARD J. McMILLAN, CPA, CAE

WILEY

John Wiley & Sons, Inc.

For general information on our other products and services or for technical support, please contact our Customer Care Department within the United States at (800) 762-2974, outside the United States at (317) 572-3993 or fax (317) 572-4002.

Wiley also publishes its books in a variety of electronic formats. Some content that appears in print may not be available in electronic books. For more information about Wiley products, visit our web site at www.wiley.com.

Library of Congress Cataloging-in-Publication Data:
McMillan, Edward J., 1949-
   Not-for-profit accounting, tax, and reporting requirements / Edward J. McMillan. — 2nd ed.
      p. cm.
   Includes index.
   ISBN 978-0-470-57538-3 (pbk.)
   1. Nonprofit organizations—United States—Finance. 2. Nonprofit organizations—United States—Accounting. 3. Nonprofit organizations—Taxation—United States. 4. Financial statements—United States. I. Title.
   HG4027.65.M363 2010
   657'.980973—dc22

                                                                        2010003129

Printed in the United States of America.

10 9 8 7 6 5 4 3 2 1

To my beautiful daughter, Terryn, Spencer,
her dedicated husband, David,
and their three terrific boys,
Patrick, Benjamin, and John

About the Author

Edward J. McMillan, CPA, CAE, has spent his entire career in not-for-profit financial management. He has served as the controller of the national office of the Associated Builders and Contractors and as the finance and membership director of the American Correctional Association. In 1993, McMillan was appointed faculty chair for finance for the United States Chamber of Commerce's Institutes for Organization Management program.

McMillan has written several books on not-for-profit financial management. His publishers include the American Society of Association Executives, McGraw-Hill, the U.S. Chamber of Commerce, and the American Chamber of Commerce Executives.

McMillan now concentrates solely on speaking, writing, and consulting on financial management topics for associations and chambers of commerce. He lives near Baltimore, Maryland. In his free time, he enjoys coaching youth sports and motocross racing. You may contact McMillan at P.O. Box 771, Forest Hill, MD 21050; phone/fax: (410) 893–2308; e-mail: emcmillan@sprintmail.com. Also see his web site at www.nonprofitguru.com.

Contents

Acknowledgments xiii

Preface xv

Disclaimer xvii

Chapter 1
Classification of Tax-Exempt Organizations 1

Chapter 2
Financial Responsibilities of Not-for-Profit Board Members 9

Chapter 3
The Basics of Form 990, Form 990-EZ, and Form N 15

Chapter 4
Tax on Unrelated Business Income and Form 990-T 25

Chapter 5
Other IRS Issues 33

Chapter 6
Disclosure of Information 39

Chapter 7
Conditions of Employment Agreement 47

Chapter 8
Wholly Owned Taxable Subsidiaries 55

Chapter 9
Internal Revenue Service Audits   59

Chapter 10
Developing Strong Internal Controls and Documenting a Fraud Action Plan   69

Chapter 11
Using CPA Firms and Understanding Their Functions   87

Chapter 12
Grant Accounting and Auditing   111

Chapter 13
Implications of Lobbying Expenditures   127

Chapter 14
Campaign Contributions, PACs, and 527s   141

Chapter 15
Internal Audit Committees   149

Chapter 16
The Accounting Policies and Procedures Manual   153

Chapter 17
Restricted-Fund Transactions   159

Chapter 18
The Basics of Intermediate Sanctions   167

Chapter 19
The Basics of Not-for-Profit Accounting and Financial Statements   171

Chapter 20
Private Foundations   179

Appendixes
Appendix A. Statement of Financial Accounting Standards #117:
Financial Statements of Not-for-Profit Organizations   183

Appendix B. Statement of Financial Accounting Standards #116:
Accounting for Contributions Received and Contributions Made   215

Appendix C. Statement of Financial Accounting Standards #124:
Accounting for Certain Investments Held by Not-for-Profit Organizations   233

Appendix D. Statement of Financial Accounting Standards #136:
Transfer of Assets to a Not-for-Profit Organization or Charitable Trust that Raises or Holds
Contributions for Others   239

Glossary   245

Index   255

Acknowledgments

The publisher and author would like to take this opportunity to gratefully thank and recognize Lynn M. Craig, CPA and Patrick R. Blanda, CPA for the generous contributions of their time and expertise incorporated in this handbook.

Lynn is a senior manager for the S & F Company, CPAs and Business Advisors located in Wormleysburg, PA. Lynn is recognized as an authority on not-for-profit auditing, taxation and reporting requirements. Her contact information is:

Lynn M. Craig, CPA
Seligman, Friedman & Company, P.C.
1027 Mumma Road
Wormleysburg, PA 17043
(717) 761–0211

Pat Blanda is currently the Controller of ROSECOR, Inc., and has extensive experience in business analysis, improving accounting operations and fraud investigation among several other essential business applications. Additionally, Pat served five years as an Adjunct College Instructor: Accounting, Tax & Auditing. Also, Pat is a current member of the Leadership Cabinet of the Indiana CPA Society.

Pat's contact information is:

Patrick R. Blanda, CPA
10949 Gorden Setter Drive
Osceola, IN 46561
(260) 494–7608

Preface

The accounting principles, tax issues, reporting requirements, and general work environment of not-for-profit organizations are remarkably different from similar issues affecting commercial organizations. This handbook is designed to help bookkeepers, managers, volunteers, and auditing CPA firms working with trade associations, professional associations, charities, chambers of commerce, and other not-for-profit organizations in their various financial responsibilities. It provides guidance and assurance in understanding and addressing their fiduciary obligations.

The accounting standards addressed herein are in accordance with applicable standards promulgated by the American Institute of Certified Public Accountants (AICPA) and the Financial Accounting Standards Board (FASB), as of the date of this publication. Additionally, all tax issues and reporting requirements are similarly current.

Edward J. McMillan, CPA, CAE
June, 2010

Disclaimer

The contents of this book should not be construed as legal advice, and in that respect the publisher and author assume no liability or responsibility accordingly.

Before implementation, the internal controls, accounting standards, policies and forms suggested in this book should be reviewed by a competent attorney and independent CPA to assure compliance with federal, state, and local laws.

CHAPTER 1

Classification of Tax–Exempt Organizations

ORGANIZATIONS QUALIFYING FOR EXEMPTION from federal income tax are granted exemption under the Internal Revenue Code (IRC), Section 501(a).

The qualification process starts by completing one of these forms:

➢ Form 1023, Application for Recognition of Exemption Under Section 501(c)(3) of the IRS Code, for 501(c)(3) organizations

➢ Form 1024, Application for Recognition of Exemption, for all other not-for-profit organizations

Tax-exempt status applications are open for public inspection and must be retained for this purpose permanently. This issue is discussed in detail in Chapter 6, "Disclosure of Information."

Essential IRS Classifications

Of the many types of tax-exempt organizations, six are particularly important to not-for-profit professionals. They are listed in Exhibit 1.1 by type, advantages, and disadvantages. Exhibit 1.2 lists other 501(c) organizations, and Exhibit 1.3 lists other important IRS classifications of organizations.

EXHIBIT 1.1

IRS Classifications and Types of Tax-Exempt Organizations

IRS Classification: 501(c)(3) (Public Charities)

Qualifying Entities or Organizations
- Religious
- Charitable
- Scientific
- Educational
- Public safety testing
- Literary
- National or international amateur sports
- Organizations formed to prevent cruelty to children or animals

Advantages
- Contributions are deductible by the donors.
- Postal rates are favorable.
- Organizations are exempt from the Federal Unemployment Tax Act (FUTA).
- State sales tax and other local tax exemptions are possible if allowable under state law.
- Foundations often require 501(c)(3) status before issuing grants.
- Exemption from Federal Insurance Contributions Act (FICA) tax election is available to clergy.

Disadvantages
- Insubstantial amounts can be spent on lobbying to influence legislation.
- There is absolute prohibition from lobbying in election campaigns.
- Earnings cannot inure to individuals.

IRS Classification: 501(c)(3) (Private Foundations)

501(c)(3) organizations are further classified as either public charities or private foundations. This distinction is decided when completing Form 1023, the application for exemption. The major differences for private foundations are as follows:

Disadvantages
- More reporting requirements on Form 990-PF
- Limitations on deductions for charitable contributions
- IRS-imposed operating restrictions

IRS Classification: 501(c)(4)
- Social welfare organizations
- Local associations of employees for charitable purposes

EXHIBIT 1.1 *(Continued)*

Advantage
➣ Lobbying activities are unrestricted.

Disadvantages
➣ Charitable contributions are not deductible by donors.
➣ There are no exemptions for FUTA, FICA, or state and local taxes.
➣ Earnings cannot inure to individuals.
➣ Foundations cannot participate in political activities.
➣ Postal rates are less favorable.

IRS Classification: 501(c)(5)
➣ Labor
➣ Agriculture
➣ Horticulture
➣ Unions

Advantage
➣ There is no restriction on lobbying activities, including participation in political activities, which is not available to 501(c)(3) and 501(c)(4) organizations.
  Note: Under the Hatch Act, unions of federal government employees may not engage in political activities. See Section 527 (political action committees).

Disadvantages
➣ Charitable contributions are not deductible by donors.
➣ No exemptions are available for FUTA, FICA, or state and local taxes.
➣ Earnings cannot inure to individuals.
➣ Postal rates are less favorable.

IRS Classification: 501(c)(6)
➣ Business leagues
➣ Trade associations
➣ Professional associations
➣ Chambers of commerce
➣ Boards of trade
➣ Real estate boards
➣ Professional football leagues not organized for profit

Advantages
➣ There are no restrictions on engaging in lobbying or political activities.
➣ Contributions may be deductible as business expenses.

EXHIBIT 1.1 *(Continued)*

Disadvantages
- ➢ Charitable contributions are not deductible by the donors.
- ➢ There are no exemptions for FUTA, FICA, or state and local taxes.
- ➢ Postal rates are less favorable.

IRS Classification: 501(c)(7)
- ➢ Social clubs

Advantages
- ➢ Advantages are essentially the same as for 501(c)(6) organizations.

Disadvantages
- ➢ Disadvantages are essentially the same as for 501(c)(6) organizations, with the exception that there are strict limits on revenues from nonmembers; nonmember activity could result in conversion to a taxable entity.

IRS Classification: 501(c)(19)
- ➢ Armed forces organizations (at least 75 percent of the members must be present or past members of the armed forces).

Advantages
- ➢ Advantages are essentially the same as for 501(c)(6) organizations, except that contributions are deductible as charitable contributions by the donors.

Disadvantages
- ➢ Disadvantages are essentially the same as for 501(c)(6) organizations.

EXHIBIT 1.2

Other 501(c) Classifications

IRS Classification	Qualifying Entities or Organizations
501(c)(1)	Organizations organized by an act of Congress
501(c)(2)	Title-holding corporations for other 501(c) organizations
501(c)(8)	Fraternal organizations producing life, sickness, accident, or other benefits to members or dependents
501(c)(9)	Employee beneficiary organizations providing life, sickness, accident, or other benefits to members, dependents, or beneficiaries
501(c)(10)	Fraternal societies devoted to religious, charitable, educational, scientific, or literary purposes, excluding life, sickness, and accident benefits
501(c)(11)	Local teacher retirement fund associations
501(c)(12)	Local ditch, irrigation, telephone, and life insurance associations
501(c)(13)	Cemetery, burial, and cremation organizations
501(c)(14)	Credit unions without capital stock
501(c)(15)	Insurance companies other than life or marine with receipts under $150,000
501(c)(16)	Farmers cooperative associations
501(c)(17)	Supplemental unemployment benefits trusts
501(c)(18)	Pension plans funded by employees and organized before June 25, 1959
501(c)(20)	Legal services plans
501(c)(21)	Black Lung Acts benefits
501(c)(22)	Employment Retirement Income Security Act of 1974 benefits
501(c)(23)	Organizations of past or present members of the armed forces
501(c)(24)	Employee Retirement Income Security Act of 1974 trust described in Section 4049
501(c)(25)	Other title-holding trusts or corporations

EXHIBIT 1.3

Other Important IRS Classifications

IRS Classification	Qualifying Entities or Organizations
Section 527	Political organizations
Section 528	Homeowners' associations
Section 501(d)	Religious and apostolic organizations
Section 501(e)	Cooperative hospital service organizations
Section 501(k)	Child care organizations

Private Foundations

There are two types of 501(c)(3) organizations: publicly supported organizations and private foundations.

Typically, private foundations are associated with large corporations and wealthy families that don't find it necessary to solicit the public for support.

There are several rules that affect private foundations, the most important of which are as follows:

➢ Private foundations are prohibited from lobbying.

➢ There is significantly more paperwork and reporting involved.

➢ There is an excise tax on net investment income.

Private foundations file Form 990-PF.

CHAPTER 2

Financial Responsibilities of Not-for-Profit Board Members

IT IS VERY COMMON FOR POTENTIAL AND CURRENT MEMBERS of not-for-profit boards to experience trepidation with regard to their financial oversight role and possible personal liabilities. This chapter addresses these concerns and suggests recommended responsibilities and action. If followed properly, personal liability is highly improbable.

Basic Duties

Current members of nonprofit boards must comply with three basic duties:

➢ The duty of loyalty

➢ The duty of obedience

➢ The duty of care

Explanations of these duties follow.

Loyalty

Loyalty requires board members not to have conflicts with regard to the mission of the organization, act in the best interest of the organization, avoid fraud, act in good faith, and avoid unfair personal enrichment due to their position of authority.

Obedience

Obedience requires board members to follow federal and state not-for-profit laws, and follow the organization's by-laws, articles of incorporation and adhere to organization policies.

Care

Care requires board members to make prudent business decisions that are in the best interest of the organization and protect confidential information.

With regard to fiduciary financial obligations, the duties of obedience and care are the areas that primarily affect the financial operation. The following actions apply to both of these duties and, if followed, highly isolate board members from potential personal liability.

1. Become knowledgeable of federal not-for-profit requirements.
   There are many books and other resources that explain these responsibilities. Also, many not-for-profit organizations have annual board retreats with presentations by knowledgeable accountants and lawyers, thereby educating board members of their responsibilities and providing an opportunity to ask questions.

   For example, the board should promulgate policies with regard to disclosure of records to members and the public. (See the Disclosure of Information chapter of this book for detailed information and sample policies.)

2. Become knowledgeable of state not-for-profit requirements.
   There are three primary resources for state issues:
   - ➤ The organization's CPA
   - ➤ The organization's general counsel
   - ➤ The Internet. Typically, this is accessible by going to the state's web site and referring to the state's Secretary of State link and downloading the law.

   Most of the information is boilerplate, such as the requirement to have a registered agent, but other information may be state specific. Areas that need addressing include, but are not limited to:
   - ➤ Member rights to inspect records such as minutes, etc.
   - ➤ Allowable executive session areas, typically to discuss personnel issues, to discuss current or pending legislation and to discuss real estate issues
   - ➤ Open meeting requirements
   - ➤ State filings subject to public inspection

3. Competent understanding of the two primary financial statements.
   Basic understanding of the two primary financial statements, the Statement of Financial Position (Balance Sheet) and the Statement of Activity (Income Statement), can easily be accomplished by having a financial statement understanding at the board retreat or stand-alone seminar.

4. Ensure that internal financial statements are prepared *monthly* and *timely*.

   It is extremely important that the internal financial statements be prepared on a *monthly* basis and prepared *timely*. It is reasonable for internal statements to be prepared 10 to 15 work days after the close of the prior month. Statements that are prepared quarterly and take 30 or more days to compile are relatively meaningless because the data is so old. It could be months before a serious problem is discovered, and valuable time that could have been used to correct the problem is lost and can never be made up.

5. Be certain that the organization's budget is well-thought-out and reasonable and that financial goals are attainable.

   The board is generally not involved in the detailed preparation of the annual budget, with the exception of requesting that new programs are investigated and obsolete programs eliminated.

   Generally, the board typically approves or denies the budget compiled by the organization's staff after review and discussion. Be certain to note that the budget was reviewed and action taken *in the organization's minutes.*

6. Ensure the internal statements compose actual versus budget for all revenues and expenses.

   When staff compiles internal financial statements, these statements should present both current month and year-to-date data comparing actual versus budget for all revenues and expenses.

   Additionally, staff should be directed to include an Executive Summary that addresses the most important items of the statements.

7. The internal financial statements should be forwarded to the board on a monthly basis.

   Even if the board does not meet monthly, the internal statements are distributed and board members are encouraged to ask questions.

   For months that the board does meet, ensure that the statements were distributed, questions encouraged and any action taken *in the minutes.*

8. Ensure that the organization retains a competent CPA firm that specializes in or includes among the specialities not-for-profit accounting and tax.

   Whether the organization receives an audit, review, or compilation by an independent CPA, the board should have a member, typically the Treasurer, involved in the interview and the recommendation to the board on which firm to select.

   Once the board approves the selection of the firm, make sure that this action is *included in the minutes.*

9. Ensure that documents prepared by the independent CPA are forwarded to the board and the board meets with the CPA at a board meeting to review the statements and ask questions to representative of the firm.

   The board should meet with the independent CPA firm at the board meeting immediately following the distribution of the CPA's audited financial statements and ask questions.

   Details of this meeting should be noted *in the minutes*.

10. Review of the CPA's Management Letter

    While the independent CPA firm is not on-site to uncover problems, they often do. If the problems arise to the importance of reportable conditions, they are required to advise the *board* in the form of a Management Letter.

    The Management Letter is a vitally important document and is the primary avenue for the board to be advised of serious issues and corrective action.

    Once again, it is very important for the board to note that they discussed the Management Letter with the CPA firm *in the minutes*.

11. Assure internal control policies are adequate.

    Effective internal control policies, like the Management Letter, are extremely important, and it is the duty of the board to ensure they are followed. (See the Chapter 10, Developing Strong Internal Controls and Documenting A Fraud Action Plan.)

12. Review the adequacy of insurance coverage.

    It is suggested that the board meet with the organization's insurance agent prior to reviewing the policies to review if their adequacy is acceptable. Of particular importance relating to financial issues is the review of the Fidelity Bond (Employee Dishonesty Insurance).

    Whether the board meets with the insurance agent or simply reviews insurance coverage, make sure the actions and discussion are *in the minutes*.

13. Investment policies.

    It is strongly suggested that the board form an investment committee composed of knowledgeable investment advisors to promulgate proper investment policies. Note the committee's suggestion on investments and action approved *in the minutes*.

14. Financial and accounting policies.

    Financial staff should prepare and review financial policies with the independent CPA and present the policies to the board for discussion and approval. Board approved financial and accounting policies are essential as they eliminate misunderstandings among the board, organization staff, and the independent CPA firm. They are also valuable in the event of an IRS audit.

Ensure that the approval and amendments of financial and accounting policies are noted *in the minutes.*

15. Reserves policy.

    It is important that the board reviews the current ratio and acid test ratio to arrive at an acceptable amount of money that is not used for day-to-day transactions and perhaps invested.

    This discussion and action should be noted *in the minutes.*

16. Noncomingling of funds.

    If the organization has grant funds, temporarily restricted funds, permanently restricted funds, etc., the board should direct the staff that comingling of these funds with unrestricted funds is disallowed.

    If these funds are comingled with unrestricted funds and an embezzlement or other serious issue affects monies held in trust, serious consequences could result.

    Note that this direction was reviewed and note this review *in the minutes.*

17. Review of tax and information returns.

    It is suggested that the board be provided with individual copies of Form 990, Form 990-T, state returns, and the like. The board should review these documents at the annual meeting with the independent CPAs and ask questions. It is *very* important to note this *in the minutes.*

Summary

It would appear that the financial responsibilities accepted by board members are complex and burdensome, but in reality they are very easy to follow.

As long as board members follow the following important points, the probability of personal liability is very low:

➢ Note all financial discussions and actions in the minutes.

➢ Don't engage in willful ignorance or intentional wrongdoing.

➢ Don't make decisions with the *intention* of causing injury or damage.

➢ Don't make decisions outside of their authority.

Other Important Areas

While not all of the following is directly connected with financial responsibilities, it is advisable that board members consider the following action to further reduce any liabilities:

➢ Ensure the organization's general counsel specializes in not-for-profit law.

➤ Ensure that insurance policies for Officers and Directors Errors and Omissions and other liabilities are in place.

➤ Understand state volunteer protection laws.

➤ Ensure that board members are protected individually by an Indemnification Agreement.

➤ Ensure there are written policies in the areas of financial and accounting, investments, personnel, internal controls, officers and administration, and so on.

3

The Basics of Form 990, Form 990-EZ, and Form N

THE IRS FORM 990 WAS COMPLETELY REDESIGNED and is effective December 31, 2008. The new form consists of 11 pages with 75 pages of instructions! Additionally, the new Form 990 now has 16 possible schedules to complete as well as two indexes with many more pages of instructions! The purpose of this chapter is to apprise not-for-profit organizations' key employees and boards of directors of the basic information that they need to know. (It is *not* intended to thoroughly educate independent CPAs and tax attorneys on their responsibilities.) The reader will quickly learn that there are very few questions regarding financial information versus a great many questions on governance.

Important Items for Consideration

Who Is Affected?

Any organization with a 501(c)( ) classification must file either the new Form 990, Form 990-EZ or Form 990-N.

Effective Date

Calendar year ended 12/31/2008 and fiscal years thereafter.

When Are Form 990s Due?

The 15th day of the 5th month following the end of their year.

Where Are Form 990 and Form 990-EZ Filed?

Department of the Treasury
Internal Revenue Service Center
Ogden, UT 84201–0027

What Are the Penalties for Not Filing?

$20 per day to a maximum of $10,000 or 5 percent of gross receipts.

Important: IRS will send a letter and final due date to the organization. The *individual* failing to comply will be charged $10 per day to a maximum of $5,000.

Where Can an Organization Get the Complete Set of Form 990, Form 990-EZ, and Form 990N?

For the forms and related, as well as instructions, schedules, and attachments, go to the IRS web site, www.irs.ustreas.gov:

1. Click "More Forms & Publications" on the home page.

2. Click "Forms & Instructions number (PDF)" on next screen.

3. Click pages 5 and 6 for various Form 990, etc. information.

New Form 990-N (e-Postcard)

Small not-for-profit organizations whose gross revenues are typically under $25,000 may be required to submit Form 990-N, also known as the e-Postcard.

This new form *must be submitted electronically* on the following IRS web site: http://epostcard.form990.org.

What Information Is Required?

➢ Employer Identification Number (EIN) or Taxpayer Identification Number (TIN)

➢ Tax year

➢ Legal name and mailing address

➢ Name and addresses of principal officers

➢ Confirmation that gross receipts are typically $25,000 or less

➢ Web site address (URL) if one exists

Note: If the not-for-profit organization fails to file Form 990-N, it may lose its tax-exempt status. Also, most churches are exempt from filing. Finally, Private Foundations must file Form 990-PF.

Form 990-EZ

What Not-for-Profit Organizations May File Form 990-EZ?

Year	Gross Receipts	Total Assets
2008	>$25,000 and <$1 million	<$2.5 million
2009	>$25,000 and <$500,000	<$1.25 million
2010	>$25,000 and <$200,000	<$500,000

When Is Form 990-EZ Due?

The 15th day of the 5th month following the end of the calendar or fiscal year.

Where Should Form 990-EZ Be Mailed?

Department of the Treasury
Internal Revenue Service Center
Ogden, UT 84201–0027

Are Extensions Allowed?

Yes, Form 8868 should be used.

What Are the Penalties of Failure to File?

$20 per day or the smaller of $10,000 or 5 percent of yearly gross receipts.

Can Individuals Be Held Personally Responsible for Failure to File?

Yes, at a rate of $10 per day to a maximum of $5,000.

Does Form 990-T (Unrelated Business Income Tax) apply to Form 990-EZ?

Yes, if the gross receipts from an Unrelated Business Source exceeds $1,000.

Is Form 990-T Open to Public Inspection?

Only if the organization has 501(c)(3) status.

What Are Possible Required Schedules or Attachments Supporting Form 990-EZ?

Schedules

Schedule A, Public Charity Status & Public Support

Schedule B, Schedule of Contributors

Schedule C, Political Campaign & Lobbying Activities

Schedule E, Schools

Schedule G, Supplemental Information Regarding Fundraising or Gaming Activities

Schedule L, Transactions with Interested Persons

Schedule N, Liquidation, Termination, Dissolution or Significant Disposition of Assets

Attachments

1. Form 1128 for change of accounting period
2. Reasons for late filing

3. Description of amendments in amended return

4. Name change amendment to organizing document

5. Additional "also known as" (a.k.a.) names (see heading, Item C, Name & Address)

6. Explanation of why an organization that reports more than $15,000 in Part 1, line 6a is not required to complete schedule G

7. Schedule of grants made

8. Explanation of other changes in net assets or fund balances

9. Schedule listing other program services

10. Statement regarding personal benefit contracts

11. Description of activities not previously reported

12. Conformed copy of changes to organizing or governing document

13. Reasons for not reporting income from business activities on Form 990-T

14. Request and determination letter regarding termination of exempt status

15. Articles of merger or dissolution, resolutions, and plans of liquidation or merger

What Is a "Disqualified Person"?
Someone who benefits financially unfairly due to their position with the organization.

Who Must Sign the Return?
Paid preparers and an officer of the organization.

Is Form 990–EZ Open to Public Inspection?
Yes. See Chapter 6 of this book.

Form 990

What Organization's Must File Form 990?

Fiscal Year	Gross Receipts	Total Assets
2008	≥$1 Million	≥$2.5 Million
2009	≥$500,000	≥$1.25 Million
2010	≥$200,000	≥$500,000

This phase-in period substantially increases the number of not-for-profit organizations required to file Form 990. Considering that effective with calendar year 2010 and fiscal years thereafter, if gross receipts are $200,000 or more and total assets are $500,000, the not-for-profit organization must file Form 990.

Important Items

Tax Accounting Methods

Simply, Form 990 states that the organization should use the same accounting method that it uses to maintain its books and records.

Typically, most new not-for-profit organizations start with using the cash basis and switches to accrual. To change the method, Form 3115 must be filed.

Professional Accounting Standards

Most not-for-profit organizations eventually retain the services of an independent CPA. Auditing CPAs are required to follow Not-For-Profit Professional Accounting Standards as follows:

➢ SFAS #116

➢ SFAS #117

➢ SFAS #124

➢ SFAS #136

Please see the chapters in this handbook that fully explain these not-for-profit specific standards.

Other standards that are not specific to not-for-profit organizations must also be followed.

Page 1

E. Note the organization's public telephone number.

F. Note name and address of Chief Elected Officer or Chief Staff Executive.

Part I, Summary

1. Note the organization's mission statement.

4. Note number of "independent" voting members:

➢ No compensation

➢ No corporations

➢ No accrual financial benefits

➢ No family members

Part II, Signature Block

The signature block now appears at the bottom page rather than the last page.

An officer must sign the return. The paid preparer must also sign the form.

Important: The new Form 990 has a check box that automatically allows IRS to contact the preparer directly by checking the YES box.

Page 2:
Part III, Statement of Program and Service Accomplishments

1. Note the organization's mission statement. It is preferable but not necessary to have this in writing.

2. New programs should be listed on Schedule O.

3. Termination of significant programs should be listed on Schedule O.

4. The three largest expense programs should be listed on lines 4a, 4b, and 4c.

Page 3:
Part IV, Checklist of Required Schedules

This checklist has 37 questions that require the organization to complete certain schedules of the 16 existing schedules. The question response will dictate what schedules must be completed.

Page 5:
Part V, Statements Regarding Other IRS Filings and Tax Compliance

This part asks questions that determine if the organization is in compliance with and has filed other tax forms.

Page 6:
Part VI, Governance, Management and Disclosure

This part requires the organization to answer 20 questions in the follows areas:

➤ Section A, Governing Body and Management

➤ Section B, Policies

➤ Section C, Disclosure

Most of the questions require an explanation on Schedule O with the exception of lines 1b, 9a, 13, 14, 17, and 20 that require no explanation.

Section A, Governing Body and Management

As stated earlier in this chapter, it is important to recognize independent versus non-independent. To summarize this important area:

Independent Board Member

1. Was not compensated by the organization or related organizations.

2. The individual did not receive compensation of $10,000 or more from the organization or related organizations other than expenses.

3. Neither the individual or the individual's family were involved with the organization or affiliated organizations that is required to be reported in Schedule G, Transactions with Interested Persons.

There are three factors that do *not* cause nonindependence:

1. Any donor regardless of the amount.

2. A religious order member who has taken a vow of poverty.

3. Members who receive financial benefits indirectly of a member merely receive the benefits by virtue of a charity or class served by the organization.

Section B, Policies

The most important lines are as follows:

Line 12a asks if the organization has a written Conflict of Interest Policy.

Line 13 asks if the organization has a written Whistle Blower Policy.

Line 14 asks if the organization has a written Document Retention and Reduction Policy.

Note: Most CPAs and attorneys have the position that these policies are not *required* to be in writing but encourage not-for-profit organization's to formalize them in writing to avoid confusion and misunderstandings.

Section C, Disclosure

The purpose of this section is to inquire:

Line 17, What states the organization's Form 990 is required to be filed.

Line 18, How documents that are open for public inspection are made available, through web sites or upon request.

Documents that are subject to inspection include:

➤ Form 990

➤ Form 990-T (501(c)(3) organizations)

➤ Possibly Forms 1023 or 1024 (applications for tax-exempt status)

Note: Please see the Disclosure of Information chapter of this handbook.

Line 19, State in Schedule O how the organization makes governing documents, conflict of interest policy and documents answered on line 18 available to the public.

Line 20, Requires the name, physical address and telephone number of the person to contact who possesses the books and records of the organization.

Page 7:
Part VII, Compensation of Officers, Directors, Trustees, Key Employees, Highest Compensated Employees and Independent Contractors.
This part addresses Intermediate Sanctions of payments paid to disqualified persons (see Chapter 18, The Basics of Intermediate Sanctions).

The compensation that must be reported of the individuals noted on Part VII are as follows:

➤ Current officers, directors and trustees:

  ➤ Report all even if compensation is zero.

➤ Current key employees:

  ➤ Report those who receive $150,000 or more

➤ Current five highest compensated employees who are not key employees:

  ➤ Report those five receiving $100,000 or more

➤ Independent Contractors:

  ➤ Report those receiving $100,000 or more

➤ *Former* officers, key employees and five highest compensated employees:

  ➤ Report those receiving $100,000 or more

➤ *Former* directors and trustees:

  ➤ Report those receiving $10,000 or more

Page 9:
Part VIII, Statement of Revenue
This section requires statement of gross revenues originating from:

1. Contributions, gifts, grants, and other similar amounts

2. Program service revenue

3. Other revenues

Additionally, revenues are separated into:

A. Total revenue

B. Related or exempt function revenue

C. Unrelated business revenue

D. Revenue excluded from tax under sections 512, 513, or 514

Page 10:
Part IX, Statement of Functional Expenses
This section is broken down to:

a. Total expenses

b. Program service expenses

c. Management and general expenses

d. Fundraising

The purpose of this section is to reveal how much of the organization's expenses are spent on the benefits and services of the organization versus expenses for overhead and fundraising.

Page 11:
Part X, Balance Sheet
This statement is titled Statement of Financial Position (and the income statement is titled Statement of Activity) by CPAs following the Statements of Financial Accounting Standard applying to the not-for-profit organizations.

It is important to note that the Balance Sheet requires comparing assets, liabilities, and net assets for the prior and current year.

Page 11:
Part XI, Financial Statements and Reporting
This part asks simple questions regarding the accounting method the organization uses (cash, accrual, or other), relationship with independent accountants, auditing by independent CPAs, and Single Audit Act and Circular A-133 requirements.

Related Schedules

The following schedules may be required to be filed with Form 990:

1. Schedule A: Public Charity Status and Public Support

2. Schedule B: Schedule of Contributors

   Note: Generally must indicate contributions of $5,000 or more. This schedule may be removed when disclosing information with the exception of private foundations.

3. Schedule C: Political Campaign and Lobbying Activities

4. Schedule D: Supplemental Financial Statements

5. Schedule E: Schools

6. Schedule F: Statement of Activities Outside the U.S.

7. Schedule G: Supplemental Information Regarding Fundraising or Gaming Activities

8. Schedule H: Hospitals

9. Schedule I: Grants and Other Assistance to Organizations, Governments, and Individuals in the U.S.

10. Schedule J: Compensation Information

11. Schedule K: Supplemental Information on Tax-Exempt Bonds

12. Schedule L: Transactions With Interested Persons

13. Schedule M: Non-Cash Contributions

14. Schedule N: Liquidation, Termination, Dissolution or Significant Dispositions of Assets

15. Schedule O: Supplemental Information to Form 990

    Note: This is the "catch-all" schedule that coordinates narrative descriptions and freeform attachments are no longer permitted.

16. Schedule R: Related Organizations and Unrelated Partnerships

Appendixes

This section consists of two appendixes that may also be required to file with Form 990:

Appendix 4A: State Unified Registration Statement

This is an important appendix, as it details required reporting *by state*!

Appendix 4B: Interested Party by Part and Type

Summary

As stated at the beginning of this chapter, this is to apprise boards of directors and key employees of the *basic* information on the new Form 990 and is *not* intended to instruct tax preparers or attorneys on full understanding.

The most important action that the not-for-profit organization should take is to ensure that they have:

➤ A Mission Statement

➤ A Conflict of Interest Policy

➤ A Whistle Blower Protection Policy

➤ A Records Retention and Destruction Policy

CHAPTER 4

Tax on Unrelated Business Income and Form 990-T

THIS CHAPTER DISCUSSES tax on unrelated business income, first presented in questions and answers, then in a series of examples showing taxable and nontaxable income.

Who Must File Form 990-T?

Generally, tax-exempt organizations with *gross* income of $1,000 or more for the year from an unrelated trade or business.

What Form Is Filed?

Form 990-T, Exempt Organization Business Income Tax Return, and, generally, a state form.

When Is Form 990-T Due?

Form 990-T must be filed by the fifteenth day of the fifth month after the tax year ends.

Are Extensions of Time to File Granted?

Corporations can request an automatic extension of six months to file a return by submitting Form 7004, Application for Automatic Extension of Time to File Corporation Income Tax Return.

Are 990-T Returns Available for Public Inspection?

Although the annual *information* return filed by an exempt organization (Form 990) is available for public inspection, an exempt organization's *income tax* return (Form 990-T) is not available for public inspection. See Chapter 6, "Disclosure of Information."

What Are the Tax Rates?

All organizations subject to the tax on unrelated business income are taxed at prevailing corporate tax rates.

Are Estimated Tax Payments Required?

Tax-exempt organizations must make quarterly payments of estimated tax on unrelated business income under the same rules as corporations. Generally, if an organization expects its tax to be $40 or more, estimated tax payments are required.

When Are Estimated Tax Payments Due?

Estimated tax payments are due on the fifteenth day of the fourth, sixth, ninth, and tenth months of the tax year.

How Are Estimated Taxes Computed?

Tax-exempt corporations should use Form 1120-W, Corporate Estimated Tax, to estimate taxes.

How Are Estimated Tax Payments Made?

Organizations should deposit all estimated tax payments with Form 8109, the Federal Tax Deposit Coupon. These deposits must be made with an authorized financial institution or a Federal Reserve bank in accordance with the instructions on the coupon.

How Much of the Final Tax Liability Must Be Paid via Estimated Tax Payments?

To avoid an estimated tax penalty, the amount of estimated tax payments required by the organization is 90 percent of the final tax liability.

What Is the Penalty for Underpayment of Estimated Taxes?

An interest penalty is assessed for underpayment of estimated taxes; it is effective on the due date of the tax. This interest rate is adjusted quarterly by the IRS.

Is There a Penalty for Not Filing Form 990-T?

The penalty for not filing Form 990-T by the deadline is 5 percent of the tax due per month, to a maximum of five months, or 25 percent of the tax due.

What Is Unrelated Business Income?

Unrelated business income is revenues generated by a tax-exempt organization that possess *all three* of the following characteristics:

1. The income must be from a *trade or business.*
2. It must be from a trade or business that is not substantially related to carrying out the exempt purpose for which the organization exists.
3. The trade or business must be *regularly carried on.*

What Is Considered a Trade or Business?

The term *trade or business* generally includes any activity carried on for the production of income from selling goods or performing services.

What Does "Substantially Related" Mean?

To determine whether a business activity is or is not substantially related requires an examination of the relationship between the business activities that generate the particular income in question and the accomplishment of the organization's exempt purpose.

Trade or business is related to exempt purposes, in the statutory sense, only when the conduct of the business activities has a causal relationship to the achievement of exempt purposes (other than through the production of income). The causal relationship must be substantial. The activities that generate the income, to be substantially related, must contribute importantly to the accomplishment of the organization's exempt purpose. In determining whether activities contribute importantly to the accomplishment of an exempt purpose, the size and extent of the activities involved must be considered in relation to the nature and extent of the exempt function they intend to serve.

For example, if there is income from activities that are in part related to the performance of an organization's exempt function, but the activities are conducted on a larger scale than is reasonably necessary for the performance of the function, the gross income attributable to that portion of the activities in excess of the needs of the exempt function is income from an unrelated trade or business. This income is not from the production or distribution of goods or the performance of services that contribute importantly to the accomplishment of any exempt purpose of the organization.

What Does "Regularly Carried On" Mean?

Business activities of an exempt organization ordinarily will be considered to be regularly carried on if they show a frequency and continuity and are pursued in a manner similar to comparable commercial activities of nonexempt organizations.

Are Any Revenue Sources Specifically Excluded from Unrelated Business Income?

The following revenue sources are specifically excluded from tax on unrelated business income:

> ➢ Dues (excluding associate member dues)
> ➢ Dividends and interest
> ➢ Annuities
> ➢ Royalties
> ➢ Gains from the disposition of property
> ➢ Contributions
> ➢ Proceeds from the sale of goods or services produced in the course of the organization's exempt function
> ➢ Income from any trade or business in which substantially all the work is performed by volunteer labor
> ➢ Any trade or business carried on for the convenience of members
> ➢ Selling donated merchandise or gifts
> ➢ Rental of mailing lists by two 501(c)(3) organizations

Are Any Revenue Sources Specifically Included in Unrelated Business Income?

The following revenue sources are specifically included in the computation of unrelated business income and are the most common:

> Advertising

> Rental income from debt-financed property

> Income from controlled organizations

What Does the IRS Consider Advertising Income?

Advertising income is revenue generated by an exempt organization from the sale of any paid commercial advertising in its publications, on its Web site, and so forth.

What Does "Debt-Financed Property" Mean?

The term *debt-financed property* means any property that is held to produce income and for which there is an organizational indebtedness at any time during the tax year; this includes real estate and personal property. Tax-exempt organizations that acquire or improve income-producing property with borrowed funds or with existing debt have acquisition indebtedness on the property.

Are Gross Revenues Produced from Debt-Financed Property Taxable in Their Entirety?

For each debt-financed property, the unrelated debt-financed income is a percentage of the gross income derived during the tax year from the property. The percentage is the debt/basis percentage. The formula for deriving unrelated debt-financed income is as follows:

$$\frac{\text{Average Acquisition Indebtedness}}{\text{Average Adjusted Basis}} \times \text{Gross Income from Debt-Financed Property}$$

What Is Income from Controlled Organizations?

The exclusion of interest, annuities, royalties, rents, and so forth, does not apply when an exempt organization receives them from a controlled organization. The organization from which the interest, annuities, royalties, and rents are received is called the controlled organization; the exempt organization receiving these amounts is called the controlling organization. If the controlled organization is a stock corporation, control generally means stock ownership of at least 80 percent of the total combined voting power of all classes of stock entitled to vote and at least 80 percent of the total number of shares of all other classes of stock in the corporation.

Is Tax on Unrelated Business Income Computed on Gross or Net Revenues?

This tax is computed on *net* revenues, not gross. Net income is that derived from any unrelated trade or business, less deductions directly connected with carrying on the trade or business.

Optional Proxy Tax on Lobbying Expenditures

If an organization elects to pay the optional proxy tax on lobbying expenditures, the tax is noted on Form 990-T. Write the words "Sec. 6033(e) Proxy Tax" to the left of the entry space. Attach a schedule supporting the computation.

Are There Other Considerations I Should Be Aware of?

Other, more complex, issues you should discuss with your tax adviser are as follows:

➢ Trusts

➢ Title-holding corporations

➢ Hospital services

➢ Dual use of assets or facilities

➢ Out-of-state sales

➢ Exploitation of exempt activities

➢ Special rules for social clubs, voluntary employees, beneficiary associations, veterans organizations, and other such groups

➢ Net operating losses

➢ Securities

Tax on Unrelated Business Income: Examples

	Taxable?	
	Yes	**No**
1. An agricultural organization whose primary purpose is to promote better conditions for breeders of cattle and to improve the breed generally sells cattle for its members on a commission basis.	x	
2. An exempt educational organization regularly sells membership mailing lists to business firms.	x	
3. A hospital with exempt status operates a gift shop patronized by patients, visitors making purchases for patients, and employees; a cafeteria and coffee shop primarily for employees and medical staff; and a parking lot for patients and visitors only.		x
4. An exempt organization engages primarily in activities that further its exempt purposes. It also owns the publication rights to a book. The publication and distribution of the book do not contribute to the organization's accomplishing its exempt purposes, except for its need for the income from the sale of the book. The organization exploits the book in a commercial manner. It arranges for printing, distribution, publicity, and advertising in connection with the sale of the book.	x	
The same organization transfers publication rights to a commercial publisher in return for royalties.		x
5. An exempt vocational school operates a handicraft shop where articles made by students, as part of their regular courses of instruction, are sold. The students are paid a percentage of the sales price.		x
The same organization also sells products produced by former students at home under the direction of the school.	x	
6. An exempt school has tennis courts and dressing rooms that it uses during the regular school year in its educational program. During the summer, the school operates a tennis club open to the general public. Employees of the school conduct the affairs of the club, including collecting membership fees and scheduling court time.	x	
7. An exempt organization, organized and operated for the prevention of cruelty to animals, receives income from providing pet boarding and grooming services for the general public.	x	
8. A volunteer fire company conducts weekly public dances. The work at the dances is done by unpaid volunteers.		x

		Taxable?	
		Yes	**No**
9.	A halfway house organized to provide room, board, therapy, and counseling for persons discharged from alcoholism treatment centers also operates a furniture shop to provide full-time employment for its residents. The profits are applied to the operating costs of the halfway house.		x
10.	A business league publishes an annual directory that contains a listing of all its members, their addresses, and their areas of expertise. Each member has the same amount of space in the directory, and its format does not emphasize the relative importance or reputation of any member. The directory contains no commercial advertising and is sold only to the organization's members.		x
11.	A business league operates a fringe parking lot and shuttle bus service for a fee.		x
	The same organization also operates, as an insubstantial part of its activities, a park-and-shop plan. The plan allows customers of particular merchants to park free at certain parking lots in the area. Merchants participating in this plan buy parking stamps, which they distribute to their customers to use to pay for parking.	x	
12.	An exempt organization, whose purpose is to provide for the welfare of young people, rents rooms primarily to people under age 25.		x
	In addition, the organization has a health club program that its members can join for an annual fee. The annual fee is comparable to fees charged by similar local commercial health clubs and is sufficiently high to restrict participation in the program to a limited number of community members.	x	

5

Other IRS Issues

NOT-FOR-PROFIT ORGANIZATIONS are held to a higher degree of IRS reporting requirements because of tax-exempt status, favorable postal rates, sales tax exemptions, and other benefits of their status. Five specific IRS areas are unique to not-for-profit organizations:

➤ Unrelated business income tax

➤ Deductibility of lobbying expenditures

➤ Issues regarding employee versus independent-contractor status

➤ Required statement on membership forms

➤ Restrictions on deductions for charitable contributions

The issues regarding unrelated business income tax and deductibility of lobbying expenditures are substantial and are explained in other chapters of this book.

Issues Regarding Employee versus Independent-Contractor Status

The IRS is encouraging employers, including not-for-profit organizations, to comply with rules and regulations on the proper classification of employees and independent contractors. In the past, employers were generally isolated from IRS penalties for improper classification. Because the independent contractors were issued Form 1099 if they received $600 or more, they were held responsible for improper tax reporting.

Abuses by both employers and independent contractors have resulted in payroll tax deficiencies in several areas, including:

➤ Federal income tax

➤ State and local income taxes

➤ FICA (Social Security) taxes

➤ Medicare taxes

➤ Federal unemployment taxes

➤ State unemployment taxes

Payroll tax deficiencies have prompted the IRS to shift the burden of compliance from individuals to employers. Employers now must determine the proper classification of individuals as either employees or independent contractors. To help employers make the classification decision, the IRS issued Revenue Ruling 87-41, a criterion of 20 questions regarding the relationship between the employer and individuals. (See Exhibit 5.1.)

EXHIBIT 5.1

Revenue Ruling 87–41: 20 Criteria

Next to each number, write "E" if employee, "S" if self-employed, or "U" if uncertain.

_ 1. ***Instructions.*** A person who is required to comply with instructions about when, where, and how to work is ordinarily an employee.

_ 2. ***Training.*** Training of a person by an experienced employee or by other means is a factor of control and indicates that the worker is an employee.

_ 3. ***Integration.*** Integration of a person's services into the business operations generally shows that the person is subject to direction and control and accordingly is an employee.

_ 4. ***Services rendered personally.*** If the services must be rendered personally by the person employed, it suggests an employer-employee relationship. Self-employed status is indicated when a person has the right to hire a substitute without the employer's knowledge.

_ 5. ***Hiring, supervising, and paying assistants.*** The hiring, supervising, and paying of assistants by the employer generally indicate that all workers on the job are employees. Self-employed persons generally hire, supervise, and pay their own assistants.

_ 6. ***Continuing relationship.*** The existence of a continuing relationship between a worker and the organization for whom the worker performs services is a factor tending to indicate the existence of an employer-employee relationship.

_ 7. ***Set hours of work.*** The establishment of set hours of work by the employer is a factor indicating control and, accordingly, the existence of an employer-employee relationship. Self-employed persons are masters of their own time.

_ 8. ***Full time required.*** If the worker must devote full time to the business of the employer, he or she ordinarily will be considered an employee. A self-employed person, on the other hand, may choose for whom and when to work.

_ 9. ***Doing work on employer's premises.*** Doing the work on the employer's premises may indicate that the worker is an employee, especially if the work could be done elsewhere.

_10. ***Order or sequence of work.*** If a worker must perform services in an order or sequence set by the organization for whom he or she performs services, it indicates that the worker is an employee.

_11. ***Oral or written reports.*** A requirement that workers submit regular oral or written reports to the employer is indicative of an employer-employee relationship.

_12. ***Payment by hour, week, month.*** An employee usually is paid by the hour, week, or month, whereas a self-employed person usually is paid by the job on a lump-sum basis (although the lump sum may be paid in intervals in some cases).

_13. ***Payment of business expenses.*** Payment by the employer of the worker's business or travel expenses suggests that the worker is an employee. Self-employed persons usually are paid on a job basis and take care of their own business and travel expenses.

_14. ***Furnishing of tools and materials.*** The furnishing of tools and materials by the employer indicates an employer-employee relationship. Self-employed persons ordinarily provide their own tools and materials.

_15. ***Significant investment.*** The furnishing of all necessary facilities (equipment and premises) by the employer suggests that the worker is an employee.

EXHIBIT 5.1 *(Continued)*

_16. ***Realization of profit or loss.*** Workers who are in a position to realize a profit or suffer a loss as a result of their services generally are self-employed, while employees ordinarily are not in such a position.

_17. ***Working for more than one firm at a time.*** A person who works for a number of persons or organizations at the same time is usually self-employed.

_18. ***Making services available to the general public.*** Workers who make their services available to the general public are usually self-employed. Individuals ordinarily hold their services out to the public by having their own offices and assistants, hanging out a shingle in front of their office, holding a business license, and advertising in newspapers and telephone directories.

_19. ***Right to discharge.*** The right to discharge is an important factor in indicating that the person possessing the right is an employer. Self-employed persons ordinarily cannot be fired as long as they produce results that measure up to their contract specifications.

_20. ***Right to terminate.*** An employee ordinarily has the right to end the relationship with the employer at any time he or she wishes without incurring liability. A self-employed person usually agrees to complete a specific job and is responsible for its satisfactory completion or is legally obligated to make good for failure to complete the job.

TOTALS: Employee _____ Self-Employed _____ Uncertain _____

If, after completing the questionnaire, a genuine question exists as to employment status, it is generally best to opt for employee status because monetary punishment for noncompliance can be severe. When an employer has decided a worker qualifies for independent contractor status, it is in the employer's best interest to document the rationale of the decision. This documentation should be filed permanently with other tax records of the independent contractor and with the examiner in case of an IRS audit.

If an employer is found not to be in compliance, the employer will be assessed the full employer's share of Social Security and Medicare on the total payments, plus penalties and interest. Additionally, it is common for independent contractors who have been incorrectly classified to take action against the employer and recover damages. Damages include all employee benefits that the independent contractor would have received under employment, which may include:

➢ Holiday leave

➢ Vacation leave

➢ Sick leave

➢ Personal leave

➢ Health insurance benefits

➢ Life insurance benefits

➢ Dental insurance benefits

➢ Disability insurance benefits

➢ Pension contributions

➢ Unemployment benefits

➢ Employer's share of Social Security and Medicare contributions

➢ Child care benefits

Required Statement on Membership Forms

Not-for-profit organization membership forms are required to include the following statement: "Dues are not deductible as Charitable Contributions for Income Tax Purposes." Dues may be considered ordinary and necessary business deductions.

This statement corrects the general public's misunderstanding that dues are deductible as charitable contributions. Only contributions made to 501(c)(3) organizations are deductible.

Restrictions on Deductions for Charitable Contributions

Taxpayers who make a separate charitable contribution of $250 or more must obtain written substantiation from the organization for the contribution to qualify as a charitable contribution deduction for income tax purposes. The IRS will no longer accept cancelled checks as substantiation.

Additionally, organizations that receive quid pro quo contributions in excess of $75 (payments in excess of $75 made partly as a gift and partly as consideration for goods or services) are required to inform contributors in writing of the value of the goods or services furnished and that only the portion exceeding the value is deductible as a charitable contribution.

CHAPTER 6

Disclosure of Information

A NOT–FOR–PROFIT ORGANIZATION'S disclosure of information policies are arguably *the* most important policies to formalize because it is inevitable that the organization will have records requested for review by members, contributors, the media, staff, researchers, or the general public. Furthermore, it is absolutely essential to research current federal and state law with regard to statutory requirements.

After federal and state requirements have been researched, consider formalizing policies in the following areas:

1. Requests made by current members/contributors in person

2. Requests made by current members/contributors in writing

3. Requests made by current members/contributors via telephone

4. Requests made by the general public (including media, researchers, and the like) in person

5. Requests made by the general public in writing

6. Requests made by the general public via telephone

It is recommended that the organization *draft* its disclosure of information policies first and have them reviewed by a competent attorney or CPA before adoption.

Disclosure of Information

Two of the most important policies a not-for-profit organization should have are those concerning disclosure of records to the general public and those concerning disclosure of records to members or contributors.

Very Important: This manual addresses *federal* law only. Before implementing policies, it is imperative to research prevailing *state* law inasmuch as most states have additional requirements to provide documents to the general public as well as to members or contributors. One way to research state law typically is to go to the state government web site, access the State Secretary of State, and download the state not-for-profit law, which should contain requirements for disclosure of records.

This issue is so important that a brief outline of federal requirements must be addressed. As of this writing, a summary of federal requirements concerning disclosure of records follows:

As part of their tax-exempt status, most not-for-profit organizations are required to make certain records available to public inspection. The requirement does not apply to churches, certain church-related religious organizations, or private foundations having separate inspection requirements.

For the majority of not-for-profit organizations required to disclose information, the law addresses the following, all of which are discussed in this chapter:

1. Effective date

2. Who has the right to inspect records

3. Which records must be made available for inspection

4. Group returns

5. Which records are exempt from inspection

6. Place of inspection

7. Requests made in person

8. Requests made in writing

9. Penalties for noncompliance

10. Reimbursement of expenses

11. Inspection of records through the IRS

12. State requirements

13. Exemptions

Who Has the Right to Inspect Records?

Anyone requesting to review applicable documents must be given access. Additionally, individuals are not required to reveal why they are making the request.

Which Records Must Be Made Available for Inspection?

Records that must be made available for inspection include the following:

1. Form 990, Form 990-EZ, Form 990-BL, and Form 1065, including all schedules and attachments. Requesters can ask for certain specific information only, such as Part V of Form 990, List of Officers, Directors, Trustees, and Key Employees. The

organization must furnish the most current three years of these forms. *Note:* If the tax-exempt organization has chosen to include the names and addresses of contributors to the organization with these returns, the organization may elect not to disclose this information.

2. Form 1023, Application for Recognition of Exemption under Section 501(c)(3), or Form 1024, Application for Recognition of Exemptions under Section 501(a). If the tax-exempt organization was founded before July 15, 1987, the organization must make this information available if it still has a copy of the form.

3. All correspondence submitted by the tax-exempt organization supporting these documents, as well as correspondence issued by the IRS with respect to these documents.

Group Returns

If a not-for-profit organization does not file Form 990 because it is included in a group return, it must acquire a copy of the group return and make the material available for inspection. The requester has the right to request the inspection directly from the parent organization.

Which Records Are Exempt from Inspection

Not-for-profit organizations are not required to provide public access to the following:

1. Form 990-T, Exempt Organization Income Tax Return (except for 501(c)(3) organizations)

2. Form 1120-POL, U.S. Income Tax Return for Certain Political Organizations

3. Names and addresses of contributors

If names and addresses of contributors have been included in schedules submitted with Form 990 and Form 990-EZ, this information can be deleted from the package of information provided to the inspector.

Place of Inspection

If a not-for-profit organization has a permanent headquarters, the documents being inspected must be made available at that location. If the organization does not have a permanent headquarters, the documents must be made available at a reasonable location of the organization's choice. The organization can mail the information requested if the requester agrees to forgo an on-site inspection.

If an organization has more than one location, such as regional offices, a copy of the applicable documents must be made available for inspection at the other locations. Service facilities, such as warehouses, need not retain the applicable documents.

Requests Made in Person

Documents required to be disclosed must be provided on the day of request, or the next business day if unusual circumstances exist. The time cannot exceed five days.

Requests Made in Writing

Written requests for documents must be fulfilled within 30 days of the request or within 30 days after receiving payment for expenses.

Penalties for Noncompliance

Responsible persons of a tax-exempt organization who do not provide informative returns required may be subject to a penalty of $20 per day for as long as the failure continues for a maximum of $10,000. There is no maximum penalty for failure to provide a copy of an exemption application.

An individual denied access to applicable records can alert the IRS and request enforcement action through the director of the Exempt Organizations Division.

Reimbursement of Expenses

A not-for-profit organization can charge the inspector for photocopying and postage expenses. Reimbursable expenses include the following:

➢ Photocopying: $1 for the first page and 15 cents for subsequent pages

➢ Postage: actual costs.

Inspection of Records through the IRS

Copies of Forms 990, 990-EZ, and 990-PF and applications for exemption are available for public inspection and copying on request directly through the IRS. A request for inspection must be in writing and must include the name and address of the organization that filed the return. A request to inspect a return also should indicate the number of the return and the years involved. The request should be sent to the director (and to the attention of the "Disclosure Officer") of the district where the requester desires to inspect the return or application. If an inspection at the IRS national office is desired, the request should be sent to the Commission of Internal Revenue (attention: "Freedom of Information Reading Room"), 1111 Constitution Ave., N.W., Washington, DC 20024).

An inspector can request a copy of the documents by using Form 4506-A. There is a fee for photocopying.

State Requirements

This chapter deals exclusively with federal regulations. The organization probably also must meet additional state disclosure of information requirements. This information usually can be found in the state not-for-profit organizations law handbook.

This chapter discusses information and documents that must be disclosed by law. If a not-for-profit organization elects to allow access to other records, an applicable policy on who may inspect which records should be included in the organization's board-approved manual on accounting and financial policies and procedures.

Exemptions

Organizations may be exempt from the requirement of providing copies if:

1. The organization has already made the copies widely available through the Internet. The organization must make available its URL address.

2. Most Form 990s are also posted on the following web site: www.Guidestar.org.

3. The Secretary of the Treasury determines, on application by the tax-exempt organization, that the organization is the object of a harassment campaign.

Sample Policies

Providing Records to Members or Contributors

Once again, state laws almost always grant members or contributors additional rights to documents over the general public's rights, and it is essential to research prevailing state law accordingly. Obviously there are also political realities to deal with when members or contributors are involved. It is also the author's opinion that, if the organization is audited by a CPA firm, audited statements (but not the management letter) should be provided to members or contributors on request. Another consideration is to direct members or contributors to the appropriate web site or to provide hard copies.

Because of the complexity of combining the various aspects of both federal and state laws, not-for-profit organizations have a variety of possible policies.

Disclosure of Records

General Public: Requests Made in Person

Sample Policy

It is the policy of the organization that members of the general public will be provided copies of the most current three years of Form 990 filed as well as required state documents by close of business on the day of request. Appropriate photocopying expenses must be paid before the documents are released. (State issues must also be addressed.)

Or

It is the policy of the organization that members of the general public requesting to receive documents will be directed to the following web site rather than being provided copies: www.Guidestar.org. (State issues must also be addressed.)

General Public: Requests Made in Writing

Sample Policy

It is the policy of the organization that the general public requesting records in writing will be advised that the information is available on the following web site: www.Guidestar.org.

Or

It is the policy of the organization that the general public requesting records in writing will be provided the documents upon reimbursement of photocopying expense and postage expense within the required 30-day period or 37 days if prepayment of expenses is required.

Note: Under both policies, appropriate state law must be incorporated.

Members or Contributors: Requests Made in Writing

Sample Policy

It is the policy of the organization that members or contributors requesting documents in writing will be provided copies of the most current three years of Form 990, copies of credited financial statements, and (documents required by state law) within 30 days of the request.

Or

It is the policy of the organization that members or contributors requesting documents in writing will be directed to the appropriate Web site. Additionally, copies of audited financial statements and (documents required by state law) will be mailed within 30 days.

Members or Contributors: Requests Made in Person

Sample Policy

It is the policy of the organization that members or contributors requesting documents in person will be provided copies of the most current three years of Form 990 filed, copies of audited financial statements, and (documents required by state law).

Or

It is the policy of the organization that members or contributors requesting documents in person will be directed to the appropriate Web site. Additionally, copies of audited financial statements and (documents required by state law) will be provided on request.

Board of Directors' Examination of Records

Discussion

In order for members of the board of directors to adequately direct the organization and to adhere to their fiduciary responsibilities, the board has the right to examine *all* organization records unless protected by privacy laws, such as medical information.

Sample Policy

> It is the policy of the organization to allow individuals currently serving on the board of directors access to all organization records upon request with the exception of records protected by privacy laws.

Form 990-T

Discussion

There has been a recent change with regard to public disclosure that affects *501(c)(3) organizations only* as of the publication of this book. Briefly, 501(c)(3) organizations are required to make Form 990-T available for public inspection as well as Form 990. It is suggested that this requirement be incorporated in the disclosure of records policies for 501(c)(3) organizations.

Sample Policy

> It is the policy of the organization, a 501(c)(3) organization, to include Form 990-T among the documents that are open to public inspection.

CHAPTER 7

Conditions of Employment Agreement

THE CONDITIONS OF EMPLOYMENT AGREEMENT is another important employment documents that employees should sign before hire.

The most important elements to be included in this document are described in the following section.

Elements of the Conditions of Employment Agreement

Termination for Erroneous Statements

A potential employee's application and résumé will typically include education information, prior employment positions, professional credentials, references, and other important information. Additionally, the application form should ask the applicant if he or she has ever been convicted of a felony. Once the potential employee signs the application, that person attests that the information is truthful.

Part of the Conditions of Employment document should clearly state that the organization has reserved the right of termination of employment if any of this information is later proven false.

Offers and Acceptance of Gifts

It is common for an unscrupulous vendor to unethically or even illegally influence employees by offering them gifts. Obviously, trivial gifts, such as candy during the holidays, is no cause for concern, However, offers of expensive gifts and cash constitute bribes, and it is important to include in the Conditions of Employment agreement that such gift offers must be reported to management.

Management Day

The Conditions of Employment agreement should state that management has reserved the right to direct an employee not to report to work on a day at *management's* discretion (with pay). The employee acknowledges that management has reserved the right to have another employee assume his or her responsibilities on this day, sit at his or her desk and review mail, and the like.

Additionally, a management representative (and a witness) has reserved the right to inspect the contents of the employee's desk, review web sites the employee visits, review e-mails, and so on.

Uninterrupted Vacation

The Conditions of Employment agreement should state that management has reserved the right to *require* employees to take at least one full week of vacation per year.

Additionally, as noted for Management Day, during this week management may have another employee sit at the absent employee's desk, inspect desk contents, turn on the computer, and so forth.

Sick Days

The Conditions of Employment agreement should also note that the same actions that management may take on the Management Day and during Uninterrupted Vacation also apply to sick days.

Involuntary Terminations/Leaves of Absence

The Conditions of Employment agreement should state clearly the following:

➢ Discussions regarding involuntary terminations and leaves of absence will *not* take place in the employee's office, cubicle, or similar location. Rather, the discussion will be held in an office of the management team or a neutral location such as a conference room, library, or the like. Remember that the offender's office probably contains important evidence that the offender should not have access to.

➢ At a minimum, termination discussions should *always* include a witness selected by management to verify exactly what was said during the discussion, and the manager and witness should prepare notes immediately after the discussion and record important statements, actions, and so on. Additionally, management should reserve the right to have other parties attend, if deemed necessary, such as a lawyer, CPA, police officer, and the like.

If a man has to confront a woman, the witness should be another woman. If a woman finds it necessary to confront a man, the witness should be another man. This, of course, lessens the chance of being accused of any impropriety.

Surrender of Organization Intellectual Property

Work produced by an employee during the course of employment, such as correspondence, reports, studies, books, and articles, is considered intellectual property and *is the property of the organization*. This fact should be communicated to the prospective employee to avoid any misunderstandings at termination.

Surrender of Customer Information

Many employees have access to sensitive customer information such as credit card numbers, checking account numbers, Social Security numbers, addresses, telephone numbers, and the like. The Conditions of Employment agreement should state this information may not be removed from the office under any circumstances, but particularly at termination of employment.

Immediate Removal from Office

The Conditions of Employment agreement should be clear in stating that, immediately upon termination:

➢ The employee will surrender such items as door keys, credit cards, and the like.

➢ The employee will not be allowed to return to his or her office, cubicle, or other work area. If the employee needs essential personal items such as a purse, wallet, car keys, *two* other employees will retrieve them for the employee (requiring two other employees to retrieve these items eliminates accusations such as theft).

➢ The employee will then be escorted directly out of the building.

➢ Other personal effects (photos, pictures, etc.) will be gathered by *two* other employees, and these items will be later delivered to the employee's residence via courier.

Prosecution

The document should state very clearly that in the event an embezzlement or fraud is proven, the organization *will prosecute* the offending employee, regardless of the dollar amount involved, to the full extent of the law.

This threat of prosecution is an effective deterrent against fraud. If the employee has any questions concerning prosecution, explain that a prosecution may result in a criminal record, and this would obviously affect future employment at other organizations.

A Conditions of Employment agreement document may appear as shown in Exhibit 7.1.

EXHIBIT 7.1

Conditions of Employment Agreement Form

I, [Employee Name], an employee of [Organization],   acknowledge, and agree, to the following Conditions of Employment:

1. Termination for Erroneous Statements

   I understand that if any information provided by me and noted on my original APPLICATION FOR EMPLOYMENT or related documents provided by me such as a RÉSUMÉ or CURRICULUM VITAE is later proven to be false, these misstatements are grounds for termination of employment.

   These misstatements include, but are not limited to, education, professional credentials, prior employers, prior positions, job responsibilities, references, arrest record, etc.

2. Offers of Gifts by Vendors

   I understand that acceptance of offers of expensive gifts or cash by vendors will be considered acceptance of a bribe and may be cause for disciplinary action or termination of employment.

   I also understand that I have a responsibility to report such offers to the appropriate level of management.

3. Management Day

   I understand that management has reserved the right to direct me not to report to work on a day of management's discretion (with pay).

   I also understand that management has reserved the right to direct another employee to assume my responsibilities, sit at my desk, review mail, etc.

   I further understand that a management representative and a witness may inspect the contents of my desk, review my computer files including web sites I have been visiting, e-mail messages, etc.

   I agree to abide by the provisions of the EMPLOYEE HANDBOOK and if unallowable items such as alcohol, illegal drugs, pornography, etc. are discovered, this will be grounds for immediate termination of employment for cause.

4. Uninterrupted Vacation

   I understand that I am required to take at least one full week of uninterrupted vacation per year and that management may mandate this vacation if I fail to schedule it voluntarily.

   On this time off, I also understand that management has reserved the right to have another employee assume my responsibilities, inspect the contents of my desk as well as other action noted in Item 3 above.

5. Sick Days

   I understand that the actions management has reserved the right to take in Items 3 and 4 noted in this document also apply to any sick days I may take.

6. Involuntary Terminations/Leaves of Absence

   I understand that discussions concerning my involuntary termination or leave of absence will take place at a location other than my office, cubicle, etc., such as an office of management, conference room, library, etc.

   I also understand that this discussion will include a witness and management has reserved the right to also include attorneys, CPAs, police officers, etc. at their discretion.

EXHIBIT 7.1 *(Continued)*

7. Surrender of Organization Intellectual Property

I understand that all work products that I produce during my employment, as well as works-in-progress, are the organization's intellectual property. Upon my termination, whether voluntary or involuntary, this property and supporting documents will not be removed from the office under any circumstances, and I may not use this information for any purpose without the express written permission of management.

This property includes, but is not limited to:

➢ Correspondence

➢ Reports

➢ Studies

➢ Books

➢ Articles

➢ Accounting Records

➢ Videos

8. Surrender of Customer/Employee Information

I understand that I may come into contact with sensitive information regarding customers and employees, and in this respect I agree to keep this information confidential and I understand this information may not leave the office for any reason.

This information includes, but is not limited to:

➢ Credit card information

➢ Bank account information

➢ Social Security numbers

➢ Telephone numbers

➢ Addresses

➢ Mailing lists

➢ Prospect lists

9. Immediate Removal from Office

I understand and agree to the following in the event of my involuntary termination or leave of absence:

➢ I will surrender such items as organization door keys, credit cards, etc. at management's request.

➢ I will be escorted directly out of the office and will not be allowed to return to my personal office, cubicle, etc.

➢ In the event I require essential personal items such as a purse, wallet, car keys, etc., two employees will recover these items from my office for me.

➢ Non-essential personal effects such as photographs, etc. will be gathered by two employees and these items will be delivered to my residence via courier.

10. Prosecution

I understand that if fraud or embezzlement are proven, management may proceed with prosecution to the full extent of the law, regardless of the dollar amount of the incident.

I also understand that prosecution may result in a criminal record that may affect my prospects for future employment elsewhere.

EXHIBIT 7.1 *(Continued)*

11. Background Check

I understand that, in accordance with the Permission to Conduct Background Checks Form, the organization has reserved the right to conduct background checks anytime subsequent to my unemployment.

I hereby state that I have read and understand this Conditions of Employment agreement and Employee Handbook and agree to abide by the conditions therein.

Employee Name _____

Employee Signature_____

Date _____

Management Representative Name _____

Note: This material is not intended as legal advice. Before implementing these suggestions, be certain to have them reviewed by a competent employment law attorney familiar with your state and federal employment laws.

Tip: When the employee signs and dates the agreement, have Human Resources make a copy of it and place the *copy* in the employee's personnel file. Place the original in a location to which the employee has no access, such as a safe deposit box or safe.

As stated elsewhere in this handbook, it is very important to protect the original document because it may be evidence in the event of a criminal proceeding. In the event of an incident, if the offending employee removed this document, it could weaken a criminal case because a defense attorney could assert that the employee was never made aware of the ramifications of his or her actions and would not have proceeded with the fraud if he or she had known it would result in dire consequences.

Binding Arbitration

Many not-for-profit organizations have come to the conclusion that implementing a Binding Arbitration agreement with employees is a reasonable alternative for employees retaining legal representation in the event of disagreements between management and staff. Having legal representation is expensive for both the organization and the employee and often drags out over time.

Briefly, the employee and the organization agree that all issues between the organization and the employee would be submitted to a mutually agreed upon arbitrator and the decision of the arbitrator would be *binding and final to both parties.*

This system is fair and typically saves both parties expensive legal representation.

Important: The Disclaimer Statement noted in this handbook obviously applies to all issues addressed in this handbook. However, it is *vitally* important to have your Conditions of Employment Agreement and your Binding Arbitration Agreement reviewed by a competent labor attorney.

Wholly Owned Taxable Subsidiaries

IF AN ORGANIZATION has excessive amounts of unrelated business income in relation to its total revenues, it may wish to consider creating a wholly owned taxable subsidiary. However, it is unusual for the IRS to attack the tax-exempt status of a not-for-profit organization on the basis of excessive unrelated income, because the definition is so subjective. Wholly owned taxable subsidiaries should be considered only when necessary; they are not a panacea.

Before proceeding with establishing a wholly owned taxable subsidiary, consider the advantages and disadvantages.

Advantages

> *Isolation of liability*—If set up properly, the assets of the parent not-for-profit organization can be protected from creditor problems if legal action is taken against the subsidiary. Be careful, however, of interlocking boards of directors.

> *Fewer restraints on activities*—Often a not-for-profit organization is prohibited from engaging in unrelated revenue activities because of bylaws or action taken by governing bodies. These restraints can be removed by correctly establishing a wholly owned taxable subsidiary.

Disadvantages

> *Increased administrative costs*—Creating a wholly owned taxable subsidiary will result in significantly higher overhead in terms of additional accounting requirements, audit fees, tax returns, and the like.

> *Increased IRS audit exposure*—Creating a wholly owned taxable subsidiary means creating another taxable entity subject to audit. If the subsidiary is selected for audit by the IRS, the parent not-for-profit organization is likely to be audited because of the relationship, and vice versa.

> *Loss of related benefits*—A wholly owned taxable subsidiary cannot enjoy the benefits that accompany tax-exempt status by law. This means the subsidiary cannot benefit from favorable postal rates, sales tax exemptions, tax-deferred annuities for employees, property tax exemptions, and so forth.

Setting Up a Wholly Owned Taxable Subsidiary

If, after careful analysis, it seems in the best interest of the not-for-profit organization to establish a wholly owned taxable subsidiary, this subsidiary should be set up as follows:

> Set it up as a separate corporation. In the interests of risk isolation and protection of the parent organization's assets, the business form of a wholly owned taxable subsidiary should be a corporation, not a partnership.

> Set it up so that the parent not-for-profit organization owns 100 percent of the stock of the wholly owned taxable subsidiary.

> Avoid interlocking boards of directors. The officers of the parent not-for-profit organization should not be officers of the wholly owned taxable subsidiary. If the two organizations have the same officers, the IRS may take the position that they are in reality one entity, and the corporate veil may be pierced. If the two organizations have the same officers, all of the advantages of setting up a wholly owned taxable subsidiary could be lost in the event of legal action, IRS audits exceptions, and so forth.

> Keep business transactions between the parent not-for-profit organization and the wholly owned taxable subsidiary at arm's length. When the IRS audits a not-for-profit organization, business transactions between the parent and the subsidiary will be closely scrutinized. Neither the not-for-profit organization nor the subsidiary should benefit from the relationship unfairly. For example, ensure that the subsidiary does not use the favorable postal rates enjoyed by the parent and be certain that sales taxes have been paid on purchases by the subsidiary.

Dividends

The parent not-for-profit organization benefits financially from the profits of the wholly owned taxable subsidiary through dividends. The subsidiary must maintain separate accounting records and file its own tax returns. When the subsidiary earns a profit, taxes will be paid on the profit, and the officers of the wholly owned taxable subsidiary are free to declare an after-tax dividend to be paid to shareholders. In this case, the only shareholder is the parent not-for-profit organization, and the not-for-profit organization will receive the dividend accordingly.

CHAPTER 9

Internal Revenue Service Audits

NOT–FOR–PROFIT, TAX–EXEMPT ORGANIZATIONS, considered taxpayers by the IRS, are subject to IRS audit examinations. IRS audits are often costly, time consuming, and embarrassing when the circumstances of audit exceptions are revealed.

The IRS has the advantage over the not-for-profit organization selected for an audit. The audit plan of action formulated by the organization should be designed to take the advantage away from the IRS.

Avoiding IRS Audits

A not-for-profit organization should do everything within its power to avoid being audited by the IRS. The best way to handle an IRS audit is not to be selected for one. Although avoiding an audit cannot be guaranteed, the possibility of being selected for an audit can be significantly reduced by following four basic rules:

1. File on time. Unless there is a compelling reason to apply for an automatic extension to file the tax returns, it is advisable to file on time. As part of their agreements with their independent CPA firms, it is common practice for not-for-profit organizations to have in writing the understanding that tax deadlines will be met without filing extensions.

   Not-for-profit organizations have until the fifteenth day of the fifth month after the tax year to file tax returns. An application for an extension gives the appearance that the financial records may not be in order and may trigger an audit.

2. Have the tax returns reviewed. Before sending in the tax returns, have them reviewed for accuracy and completeness by an experienced tax preparer who did not work on the return. Anyone can make a mistake, and mistakes attract IRS attention. A simple mathematical error or failure to check a box may be noticed by the IRS and may cause the organization to be selected for audit.

If the tax return preparer has professional credentials, such as CPA or attorney at law, ensure the credentials are noted on the signature line of the return. Stating that the return was prepared by a professional lends credibility to the return.

3. Do not attract the IRS's attention. Ensure that the return is complete, but do not include unnecessary notes or explanations of how figures were computed, the tax rationale, and the like. The simpler the return, the less chance it will be selected for audit. Additionally, ensure that the return is signed by a corporate officer and the tax return preparer.

4. Send a copy of the audited financial statements with the return. When a not-for-profit organization is audited by an independent CPA firm, the organization typically receives an unqualified audit opinion with no tax issues noted. If an organization receives this opinion, it is a good idea to send in a copy of the audited financial statements with the return.

IRS examiners know that an audit by an independent CPA firm suggests that the not-for-profit organization is serious about financial management. Sending in a copy of the CPA's audited financial statements is a declaration that the financial records are in order and the tax returns have been prepared professionally.

Handling IRS Audits

If the organization *has* been selected for an IRS audit, it will receive a letter stating that it is to be audited. The letter will include the following:

➢ Name and telephone number of the IRS agent

➢ Entity(s) being audited

➢ Year(s) being audited

➢ Location and time of the audit

➢ Preliminary list of materials to be examined

Once selected, the not-for-profit organization should approach the audit aggressively and follow the 14 rules of handling IRS audits.

Rule 1: Delay the Audit

The organization selected for an IRS audit has the *right* to request a delay in the examination to get organized and resolve schedule conflicts. Always exercise this right.

Call the IRS agent, state why the first date is not acceptable, and request that it be rescheduled; make notes as to the date, the IRS staff person you spoke to, and the reason for the requested postponement. If an agent shows up at the organization's office on the first date, proof of the request to reschedule should be available.

Delaying the audit often results in never hearing from the IRS again concerning the audit. Why? Anything can happen on the IRS's end, such as work backlogs, retirements, agent transfers, illnesses, and other priorities, which may result in the audit being cancelled.

Rule 2: Try to Handle the Audit Informally

Often, a not-for-profit organization is selected for an IRS audit because one or two items look suspicious. It is wise to call the agent to find out whether a particular item has triggered the examination. If it has, you may be able to resolve the issue by correspondence, and the agent may not find it necessary to conduct a field examination.

Rule 3: Try to Have the Audit Conducted at Your CPA's Office

Professional accountants and tax return preparers are experienced in dealing with the IRS. They know what information is proprietary, what to say, and, more important, what *not* to say. It is reasonable to make this request, and the IRS will often agree.

In a related matter, it is wise to change the organization's address on the IRS's records to the CPA's address. IRS field audits are often scheduled at the address on the IRS's records. Additionally, a request to have the audit conducted at the accountant's office has more credibility when that is where tax returns and other IRS correspondence are sent.

Rule 4: Get Ready

Gather everything the IRS agent may want to examine for the audit in advance. Typically, an IRS field audit involves four areas: organizational documents, financial documents, contractual documents, and publications.

Organizational Documents

Organizational documents include the following:

➢ IRS not-for-profit classification determination letter

➢ Articles of incorporation

➢ Bylaws

➢ Organizational chart

➢ Names and addresses of officers

➢ Charter or subsidiary agreements

➢ Minutes

➢ Manual on accounting and financial policies and procedures

Have these items photocopied so they will be ready for the agent if requested. Two of these items warrant further discussion: minutes and the manual for accounting and financial policies and procedures.

Concerning minutes, avoid using buzzwords, such as *political, legislation, lobbying, tax avoidance,* and similar words that suggest political activities or tax evasion. These words can lead to an in-depth examination of your organization's activities.

In regard to the policies and procedures manual, a board-approved manual on accounting and financial policies and procedures that is current with IRS tax issues and Generally Accepted Accounting Principles (GAAP) is documentation that your organization is attempting to operate in accordance with conventional accounting rules and IRS regulations. This can go a long way when negotiating the settlement of a problem.

Financial Documents

Financial documents include the following:

- ➤ Audited financial statements
- ➤ Chart of accounts
- ➤ General ledger and supporting schedules
- ➤ Tax return for the year in question and the preceding and subsequent years
- ➤ Payroll returns and documents
- ➤ Form 1099s
- ➤ Bank statements
- ➤ Employee benefit documents

Two of these items require further discussion: the chart of accounts and the Form 1099s. The chart of accounts is typically a growing and ever-changing document. Old charts of accounts should be maintained as a permanent accounting record both for IRS audits and for audits by independent CPA firms. It may look suspicious when an audit reveals accounts that do not appear on the chart of accounts.

With regard to Form 1099s, the IRS looks at these forms carefully to determine whether independent contractors should be classified as employees. You should attach the results of the IRS's 20-question questionnaire (see Chapter 11, Exhibit 11.1, Revenue Ruling 87-41) and the justification of the decision to the individual's independent-contractor agreement as substantiation for the classification. The penalties for making an error in employee versus independent-contractor classification are severe.

Contractual Documents

Contractual documents include the following:

- ➤ Office leases
- ➤ Equipment leases

➤ Job descriptions

➤ Employment contracts

➤ All other contracts

The primary purpose for reviewing contracts is to investigate contracts with members and staff of the organization to decide whether any individuals have benefited unfairly by virtue of membership. If less-than-arm's-length transactions exist, tax-exempt status may be in jeopardy. This is of particular importance considering intermediate sanctions, discussed in detail in Chapter 14.

Publications

Publications include the following:

➤ Magazines

➤ Newsletters

➤ Promotional brochures

The IRS examines publications to determine that advertising is reported on Form 990-T, to ensure that postal permits are used exclusively by the organization holding the permit, and to ensure that the organization is not engaging in improper lobbying or political activities.

When preparing for an IRS audit, you should review any prior audit exceptions to ensure that problems have been addressed and corrected.

Rule 5: Get the Staff Ready

You should appoint an audit coordinator to interact with the IRS field agent. This person should be competent and experienced in handling IRS audits. If the organization is not satisfied and comfortable with having a staff member take on this responsibility, it should contract with an outside professional. The other staff should be instructed that the audit coordinator is the *only* person allowed to discuss business with the IRS field agent.

Rule 6: Conduct a Mock Audit

After everything is assembled and staff members know their roles, hire an *outside* CPA experienced with not-for-profit organizations and IRS audits to conduct a mock audit. The CPA should assume the role of an IRS agent—request documents to be reviewed and so forth.

At the conclusion of the mock audit, audit exceptions can be examined and corrected, rationales for tax positions can be formulated, the completeness of the audit coordinator's work can be evaluated, and so forth.

Conducting a mock audit is inexpensive when considering the alternative of an extended IRS visit, tax increases, penalties, interest, and other costs.

Rule 7: Decide Where to Locate the IRS Field Agent

Many not-for-profit organizations strive to make the IRS field agent comfortable. This is a mistake, because pleasant surroundings and work conditions may lead to an extended field audit, and the IRS agent must justify this extra time. Typically, an agent justifies extended audits by uncovering additional problems.

When deciding where to locate IRS field agents:

➢ Don't locate them in the accounting department, where they can observe operations, inspect files, etc.

➢ Don't put them in a library or conference room, where minutes, publications, and other information regarding the organization may be available.

It may be best to locate the agent at a table in an open area where his or her time on the audit can be easily observed by staff.

Rule 8: Take the Offensive

Have your independent CPA present at the first meeting with the IRS field agent to discuss what the agent intends to examine, how long the audit is expected to take, when the agent intends to be on site, and other important matters related to the audit examination. Assuming that the agent agrees, the first meeting between the not-for-profit organization and the IRS auditor should be recorded, or, at a minimum, notes should be taken and retained in case problems occur.

The purpose of a meeting of this nature is to provide time to research the rights of the not-for-profit organization regarding providing proprietary information, withholding information outside the realm of the period being examined, and similar matters.

In addition to having the organization's CPA and CFO present, also consider the following: the organization's counsel, the chief staff executive, the chief elected officer, and the treasurer.

Rule 9: Put *Everything* in Writing

As part of taking the offensive, tell the IRS field agent that your organization would prefer that the agent request in writing all items to be audited. Questions posed to your organization also should be in writing. Tell the agent that the documents requested and answers to the questions asked will be provided by the next working day.

The requests for documents to be examined and questions posed should be forwarded to your organization's outside CPA. The CPA firm will evaluate and make recommendations on the formal responses. This practice gives your organization time to find out whether the agent is entitled to review the documents requested; it also gives you time to formulate official responses to questions.

When documents and answers to questions are provided, the IRS agent should be asked to sign for the documents. A permanent record of documents examined and answers to questions posed should be retained in your audit file.

Finally, written documentation of the IRS agent's time on the audits should be noted in a log and retained in your organization's audit file.

Rule 10: Don't Volunteer

Give the auditor the records he or she is entitled to review, but do not volunteer any other records and do not allow the auditor random access to files. An organization undergoing an IRS audit only *thinks* all records are in order and will withstand audit scrutiny. Unfortunately, volunteering information and allowing random access to files and records may result in the auditor's reviewing documents with problems. This may lead to an extended, more in-depth audit.

Rule 11: Keep Audited Records Separate

Until the audit is fully resolved, do not refile documents the auditor has reviewed. Keep the documents separate from general files, where they will be readily avalible. If the IRS audit turns up a problem, the not-for-profit organization will most likely protest the conclusions of the audit at the federal building. If the records are kept separate, it would be a simple matter to take all documents reviewed to the meeting location.

Rule 12: Avoid the IRS "Fishing Expedition"

Keep the IRS audit confined to the year and the entity in question. IRS agents are, by law, entitled to review only certain documents, but it is possible for them to ask to review documents from different entities or different years.

Have the field agent put requests to review documents in writing. If there is any doubt about the agent's right to review documents, get professional advice before responding. Providing an IRS agent information that the IRS may not be entitled to examine may lead to extended audits, audits of different years, audits of different entities, and even audits of individuals.

Rule 13: Do Not Sign Any Documents without Professional Advice

During an IRS examination it is likely that your organization will be requested to sign documents relating to the audit. Do not sign *anything* without having an experienced professional review the request. Signing documents may:

➤ Lead to extended audits

➤ Give the IRS permission to review proprietary documents or documents it is not entitled to review

➤ Extend the statute of limitations on documents eligible to be reviewed

Rule 14: Always Have a Board-Approved Accounting Policies and Procedures Manual

Assuming the manual is current and is in accordance with accounting regulations and tax law, and the organization is operating in accordance with its policies, IRS field auditors will view the existence of an accounting policies and procedures manual as an attempt to comply with requirements, and the manual will be viewed as valuable audit documentation. For additional information on policies and procedures, see *Model Policies and Procedures for Not-for-Profit Organizations* (Edward J. McMillan, John Wiley & Sons, Inc., 2003).

Tips

Problem

The CPA firm currently retained is not the CPA firm engaged for the year being audited. Representation could be expensive.

⇨ **Tip**

As part of the engagement agreement with an independent CPA firm, ask the firm to provide a copy of the CPA working papers to your organization at the conclusion of its audit. Working papers often document tax rationale, provide detailed schedules of subsidiary records, and so forth.

Problem

Figures on audited financial statements do not agree with figures as they appear on the tax return.

⇨ **Tip**

As part of the engagement agreement, request that the independent CPA firm provide a reconciliation that coordinates items as they appear on tax returns and audited financial statements. This could be a considerable time-saver.

Problem

The not-for-profit organization is routinely selected for IRS audits.

⇨ **Tip**

Complain. Something is wrong if your organization is routinely audited. Contact the district director of the IRS, state that your organization is audited routinely, and ask to be informed why. Bringing this matter to the attention of the district director may resolve the problem.

Problem

The IRS field auditor takes extended leaves of absence during the audit.

⇨ **Tip**

Complain. Remember that the interest clock is running until the audit is concluded. Inform the field agent in writing that the extended absences are a problem and request that the audit be concluded. Send a copy of the correspondence to the district director.

CHAPTER 10

Developing Strong Internal Controls and Documenting a Fraud Action Plan

AN EFFECTIVE INTERNAL CONTROL SYSTEM ensures that the organization's assets are protected and lessens the opportunity for employee dishonesty. Strong internal control procedures are difficult to implement in very small organizations. These organizations should consult with a CPA firm to help them establish controls. Larger organizations should strive for ideal internal control conditions.

As part of their annual audit procedures, independent CPA firms *must* evaluate the effectiveness of the not-for-profit organization's internal control system and make recommendations for improvement if improvement is needed. However, a not-for-profit organization should set up its own controls over checks received and checks disbursed to strengthen the internal controls suggested at the time of the annual audit. These controls should be documented in the organization's manual on accounting and financial policies and procedures.

Four Areas of Risk

There are four areas of risk particular to not-for-profit organizations:

1. Personnel related expenses:
   - Salaries
   - Payroll taxes
   - Fringe benefits
2. Printing
3. Postage
4. Travel reimbursements

The reason these areas are particularly prone to embezzlement is because these are the areas in which a typical not-for-profit expends the bulk of their resources. Other expenses are either predictable (rent, equipment leases, depreciation and amortization for purchases made in a prior year, etc.) or somewhat immaterial. Obviously, don't ignore these four areas—but be especially vigilant to them.

While certainly not a panacea, the following Internal Control evaluation addresses most of the exposure to risk facing not-for-profit organizations:

1. Are *copies* of all bank statements forwarded off-site to someone *not* involved with check preparation and reviewed?

   ☐ Yes

   ☐ No

   This is an extremely important internal control, as it is very easy to alter checks, deposit slips, etc. Simply train someone to review the statements to ensure there are no forgeries, investigate new vendors, investigate unusual transactions and inspect the back of checks to ensure they have been deposited by the proper organization or individual. The original bank statements should be mailed to the proper individual for bank reconciliations, etc. (See Check 21 at the end of this chapter.)

2. Are debit memorandums investigated?

   ☐ Yes

   ☐ No

   Debit memorandums (DMs) are funds taken directly from the bank account. Typical examples would be insurance premiums and car payments. Check all DMs to ensure the payment is for organization purposes and not individuals.

3. Are copies of organization credit card transactions mailed or faxed off-site to someone for review?

   ☐ Yes

   ☐ No

   The only way to ensure that organization credit cards are not being abused is to have someone independently review the charges and investigate suspicious transactions.

4. Are *two* signatures required on all checks, wire transfers, etc.?

   ☐ Yes

   ☐ No

   The signatures should be of two people not involved with processing checks if possible. If two signers are required, it is possible that someone may notice something suspicious.

Also, two signatures should be required on *every* check. If one signature is allowed for checks under $1,000 for example and two are required for transactions over $1,000, all the single signers would have to do is process numerous checks under $1,000 for a transaction over $1,000 and bypass the system and intent.

5. Does accounting attach a copy of the bank reconciliation to the monthly financial statements?

    ☐ Yes

    ☐ No

    It is very important that bank reconciliations be completed immediately upon receipt to ensure bank accounts have not been compromised. Simply make sure the reconciler is working off the correct bank balances, old checks that have not cleared the bank be investigated, and so on.

6. Are finance personnel prohibited from being signers on all bank accounts?

    ☐ Yes

    ☐ No

    It is prudent business practice to *not* have finance personnel as approved check signers if possible. Individuals who prepare or have access to checks should not be signers.

7. For remittances via the mail, do you take advantage of a bank's Lock Box service?

    ☐ Yes

    ☐ No

    It is very common for not-for-profits to be widely known by their acronym rather than their formal name (American Medical Association is known by its members and staff as AMA for example). Unfortunately, many individuals paying dues and so forth make checks payable to the acronym. It is very easy for an individual having access to payments to open up an account at another bank under a variation of the acronym. For example, the hypothetical American Mother's Association has the same AMA acronym, and checks could be diverted to that account.

    It is prudent to see if the organization's bank offers Lock Box. Briefly, payments to the organization are mailed to the bank's address instead of the organization's address and the bank deposits the payment directly into the organization's account and forwards a copy of the checks, all other information and a validated deposit slip to the organization. This system eliminates employees or outsiders from having access to original checks.

8. Does the organization's restrictive endorsement stamp *not* include your account number?

    ☐ Yes

    ☐ No

A recent scam is for a dishonest person to make a small contribution or purchase an inexpensive item from a not-for-profit organization. What they want is to get their check back and hope the organization's bank account number is on the endorsement stamp. They then acquire fake ID, print checks at their home matching the fake ID and the organization's account number on the bottom and go on a shopping spree.

Check with your bank, but many banks no longer require account numbers on endorsement stamps. They know who their customers are in the event of a problem.

9. If the organization prepares manual checks, is the amount protected with a check protector machine or are the checks written with gel pens?

   ☐ Yes

   ☐ No

   It is very easy for a knowledgeable person to alter a check amount if a check is written with a common ink pen. They simply "wash" the check in a common solution that eliminates the date, payee, and amounts and they protect the check signature. They then can make the check payable to whomever they want and in any amount. It is also difficult to recover the loss from the bank as an approved check signer's signature is on the check.

   Consider writing these checks with a very inexpensive gel pen. The liquid in a gel pen cannot be "washed."

10. Are all employees bonded, and are you aware of any contractual obligations concerning the Fidelity Bond?

    ☐ Yes

    ☐ No

    It is wise to review your Fidelity Bond (Employee Dishonesty Insurance) with your insurance agent to *ensure* all people who handle checks, cash, and credit card payments are covered in your policy.

    Also, ensure there are no contractual obligations to maintain the policy at a certain level (grants, funds, etc.).

11. Does the organization require employees to take at least one full uninterrupted week of vacation annually?

    ☐ Yes

    ☐ No

    A warning sign of a possible problem employee is an employee who doesn't take vacation and is unnaturally protective of his or her work.

    Require that employee take at least one full week of vacation and reserve the right to have another employee assume those responsibilities.

    (See Chapter 7, Conditions of Employment, in this handbook.)

12. Is the check supply under lock and key, and are all checks signed manually?

    ☐ Yes

    ☐ No

    The checks should be secured for obvious reasons and be kept under lock and key to prevent stealing.

    Unless a very large organization requires pre-imprinted signatures on checks, the practice should be abolished, as it is very simple for a dishonest person to have bogus signatures imprinted on checks and divert them to their attention. Recovering from a bank would be *very* difficult.

13. Are *two* people involved in preparing payroll and remitting payroll taxes?

    ☐ Yes

    ☐ No

    Stealing through salaries, tax deposit misappropriation, and fringe benefits *is very* easy for a knowledgeable person to implement.

    Simply stated, *two* employees are involved in preparing payroll—one person does the detail and the other employee checks it for accuracy. *Both* employees sign the payroll detail for accuracy.

14. Does the organization have a mechanism in place to spot "Ghosts on the Payroll"?

    ☐ Yes

    ☐ No

    A typical nonemployee's profile would be as follows:

    ➢ The ghost will have a very common surname (Miller, Smith, etc.).

    ➢ The ghost will probably be part-time, as having full-time status complicates things such as insurance, pension, etc.

    ➢ The ghost will rarely cash the check at a bank, as an account number is necessary. They are typically cashed at check cashing services, liquor stores, etc.

    ➢ The ghost will have an excessive number of dependents on his W-4, increasing the net value of the check, as no federal or state income taxes are withheld.

    ➢ The ghost's personnel files rarely note a street address, but rather, indicate a post office box address.

15. Does the organization have a "Conditions of Employment Agreement"?

    ☐ Yes

    ☐ No

    (See Conditions of Employment Agreement, Chapter 7, in this handbook.)

16. Does the organization have a "Conflict of Interest Agreement"?

    ☐ Yes

    ☐ No

    A Conflict of Interest policy is very necessary and in fact is required in the new Form 990.

    It is good business for *all* employees and board members to be advised of the Conflict of Interest Policy in the event a conflict surfaces. This doesn't mean that a Conflict of Interest is bad, but the individual having a conflict is generally required to bring it to light and avoid votes and the like that affect the conflict.

17. Are the organization's internal control policies in writing?

    ☐ Yes

    ☐ No

    It is prudent to have the internal control policies in writing; thereby, everyone is aware of all policies and eliminate excuses.

18. Does the organization's CPA firm or Internal Audit Committee visit the office during the "window of opportunity" for embezzlement?

    ☐ Yes

    ☐ No

    Most experienced CPAs, fraud examiners, and like professionals realize that most embezzlements occur during the "window of opportunity" for embezzlement, which is between the day the auditors complete their audit field work and come back to start the following year's audit. For example, if someone has the opportunity to have a "ghost employee" on the payroll, it makes common sense to hire the ghost after the accountants finish field work and terminate the ghost before the next audit begins.

    A solution is for the auditors to make an unannounced visit to the organization during this period, preferably on a payday. The accountants will test transactions via cash, checks, or credit cards prior to the visit, check payroll accuracy and hand out the paychecks to all employees ensuring that everyone is being paid accurately and there are no ghosts.

    This is a *very effective* practice and surprisingly affordable.

19. Has the organization instructed the bank to not change authorized signers without approval of management?

    ☐ Yes

    ☐ No

    This is very simple—just have the bank include a notice in your files that a change in authorized signers must be approved by the appropriate level of management. This would prevent a dishonest person from adding his or her name as an authorized signer without approval and the like.

20. Does the organization occasionally test cash, check, and credit card transactions?

    ☐ Yes

    ☐ No

    It is very important to occasionally test cash, check, and credit card transactions as follows:

    ➤ For cash purchases, was a receipt given to the purchaser?

    ➤ Also, check to see that the transaction was not voided after the customer left.

    ➤ For checks, ensure that the checks are deposited in the organization's account. (See the Lock Box discussion in this chapter.)

    ➤ For credit card transactions, ensure that the deposits are credited to the organization's merchant number.

21. When employees terminate, does the organization require an "Exit Interview"?

    ☐ Yes

    ☐ No

    During employment, it is understandable that some employees will not bring suspected malfeasance to the attention of the proper person as some people are shy, some are frightened of retaliation and some just don't want to be involved.

    An answer to this would be an Exit Interview. The interviewer should *not* be the individual's immediate supervisor if possible and the interviewer will be provided with questions similar to the following examples:

    ➤ Are you aware of any intentional wrongdoings?

    ➤ Are you suspicious of any?

    ➤ Are there any conflicts of interest that management may not be aware of?

    ➤ Has anyone offered you a bribe?

22. Does the organization prohibit making checks payable to acronyms?

    ☐ Yes

    ☐ No

    As stated in the Lock Box discussion in this chapter, not-for-profit organizations are widely known by their acronyms. For checks disbursed, prohibit having checks made out to an acronym.

23. If the organization is known by its' acronym, does it encourage payment be made to its full legal name?

    ☐ Yes

    ☐ No

Once again, referring to the Lock Box discussion, encourage the payments made to the organization be written out as payable to the organization's legal name rather than an acronym. Obviously, a number of payments will be made payable to the organization's acronym, and this is unavoidable.

24. Does the organization take advantage of their bank's Positive Pay service?

☐ Yes

☐ No

Positive Pay is probably the most effective internal control device currently existing, but surprisingly, very few not-for-profit organizations take advantage of it.

Briefly, get the proper software from the bank and have an IT (information technology) person load it on the organization's computer. There are variations, but Positive Pay exports check data from the organization's computer to the bank's computer. The bank now knows the check numbers, payee, and check amounts. As checks are received by the bank for processing, the bank's computer matches the data to what was transmitted. If anything doesn't match exactly, the bank will not process it. The service virtually eliminates:

➢ Scanning checks and depositing them more than once

➢ Altering checks such as the name of the payee and the amounts

Banks are predicting that Positive Pay will be mandatory and exceptions will have to sign a waiver absolving the bank of responsibility.

25. Did the organization consider eliminating employee credit cards?

☐ Yes

☐ No

It is very common for not-for-profit organizations to eliminate employee credit cards except for the Chief Staff Executive and others on a must-have basis.

By having employees use their personal credit cards, it virtually eliminates credit card abuse, liability on lost or stolen cards, etc.

26. Does the organization require thorough background checks on key employees?

☐ Yes

☐ No

(See Chapter 7, Conditions of Employment Agreement, in this handbook.)

27. Does the organization have approved vendor files, and does it require investigating new vendors?

☐ Yes

☐ No

It is suggested that organizations have approved vendor files for all businesses and individuals it has an on-going relationship with.

Information in the files would list the names of businesses and individuals, street address, and mailing address, Federal Identification number or Social Security number, emergency contact information, and so on.

28. Has the organization researched check or remote deposit scanners?

☐ Yes

☐ No

Check or remote deposit scanners now enhance electronic banking to businesses beyond electronic reporting and movement of funds by bringing the bank teller to the customer. Remote deposit scanners are Web-based and can scan consumer, business, and corporate cashier checks and money orders. For a business, check scanners reduce bank fees and float, eliminate trips to the bank, and completing deposit tickets. Scanners also provide notice of returned items faster since the check deposited is turned into an electronic image/file and transferred through the Federal Reserve to the drawer bank the same night with a response the next day.

There are two general types of scanners: high speed and low speed. Low-speed scanners would be used by organizations that deposit 25 or less checks per day. The low-speed scanners process one check at a time with manual input required for customer name, business or personal check, and amount. The low-speed scanner accumulates all checks scanned during the day into one batch deposit and transmits the batch to the bank. The problem with low-speed scanners is the requirements that an amount needs to be manually entered. Entering an amount lower than the actual check amount will mean a smaller deposit for the company and possibly higher borrowings and/or being in an overdraft stage. An amount being entered that is higher than the actual check amount will cause the customer's bank account to potentially be adversely affected, especially if the customer does not have positive pay or similar program. Without proper controls in place, these errors can occur. It should be noted that until the batch is sent to the bank, amounts can be changed. If an error is caught after the file is sent to the bank, the bank can be contacted and adjustments processed through the Federal Reserve.

The major issue with low-speed scanners is the risk of fraud by entering an amount larger than the actual amount, obtaining collected funds status on that deposit and then withdrawing those funds before the drawer or drawer bank can react.

The second type of scanner is high speed. These scanners do not require manual input other than the requirement for control totals, the total amount of all checks, and the number of checks. High-speed scanners require the creation of a batch with the above control totals. As the scanner processes each check, it creates its own batch totals for number of checks and amount, which can then be verified against the batch totals entered by company personnel. Once the batch is created, the checks are scanned and the batch is closed and transmitted to the bank. Any number of batches can be created, and transmitted during the day; but once a batch is closed, it cannot be changed. The high-speed scanners therefore eliminate the risk of amount error or fraud from changing the amount.

In all cases of using a scanner, the physical checks should be locked in a secure location once they are scanned for deposit to prevent theft and fraud, even though an endorsement is applied to the back of the check as part of the scanning process. The checks should then be destroyed within 45 days from date of deposit to allow for the bank statement to be reconciled.

Remote check scanners have eliminated the need for courier services that pick up check deposits from companies to transport to the bank. Scanners give users the benefit, depending on the bank, to process deposits as late as 10 P.M. When a transaction can be turned into an image to be submitted to the Federal Reserve, it increases the speed by which the transaction is completed.

As stated in the beginning of this item, scanners use and require Web-based programs or software similar to what is required for Internet banking. Scanners are as safe as Internet banking in general, the organization's firewall, and its Internet service provider. (This also includes keeping applicable software and operating systems patched and updated.) Each user of a scanner should have his or her own user ID and password.

As with any new technology, there is a good side and bad side. Detecting check fraud may be more difficult from the examination of a copy rather than the real check as modifications and signature forgeries will be harder to prove or see. Hopefully, faster processing time will allow for identification of fraud more quickly and less paper documents will reduce the risk of loss of personal and bank information.

Summary

This checklist is, of course, just a short *managerial* evaluation of the organization's existing controls. Hopefully, the answers to most if not all of the above questions are "yes." If not, give serious consideration to a thorough analysis of your internal controls and make changes for improvement accordingly to ensure your organization's assets are protected.

The Fraud Triangle

A few disturbing facts:

> ➤ People do not know what is going on in other peoples' personal lives!

➤ In almost every situation where fraud has been discovered, the guilty party is the person *above* suspicion!

➤ And finally . . . remember that the purpose of effective internal controls is to *keep honest people honest* by removing the "opportunity" factor of the fraud triangle, as shown in Exhibit 10.1!

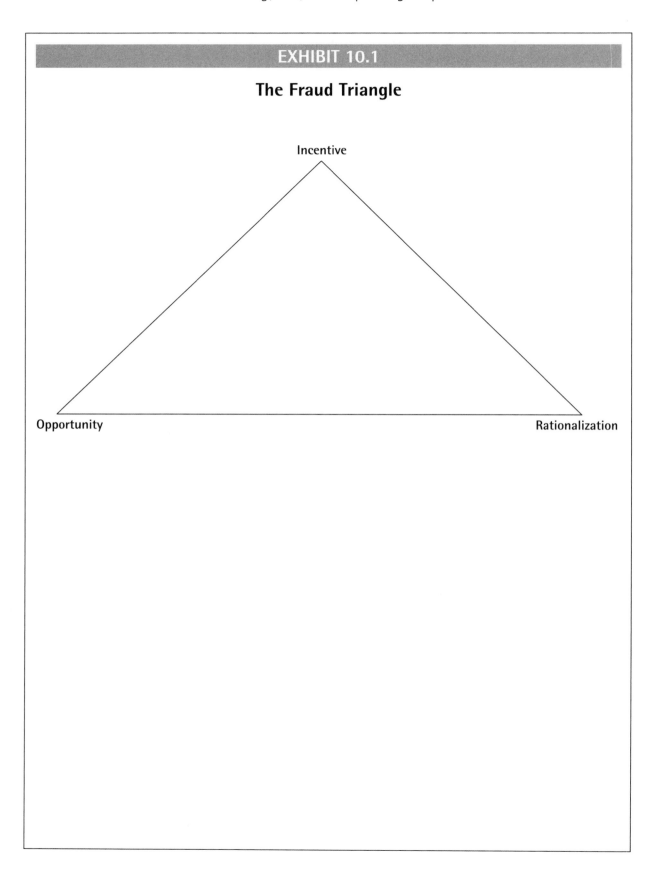

Documenting a Fraud Action Plan

Obviously, no one wants to be the victim of a fraud scheme, but possible victimization is a reality that all organizations face. A prudent business practice is to have a preplanned and well-thought-out strategy of action to take if fraud is suspected. A draft of such a plan follows:

1. Never ever accuse anyone of an impropriety—get the facts.

Remember that you may be wrong. If you are, there is a probability that you will be on the wrong end of a defamation lawsuit. Be patient and thoroughly investigate the situation before any action is taken.

2. Contact an employment law attorney.

If you suspect fraud, get advice on how to proceed from a competent employment law attorney familiar with your state and federal employment law. This is a very important step in avoiding any associated legal issues concerning termination for fraud.

3. Contact your independent CPA.

Inform your independent CPA firm that fraud is suspected and inquire if they are competent in the areas of fraud investigation, forensic accounting, and so forth. If they don't feel comfortable in this area, ask them to recommend a CPA firm that is experienced in this area.

Once you have contacted the right CPA firm, they will assist you with the investigation, help with any insurance claims, prepare for going to trial if necessary, and handle other important areas suggested in this plan of action.

4. Work from copies.

When you initially contacted your independent CPA firm, they will tell you the importance of protecting the evidence and working from copies of original documents related to the incident.

Place the original documents in a safe deposit box or safe location that the offender does not have access to. Remember that copies of documents are often not admissible as evidence in court, and if original documents are lost, stolen or altered, a valuable aspect of your criminal case, insurance claims, and the like may be compromised.

5. Take detailed, copious notes.

Again, when you initially contacted your independent CPA, you would be told of the importance of taking detailed and thorough notes of everything related to the incident.

Realistically, it may be *years* before going to trial after the incident is discovered, and anything can happen in the meantime: an understandable loss of memory, people retiring, people resigning, and so forth. When detailed notes are taken, a full record of the incident would be available to another employee, attorneys, CPAs, and the like.

6. Read your Fidelity Bond!

After review, note important provisions of your bond in this plan of action, such as police report requirements, required time frame to file a claim with the insurance company, and so forth.

7. Review the Conditions of Employment agreement.

This is always an uncomfortable situation, but the stress may be relieved somewhat if the employee was required to sign the important Conditions of Employment agreement whereby the employee has acknowledged that he or she understands what to expect in the event of a fraud investigation.

Note: Please reference and read thoroughly the "Conditions of Employment Agreement" in Exhibit 7.1.

Steps 8 through 16 are concerned with actually confronting the alleged perpetrator and are included in the agreement.

8. Do not discuss the situation in the employee's office, cubicle, or other work area.

Never have this discussion in the employee's office, but rather in an executive's office, conference room, library, or another neutral location. Remember that the offender's office almost assuredly contains vital evidence related to the incident. Never allow an offender access to this evidence because it will be important to forensic accountants, attorneys, police detectives, insurance company, and so forth.

9. Always have a witness.

At a minimum, the termination discussion should *always* include a witness selected by management, regardless of the nature of the situation. This witness is of particular importance in the event of any form of a male-versus-female confrontation. If a man finds it necessary to confront a woman, the witness should always be another woman. Conversely, if a woman has to confront a man, the witness should be another man.

Obviously, the purpose of the male/female confrontation witness is to avoid any allegations of sexual impropriety and for physical protection of the woman.

It is possible that other witnesses may be required, such as your attorney, CPA, or other persons essential to the case.

10. Protect yourself and other employees.

It is a sad commentary on our society, but realistically, violence in the work place is common.

If there is even a *hint* that this is a possibility, contact your local police department for advice. Often they will either send a uniformed officer to sit in on the discussion or allow off-duty officers to provide this service for a fee. Regardless, the police department will be prepared to offer assistance as to how to proceed.

11. Change computer passwords!

While the discussion is taking place, have an information technology (IT) representative void the suspect's computer passwords and address any other important IT issues such as email access and so forth. Failure to do this could result in the suspected offender's accessing the system off-site, compromising important data, and so forth.

12. Have the discussion during no business hours.

Ensure that the confrontation takes place before or after regular business hours. The purpose of this, of course, is to avoid an unnecessary office scene, embarrassment, and the like.

13. Ensure surrender of organization property.

The employee should be required to surrender organization property such as door keys, credit cards, and so forth. It may also be necessary to have the locks changed.

14. Employee should not collect his/her personal property from the office.

Have two employees go to the offender's office to remove important personal effects such as a purse, wallet, car keys, and the like. Two employees should always do this to avoid any accusations of theft of cash.

15. Escort the perpetrator from the office.

Never allow the employee to return to his or her office—remember, the office contains valuable evidence important to the fraud investigation, forensic accountants, and attorneys, and if the employee has access to evidence it could affect the integrity of the case.

16. Have other employee property gathered by coworkers.

Inform the offender that nonessential employee property such as photos will be gathered by two employees, and these items will be couriered to the employee's residence the following business day.

17. Make notes of the discussion.

After the discussion, the executive and the witness should compile detailed notes of the discussion. The notes should include, at a minimum, the following:

➤ Date and time of the discussion

➤ Names and contact information of the executive, witness, police officers, CPA, attorney, and the like.

➤ The offender's physical reactions to questioning

➤ Other important information as needed

The purpose of these notes is to provide detail needed by attorneys and accountants in the event that litigation is necessary.

18. Get a police report, if necessary.

On advice of your attorney, don't neglect to file a police report of the incident, as this report is required of Fidelity Bond claims, forensic accounting data, litigation strategy, and so forth.

19. Proceed with a Fidelity Bond claim.

It is very common for management to take the Fidelity Bond (employee dishonesty insurance) for granted and not know who is included on the bond, the amount of the bond, and actions to take to proceed with a claim.

20. Prosecute?

The perpetrator should be aware that the organization (or the Fidelity Bond carrier) may prosecute the offender in the event of employee dishonesty.

The Conditions of Employment agreement should clearly state that prosecution may lead to a criminal record. Criminal records are public information and discoverable by subsequent employers pursuing background checks on prospective employees, significantly damaging the offender's prospects for employment.

Obviously, the discussion to prosecute would be made on a case-by-case basis, but material dishonesty should always be prosecuted. If there is no prosecution, there is no record, and the offender could perpetrate the scam on an unsuspecting subsequent employer.

21. Decide how to relate the circumstances of dismissal to others.

Get advice of counsel on how to handle relating circumstances of the termination:

➤ Internally with staff

➤ With inquiring customers, and so forth

➤ With regard to reference checks by subsequent employers

22. And when it's all over . . .

Reconstruct the details of the occurrence and change procedures so that it cannot happen again!

Check 21

In November 2004, the U.S. Congress passed Check 21. The effect of this legislation is to allow banks to retain and forward to the bank holders *images* of checks rather than sending the original checks with the bank statement. This system is much more efficient. Also, this makes having a copy of the bank statements mailed off-site very affordable.

Check 21 is a direct result of September 11, 2001, as when commercial airlines were grounded, an unaccountable number of checks contained in their cargo holds were stalled. This directly affected worldwide cash flow.

Banks now scan an image of cashed checks for their records and forward the image to the original banks that retain the image for their records and forward the images to the account holder.

The reason this required a law is that now the images are treated as legal substitutes of the original checks and allowed to be submitted as evidence in legal proceedings. The original checks are eventually destroyed.

11

Using CPA Firms and Understanding Their Functions

THE RELATIONSHIP BETWEEN THE NOT-FOR-PROFIT organization and its independent CPA firm is important, but the function of the CPA firm is often misunderstood. Typically, a not-for-profit organization enters a relationship with an independent CPA firm because of a requirement in its bylaws or because it is forced into the relationship by a third party. Examples of third parties requiring not-for-profit organizations to be audited are lending institutions, government granting agencies, and foundations giving grants.

This chapter discusses three types of services CPA firms offer not-for-profit organizations—audits, reviews, and compilations—as well as other services firms sometimes offer.

Audits

A certified audit by an independent CPA firm is the most common service used by a not-for-profit organization. In an audit, the CPA firm expresses an opinion on the not-for-profit organization's financial statements. To be legally qualified to audit an organization and express an opinion on its financial statements, the CPA firm must have a license issued by the state board of public accountancy. By law, *only* certified public accountants are entitled to audit organizations and express an opinion on their accuracy. The objective of an audit is to assure the reader of the financial statements that the statements have been audited, that they conform to Generally Accepted Accounting Principles (GAAP), and that the audit is done according to Generally Accepted Auditing Standards (GAAS).

Once the audit fieldwork has been completed, the CPA firm issues one of four types of opinions on the financial statements: unqualified opinion, qualified opinion, adverse opinion, or disclaimer of opinion. It is important to recognize the differences in the four opinions. The various opinions affect the organization's ability to borrow money and the membership's perception of the capacity of management to professionally manage the financial operation.

Unqualified Opinion

Every not-for-profit organization should strive to receive an unqualified opinion on its financial statements from the CPA firm auditing it. Unqualified opinions state that the financial statements are "presented fairly"; these opinions are, in essence, a clean bill of health. Full assurance on the accuracy of the financial statements is provided to the reader.

Audits of financial statements issued by an independent CPA firm will include, at a minimum, the following:

1. Opinion Letter on the CPA firm's letterhead
2. Statement of Financial Position (Balance Sheet)
3. Statement of Activities (Income Statement)
4. Statement of Changes in Net Assets
5. Statement of Cash Flows
7. Footnotes to the financial statements

An example of the wording of an unqualified opinion is shown in Exhibit 11.1.

EXHIBIT 11.1

Independent Auditors' Report—Unqualified Opinion

To the Members of the Board
[Not-for-Profit Organization]

We have audited the accompanying Statements of Financial Position of [Not-for-Profit Organization, dates], and the related Statements of Activities, Functional Expenses, and Cash Flows for the years then ended. These financial statements are the responsibility of the Organization's management. Our responsibility is to express an opinion on these financial statements based on our audit.

We conducted our audits in accordance with auditing standards generally accepted in the United States of America. Those standards require that we plan and perform the audits to obtain reasonable assurance about whether the financial statements are free of material misstatement. An audit includes examining, on a test basis, evidence supporting the amounts and disclosures in the financial statements. An audit also includes assessing the accounting principles used and significant estimates made by management, as well as evaluating the overall financial statement presentation. We believe that our audits provide a reasonable basis for our opinion.

In our opinion, the financial statements referred to above present fairly, in all material respects, the financial position of ___[Not-for-Profit Organization, dates]___, and the results of its operations and its cash flows for the years then ended in conformity with accounting principles generally accepted in the United States of America.

_____

Firm's Signature

_____

Location of firm (city, state)

_____, 20_____

Date

Qualified Opinion

A qualified opinion on the financial statements suggests that there is a material problem with one or more aspects of the statements. In other words, the CPA firm is stating that except for this problem (or problems), the financial statements have been presented fairly. A qualified opinion is saying "except for" a material problem, everything else is satisfactory.

An example of the wording of a qualified opinion is shown in Exhibit 11.2.

EXHIBIT 11.2

Independent Auditors' Report—Qualified Opinion

To the Members of the Board
[Not-for-Profit Organization]

We have audited the accompanying statement of Financial Position of ___[Not-for-Profit Organization]___ as of ___[Date]___ , and the related Statements of Activities, Net Assets, and Cash Flows for the year then ended. These financial statements are the responsibility of the organization's management. Our responsibility is to express an opinion on these financial statements based on our audit.

We conducted our audit in Accordance with Generally Accepted Auditing Standards. Those standards require that we plan and perform the audit to obtain reasonable assurance about whether the financial statements are free of material misstatement. An audit includes examining, on a test basis, evidence supporting the amounts and disclosures in the financial statements. An audit also includes assessing the accounting principles used and estimates made by management, as well as evaluating the overall financial statement presentation. We believe that our audit provides a reasonable basis for our opinion.

As more fully described in Note ___ to the financial statements, the organization has valued property and equipment at a nominal value of one dollar. Also, the organization leases its premises under an agreement that provides for a nominal annual rental of one dollar. In recognition of that rental agreement, the Board of Directors established a value of $_____ for the lease in 20X0. That amount was capitalized and is being amortized over a ___-year period ending 20X0. In our opinion, property and equipment should be recorded at cost, if purchased, or at fair value, if donated or contributed, to conform with Generally Accepted Accounting Principles, and those amounts should be depreciated over the estimated useful lives of the assets. Also, in our opinion, the value to the organization of its use of space at nominal rent should be shown as a period expense with a corresponding addition to paid-in or contributed capital. The effects on the financial statements of the preceding practices are not reasonably determinable.

In our opinion, except for the effects of the matters discussed in the preceding paragraph, the financial statements referred to in the first paragraph present fairly, in all material respects, the financial position of [Not-for-Profit Organization]___ as of ___[Date]___ , and the results of its operations and its cash flows for the year then ended in conformity with United States Generally Accepted Accounting Principles.

_____
Firm's signature

_____
Location of firm (city, state)

_____, 20_____
Date

Adverse Opinion

An adverse opinion is unusual. By issuing such an opinion, the independent CPA firm is saying that the financial statements do not conform with GAAP and are not presented fairly.

An example of the wording of an adverse opinion is shown in Exhibit 11.3.

EXHIBIT 11.3

Independent Auditors' Report—Adverse Opinion

To the Members of the Board
[Not-for-Profit Organization]

As discussed in Note X to the financial statements, the organization carries its property, plant, and equipment accounts at appraisal values and provides depreciation on the basis of such values. Further, the organization does not provide for income taxes with respect to differences between financial income and taxable income arising because of the use, for income tax purposes, of the installment method of reporting gross profit from certain types of sales. Generally Accepted Accounting Principles require that property, plant, and equipment be stated at an amount not in excess of cost, reduced by depreciation based on such amount, and that deferred income taxes be provided.

Because of the departures from Generally Accepted Accounting Principles identified above, as of December 31, 20X2 and 20X1, inventories have been increased $_____$ and $_____$ by inclusion in manufacturing overhead of depreciation in excess of that based on cost, property, plant, and equipment, less accumulated depreciation, is carried at $_____$ and $_____$ in excess of an amount based on the cost to the organization; and deferred income taxes of $_____$ and $_____$ have not been recorded, resulting in an increase of $_____$ and $_____$ in retained earnings and in appraisal surplus of $_____$ and $_____$, respectively. For the years ended December 31, 20X2 and 20X1, cost of goods sold has been increased $_____$ and $_____$, respectively, because of the effects of the depreciation accounting referred to above, and deferred income taxes of $_____$ and $_____$ have not been provided, resulting in an increase in net income of $_____$ and $_____$, respectively.

In our opinion, because of the effects of the matters discussed in the preceding paragraphs, the financial statements referred to above do not present fairly, in conformity with United States Generally Accepted Accounting Principles, the financial position of X Organization as of December 31, 20X2 and 20X1, or the results of its operations or its cash flows for the years then ended.

_____
Firm's signature

_____
Location of firm (city, state)

_____, 20_____
Date

Disclaimer of Opinion

Disclaimers of opinion by independent CPA firms are unusual and generally are issued because of litigation, the unavailability of records, or other issues that would make the financial statements unreliable and unpredictable.

An example of the wording of a disclaimer of opinion is shown in Exhibit 11.4.

EXHIBIT 11.4

Independent Auditors' Report—Disclaimer of Opinion
(lawyer's letter not obtained)

To the Members of the Board
[Not-for-Profit Organization]

We were engaged to audit the accompanying Statement of Financial Position of __[Not-for-Profit__ Organization]__ as of __[Month]__ 31, 20____, and the related Statements of Financial Position, Net Assets, and Cash Flows for the year then ended. These financial statements are the responsibility of the organization's management.

We were unable to obtain a discussion or evaluation of the pending or threatened litigation described in Note X from the organization's outside legal counsel. Because of this, the scope of our work was not sufficient to enable us to express an opinion on the financial statements referred to in the first paragraph.

_____
Firm's signature

_____
Location of firm (city, state)

_____, 20____
Date

Review

Often circumstances do not require a full audit of the financial records. The next step down from an audit is a review of the financial statements.

In a review, the CPA firm does not adhere to rigid auditing standards and instead principally applies analytical procedures to financial data and its inquiries of personnel. Because the review is narrower in scope than an audit, it is not considered an opinion. Reviews provide limited assurance of the accuracy of the financial statements to the reader.

An example of the wording in a review is shown in Exhibit 11.5.

EXHIBIT 11.5

Independent Auditors' Report—Review

To the Board of Directors
[Not-for-Profit Organization]

   I (We) have reviewed the accompanying Statement of Financial Position of   [Not-for-Profit   Organization]   as of   [Date] , 20____, and the related Statements of Activities, Net Assets, and Cash Flows for the year then ended, in accordance with standards established by the American Institute of Certified Public Accountants. All information included in these financial statements is the representation of management.

   A review consists principally of inquiries of organization personnel and analytical procedures applied to financial data. It is substantially less in scope than an audit in accordance with Generally Accepted Auditing Standards, the objective of which is the expression of an opinion regarding the financial statements taken as a whole. Accordingly, I (we) do not express such an opinion.

   Based on my (our) reviews, I am (we are) not aware of any material modifications that should be made to the accompanying financial statements in order for them to be in conformity with United States Generally Accepted Accounting Principles.

_____

Firm's signature

_____

Location of firm (city, state)

_____, 20____

Date

Compilation

Often an organization wants a relationship with a CPA firm but cannot afford or does not need an audit or a review. The next step down is called a *compilation*.

In a compilation, the CPA firm does not apply any auditing standards or analytical procedures at all. It presents the financial statements in the proper financial formats, but the financial statements are the representation of management. No assurance at all on the accuracy of the statements is provided to the reader by the CPA firm. An example of the wording of a compilation is shown in Exhibit 11.6.

EXHIBIT 11.6

Independent Auditors' Report—Compilation

To the Members of the Board
[Not-for-Profit Organization]

   I (We) have compiled the accompanying Statement of Financial Position of __[Not-for-Profit Organization]__ as of __[Date]__ , 20____, and the related Statements of Activities, Net Assets, and Cash Flows for the year then ended, in accordance with standards established by the American Institute of Certified Public Accountants.

   A compilation is limited to presenting, in the form of financial statements, information that is the representation of management. I (We) have not audited or reviewed the accompanying financial statements and, accordingly, do not express an opinion or any other form of assurance on them.

_____

Firm's signature

_____

Location of firm (city, state)

_____, 20____

Date

Other Services

Not-for-profit organizations often contract with independent CPA firms for other services, sometimes not related at all to accounting or tax, where independence is required or expertise in certain areas may be needed.

An example of using a CPA firm's reputation for independence is to use the firm to count ballots in an election. If ballots are sent directly to the CPA firm and the CPA firm deals with a tellers committee directly, possible ballot tampering by management is virtually eliminated.

Examples of using CPA firms for their expertise in certain areas include data processing services, management consulting services, and the preparation of tax returns.

Choosing a CPA Firm

Because of the relationship between the not-for-profit organization and the independent CPA firm, it is important to choose the right CPA firm. The most important factor in choosing a CPA firm to audit the financial records of a not-for-profit organization is selecting a firm that specializes in not-for-profit organizations. The accounting principles and taxation issues of not-for-profit organizations are different from those for commercial organizations.

Request for Proposal

A simple and objective way to choose a CPA firm is to send a request for proposal (RFP) to CPA firms specializing in not-for-profit organizations. Reliable resources for finding names of such firms include local and state societies of CPAs and allied societies of the American Society of Association Executives.

To save time and avoid confusion for both the organization and the CPA firms, the RFP should be detailed and should state exactly the services required by the organization. A CPA firm should be told specifically what to expect if it is selected for the audit. An example of an RFP for auditing services is shown in Exhibit 11.7.

EXHIBIT 11.7

Request for Proposal for Accounting Services

[Not-for-Profit Organization Letterhead]
[Date]
Smith & Jones, Certified Public Accountants
123 Main Street
Washington, DC

Dear _____:

    Your firm has been selected as a candidate to provide tax, accounting, and auditing services for our organization and its affiliates. We encourage you to submit your proposal for consideration.

    To help you in the preparation of your response, we have enclosed information on our organization and have included our annual report, membership brochures, a magazine, a newsletter, publication brochures, training workshop brochures, and audited financial statements.

Organization Specifics

Headquarters Address: _____

IRS Classification: 501(c)(___)

Number of Members or Contributors: _____

Fiscal Year: From _____ to _____

Approximate Number of Revenue Transactions: _____

Approximate Number of Expense Transactions: _____

Affiliated Entities Requiring Audits: _____

Services Required:

Audited Financial Statements

Tax Return Preparation:

Form 990

Form 990-T

Personal Property Tax Return

State Returns

Staff Contact

Please direct your proposal to _____, our chief financial officer, at the above address.

Selection Criteria

This request for proposal is being sent to CPA firms specializing in audits of not-for-profit organizations.

Of those responding, _____ firms will be selected to interview with the organization's board of directors, who will make the final selection. The interview will last no longer than _____ minutes. The interview will consist of a presentation by the CPA firm of no more than _____ minutes, followed by _____ minutes of questions.

Notification Date

Firms selected for an interview will be noted no later than _____.
Firms not selected will be notified on the same date.

Selection of the firm to be retained will be announced no later than _____.

Information Required

Please include with your response the following information about your firm:

1. A brief history of your organization

2. Credentials of individuals who will be assigned to the audit

3. A reference listing of _____ not-for-profit organizations including contact name

4. Your written permission to contact your references

5. Anticipated fee for services

Deadline Date

To be eligible for consideration, your response must be postmarked by _____.
Deadline extensions will not be granted.

We trust the information provided in this request for proposal is sufficient, but if further information is required, please limit your inquiries to the staff contact noted.

Thank you for your time, and we are looking forward to receiving your proposal. Sincerely,

_____

Name

_____

Title

From the proposals received, the organization should select the firms for the interview with the appropriate body.

The Interview

The interview should last no longer than 45 minutes. It has two stages: a short presentation by the CPA firm and questions directed to the CPA firm.

The interview team should consist of, at a minimum, the organization's chief staff executive, chief financial officer, and representatives of the board of directors, specifically the treasurer and chief elected officer. Additionally, if an organization has an audit committee, it also should be represented.

The questions posed to CPA firm representatives are important. Prepare your questions in advance, and ask the same questions of each firm being interviewed. Note and evaluate the responses. Ask questions to help you gauge the respondent's knowledge of issues important to not-for-profit organizations. Questions may concern the following:

1. Current IRS issues affecting not-for-profits

2. Current legislation affecting not-for-profits

3. Current accounting issues affecting not-for-profits

4. The CPA firm's opinion on specific tax issues pertinent to your organization

As in any budgeting process, the most qualified firm with the lowest fee should be selected for the audit. Once a firm has been selected, the not-for-profit organization should expect the following sequence of events:

1. An engagement letter

2. Audit fieldwork

3. Issuance of audited financial statements

4. Issuance of the management letter

The Engagement Letter

Representatives of the not-for-profit should meet with representatives of the auditing firm to discuss the engagement letter. The not-for-profit can use the engagement letter as an opportunity to control audit fees and to ensure that audited financial statements will be issued by a certain date and that tax returns will be prepared by a certain date.

Audit fees can be controlled by reviewing the CPA firm's previous year's working papers to ascertain what task can be performed by staff internally instead of by the auditors and discussing how record keeping can be improved to reduce auditor involvement. One way to control audit fees is to have your organization's staff prepare every accounting schedule. Then, all the auditing firm has to do is audit the supporting schedules related to the financial statements. It is likely to be more cost effective to have your staff prepare accounting schedules at their hourly rates than to have a CPA firm do it at its hourly rate.

An example of an Engagement Letter is shown on Exhibit 11.8.

EXHIBIT 11.8

Engagement Letter

Note: The actual Engagement letter will include numerous footnotes.
[CPA Firm's Letterhead]
[Date]
[Name and Address of Nonprofit Organization]

Dear _____:

We are pleased to confirm our understanding of the services we are to provide for   [Name of Nonprofit Organization]   for the   [period, year, or years]   ended   [Date(s)] .

We will audit the statement(s) of financial position of   [Name of Nonprofit Organization]   as of [Period or Year End(s)] , and the related statements of ____ for the   [period, year, or years]   then ended. Also, the following additional information accompanying the basic financial statements [will/will not] be subjected to the auditing procedures applied in our audit of the financial statements:

    A. [ ]
    B. [ ]
    C. [ ]

We will also prepare the Organization's federal and state information returns for the   [period OR year] ended   [Date(s)] .

Audit Objective

The objective of our audit is the expression of an opinion about whether your financial statements are fairly presented, in all material respects, in conformity with U.S. Generally Accepted Accounting Principles. Our audit will be conducted in accordance with auditing standards generally accepted in the United States of America and will include tests of your accounting records and other procedures we consider necessary to enable us to express such an opinion. If our opinion is other than unqualified, we will discuss the reasons with you in advance. If, for any reason, we are unable to complete the audit or are unable to form or have not formed an opinion, we may decline to express an opinion or to issue a report as a result of this engagement.

Audit Procedures

Our procedures will include tests of documentary evidence supporting the transactions recorded in the accounts, tests of the physical existence of inventories, and direct confirmation of receivables and certain assets and liabilities by correspondence with selected individuals, funding sources, creditors, and financial institutions. We will also request written representations from the Organization's attorneys as part of the engagement, and they may bill you for responding to this inquiry. At the conclusion of our audit, we will require certain written representations from you about the financial statements and related matters.

An audit includes examining, on a test basis, evidence supporting the amounts and disclosures in the financial statements; therefore, our audit will involve judgment about the number of transactions to be examined and the areas to be tested. We will plan and perform the audit to obtain reasonable assurance about whether the financial statements are free of material misstatement, whether from (1) errors, (2) fraudulent financial reporting, (3) misappropriation of assets, or (4) violations of laws or governmental regulations that are attributable to the Organization or to acts by management or employees acting on behalf of the Organization.

Because an audit is designed to provide reasonable, but not absolute, assurance and because we will not perform a detailed examination of all transactions, there is a risk that material misstatements may exist and not be detected by us. In addition, an audit is not designed to detect immaterial misstatements or violations of laws or governmental regulations that do not have a direct and material effect on the financial statements. However, we will inform you of any material errors and any fraudulent financial reporting or misappropriation of assets that come to our attention. We will also inform you of any violations of laws or governmental regulations that come to our attention, unless clearly inconsequential. Our responsibility as auditors is limited to the period covered by our audit and does not extend to any later periods for which we are not engaged as auditors.

Our audit will include obtaining an understanding of the Organization and its environment, including internal control, sufficient to assess the risks of material misstatement of the financial statements and to design the nature, timing, and extent of further audit procedures. An audit is not designed to provide assurance on internal control or to identify deficiencies in internal control. However, during the audit, we will communicate to you and those charged with governance internal control related matters that are required to be communicated under professional standards.

We may from time to time, and depending on the circumstances, use third-party service providers in serving your account. We may share confidential information about you with these service providers, but remain committed to maintaining the confidentiality and security of your information. Accordingly, we maintain internal policies, procedures, and safeguards to protect the confidentiality of your personal information. In addition, we will secure confidentiality agreements with all service providers to maintain the confidentiality of your information and we will take reasonable precautions to determine that they have appropriate procedures in place to prevent the unauthorized release of your confidential information to others. In the event that we are unable to secure an appropriate confidentiality agreement, you will be asked to provide your consent prior to the sharing of your confidential information with the third-party service provider. Furthermore, we will remain responsible for the work provided by any such third-party service providers.

Management Responsibilities

You are responsible for making all management decisions and performing all management functions; for designating an individual with suitable skill, knowledge, or experience to oversee the tax services and any other nonattest services we provide; and for evaluating the adequacy and results of those services and accepting responsibility for them.

You are responsible for establishing and maintaining internal controls, including monitoring ongoing activities; for the selection and application of accounting principles, and for the fair presentation in the financial statements of financial position, changes in net assets, and cash flows in conformity with U.S. Generally Accepted Accounting Principles. You are also responsible for making all financial records and related information available to us and for the accuracy and completeness of that information. Your responsibilities include adjusting the financial statements to correct material misstatements and confirming to us in the management representation letter that the effects of any uncorrected misstatements aggregated by us during the current engagement and pertaining to the latest period presented are immaterial, both individually and in the aggregate, to the financial statements taken as a whole.

You are responsible for the design and implementation of programs and controls to prevent and detect fraud, and for informing us about all known or suspected fraud affecting the Organization involving (1) management, (2) employees who have significant roles in internal control, and (3) others where the fraud could have a material effect on the financial statements. Your responsibilities include informing us of your knowledge of any allegations of fraud or suspected fraud affecting the Organization received in communications from employees, former employees, grantors, regulators, or others. In addition, you are responsible for identifying and ensuring the Organization complies with applicable laws and regulations and for taking timely and appropriate steps to remedy any fraud, illegal acts, or violations of contracts or grant agreements that we may report.

Engagement Administration, Fees, and Other
We understand that your employees will prepare all cash, accounts receivable, and other confirmations we request and will locate any documents selected by us for testing.

[Name of Engagement Partner]   is the engagement partner and is responsible for supervising the engagement and signing the report or authorizing another individual to sign it. We expect to being our audit on approximately   [Date] and to complete your information returns and issue our report no later than [Date] .

We estimate that our fees for these services will range from $ ____ to $____ for the audit and $____ to $____ for the information returns. You will also be billed for travel and other out-of-pocket costs such as report production, word processing, postage, etc. Additional expenses are estimated to be $____. The fee estimate is based on anticipated cooperation from your personnel and the assumption that unexpected circumstances will not be encountered during the audit. If significant additional time is necessary, we will discuss it with you and arrive at a new fee estimate before we incur the additional costs. Our invoices for these fees will be rendered each month as work progresses and are payable on presentation. In accordance with our firm policies, work may be suspended if your account becomes ____ days or more overdue and will not be resumed until your account is paid in full. If we elect to terminate our services for nonpayment, our engagement will be deemed to have been completed upon written notification of termination, even if we have not completed our report. You will be obligated to compensate us for all time expended and to reimburse us for all out-of-pocket expenditures through the date of termination

We appreciate the opportunity to be of service to you and believe this letter accurately summarizes the significant terms of our engagement. If you have any questions, please let us know. If you agree with the terms of our engagement as described in this letter, please sign the enclosed copy and return it to us.

Very truly yours,

 [CPA Firm's Name]

RESPONSE

This letter correctly sets forth the understanding of___[Name of Nonprofit Organization]___.

Officer signature: _____

Title: _____

Date: _____

Audit Fieldwork

Once an agreement has been reached by the not-for-profit organization and the CPA firm via the engagement letter, the CPA firm starts the audit fieldwork. During this segment of the audit, the auditors work at the client's office. It is typically viewed as an inconvenience by the organization's staff, and a good auditing firm is sensitive to this fact. However, fieldwork is a necessary part of the audit sequence. The time auditors spend on-site can be reduced if records are in proper order, staff have prepared supporting schedules, and the organization is ready to be audited.

Issuance of Audited Financial Statements

Once fieldwork is complete, the audit working papers are reviewed by senior CPAs and partners before the audited financial statements are prepared. Assuming no problems exist, the statements are prepared and distributed to the not-for-profit organization.

It is the auditor's responsibility to deliver the statements to top *staff* management of the organization. The statements are, however, addressed to the board of directors. It is the responsibility of the chief executive officer, the chief financial officer, or both to distribute the audited financial statements to the board of directors.

Issuance of the Management Letter

During the audit, the CPA firm may discover problems that affect the general operational effectiveness of the not-for-profit. If, in the professional opinion of the CPA firm, these problems are material, the firm is required to report the issues to the board of directors via the CPA management letter.

The management letter is an important document and is designed to be a management tool. The not-for-profit should consider all problems noted as being important to the organization and be prepared to take corrective action. Management of the not-for-profit should view the management letter as an opportunity for the CPA firm to report to the board on problems and recommendations about which management has been unable to convince the board that action is required. Examples include understaffing, obsolete equipment, and uncompetitive salary ranges.

Typically, a representative of the CPA firm will make himself or herself available to discuss both the audited financial statements and the management letter with the organization's board of directors. It is the board's responsibility to direct staff to correct deficiencies noted in the management letter and to follow up accordingly.

Hints

Unfortunately, it is common for a not-for-profit organization to pay for an expensive and time-consuming audit by a CPA firm, and then not use the audited financial statements to the organization's advantage. Rather than just filing the audited statements, consider the following:

1. Reduce the possibility of an IRS audit by attaching a copy of the audited financial statements to the organization's IRS Form 990 and 990-T or any other document subject to audit, such as personal property tax returns. (See Chapter 4, Tax on Unrelated Business Income and Form 990-T, for further explanation.)

2. Send a copy to the organization's bank and instruct it to start a file.

3. Send a copy to the organization's insurance company.

4. Store a copy off premises in a safe deposit box with a copy of the organization's annual report. In case of a fire or other catastrophe, an organization's historical perspective could be lost if information is not stored off-site.

5. Consider publishing the audited financial statements in the organization's newsletter.

Another helpful hint concerns that common frustration of spending needless hours compiling a list of CPA firms in order to distribute the Request for Proposal. The reason is that the accounting profession is very large and many CPA firms do not work in not-for-profit auditing, tax, reporting, and so on. While it is relatively easy to compile such a listing of large firms that *specialize* in not-for-profit issues and firms located in such areas as Washington, D.C., Chicago, and other cities that host not-for-profit organizations, it can be difficult for a not-for-profit organization to contact the right CPA firm if it is located in an area with relatively few not-for-profit organizations. Remember, contacting the right CPA firm is *crucially* important, as the auditing standards, accounting, taxation, and reporting requirements are substantially different from those of commercial businesses.

Rather than compile such a list, contact the state association (or society) of CPAs. When their members renew their memberships, they check off various specialties, including not-for-profit organizations. Simply contact the state organization and request a listing of not-for-profit specialization firms. This can save considerable time and frustration.

12

Grant Accounting and Auditing

BEING AWARDED A GRANT for many not-for-profit organizations significantly improves cash flow and budget goals and enhances their presence in both the public and not-for-profit sectors. When an organization is awarded a grant, certain basic rules and guidelines pertain to grant accounting and auditing. This chapter surveys them.

Understanding the Grant

Grant awards come through a variety of sources and are provided for a wide array of purposes. The grant process begins with the grantee's application, in which the organization requests consideration for a funding to be used for a special purpose. These applications are hugely important. The larger the award, the more complex the application process and the more information is required. The application process usually involves reporting organization-wide information about the organization's operations, programs, mission, and financial position. Often a detailed narrative is required to discuss how the grant will be used, what programs are needed, and what outcome is anticipated. A budget is developed and included in the application that details the cost to implement and operate the project.

Since the grant is awarded based on the application, most granting agencies incorporate all or part of the grant application into the grant agreement. Therefore, performance is expected—based on the information provided at the onset, the kind of program or project, the budget, and the final outcome measurements—forecasted by the applicant.

It is impossible to adequately address the specifics of grants in detail, since they are so varied in their complexity. When preparing a grant, it is necessary to be accurate in the application about the time required to plan and implement, and the likely measurements of the project's initial success. New programs, particularly those geared toward hard-to-serve segments of the population or those that require community participation, often are not as successful at the onset. (On the contrary, the best of these programs have taken years to become known, accepted and utilized by the community.) Plan wisely the advertising and marketing budget, in time and expense, and be reasonable about the development of a successful project over time.

The grant agreement is the source of most of the information needed for compliance, and though the grantee believes it has an understanding of what is required, the granting agency may have defined the terms differently. As soon as the grant document is received, it should be read carefully and thoroughly. Any of the terms, conditions, or appendixes that are not clear need to be addressed before any of the awarded funds are spent. Always there is contact information for the granting agency contained in the documentation, and it is important to clear up any areas of concern by contacting the grantor. If this contact is made by telephone or by e-mail, it is important then to document, in writing, the issues involved. The recommended method of doing so is to follow up with a letter to the individual with whom you spoke, documenting the conversation and the resolution, and request that the agent of the grantor make contact if they are not in agreement with the overall resolution of the issue. As the grant project progresses, maintain contact whenever any issues arise, and similarly document the resolution in writing. Be certain to include the person and position that was contacted, the date, the issue and the resolution. Maintain this information in date order with the other documentation that accompanies the project as it progresses.

The grant agreement will often contain or reference a budget document. Usually the budget that was submitted with the original application will be incorporated as an appendix to the grant agreement. Terms of the grant may include compliance requirements that relate to the budget, such as how variances between budgeted and actual expenses should be addressed. For instance, many grants allow for amendments to the original budget in the maximum amount of 10 percent per line item, and require approval for any amendments necessary that exceed this threshold. It is therefore extremely important to monitor the actual spending with the grant budget and address variances promptly and in compliance with the agreement. Not performing these steps could result in the realization at the closeout of the grant that expenses exceeded the allowable variances, which would be considered noncompliance and may have financial implications to the grantee.

Grants are often provided to nonprofit organizations by other nonprofit agencies, such as private and community foundations, affiliated organizations, recipients of larger grants who are subcontracting all or a portion of the project. The grantor agency will develop the grant agreement in such a way that it is able to monitor the project and to, when necessary, meet the requirements at their end as well.

Government grants can be provided directly from the federal government, or through a state or local government or quasi-government agency. Often funding flows through to others. For instance, a grant may originate at a federal department, such as the U.S. Department of Health and Human Services. The U.S. Department of Health and Human Services provides funding to the state department of welfare or state health department, who then may pass those funds through to a variety of county, city or local township, or borough governments, or to large or small non-profit organizations. The complexity of this flow-through funding creates issues for a number of reasons. The original grantor, in this case, the U.S. Department of Health and Human Services, has reporting requirements to oversight agencies, based on the terms under which the funding was appropriated. Therefore, it must specify requirements to the department that received these funds. Similarly, as the funds pass-through and down to other agencies or governments, additional terms and conditions may be required in order that the agencies remain in compliance with those that funded them originally. It is important that the "end grantee" know the original source of the funding. While it may be the grantor's responsibility to provide this information, it doesn't always happen this way. In the case of funds that originated at the federal level, the end user's responsibility to report the use of federal funds cannot be relegated simply because it was not aware of the source, regardless of the fact that it may have passed through several other agencies before it was finally awarded to the end user. We recommend, therefore, that if the original source of grant funds is not immediately apparent through the reading of the grant document, that the grantor be asked to provide this information in writing.

State reporting requirements vary widely. However, grant contracts that award state funds will specify the state agency to which the grantee must report and will also usually contain a covenant that addresses the audit requirements. If the grant agreement from a state government or quasi-government agency does not specifically detail the type of financial reporting during and at the termination of the grant project, it would be prudent for the grantee to contact the grantor and obtain specific instructions with regard to these details.

Federal reporting is particularly important when an agency or organization receives a number of or significant amount of government funds, as this type of funding likely will result in different accounting, audit, compliance, and reporting requirements.

For example, a nonprofit organization, is a provider of community services and receives funding from several sources. Grants from seven different sources total $1,400,000, with each grant approximating $200,000. The nonprofit organization is not required by any direct funders to report under the federal requirements because a single grantor has not provided funding in excess of the threshold ($500,000) of federal dollars, even though half of each of these $200,000 grants is federal pass-through funds. Given this example, the grantee has received $700,000 in federal funds, in total exceeding the $500,000 threshold, and is required to report this activity under the federal reporting rules, which include an audit in accordance with the U.S. Office of Management and Budget. Now, if two of the seven grants fail to provide the information needed to recognize that the grants originated at the federal level, the nonprofit organization will unknowingly fail to comply with the requirements of the federal government.

Terminology

Since such a significant number and amount of grant funds initiated from the federal government, many of the grant agreements, whether developed by state agencies or larger nonprofit organizations for the purpose of passing funds through a subcontractor agency, contain terminology that relates to regulatory documents found in federal circulars or legislative mandates. For that reason, we will attempt to discuss some of the more common terms seen in many such contracts.

OMB

The U.S. Office of Management and Budget (OMB) is a part of the Executive Branch of the U.S. government and is responsible for federal financial management, including the federal budget, federal agency programs, policies, funding, and administration. This office issues regulatory guidance in the form of circulars, bulletins, memoranda, and reports. As relates to the administration of grant agreements, the circulars are the predominant regulatory material.

OMB Circulars

This office issues circulars that attempt to set guidance for the administration of those agencies that are included under the executive office and agencies that are funded by these departments or agencies. The circulars most frequently associated with covenants or conditions of grant agreements are as follows:

Cost Circulars

These circulars pertain to what particular costs are allowable or unallowable under grants funded by the federal agencies, based on the type of organization, as follows:

A-21: Cost principles for Educational Institutions

A-87: Cost principles for State, Local & Indian Tribal Governments

A-122: Cost principles for Nonprofit Governments

Since A-122 is specifically developed for nonprofit organization, we will delve into a more descriptive explanation of this circular. But be aware that the full text of all of the OMB circulars is available on the OMB website, www.whitehouse.gov/omb/. A-122 provides that costs under the circular, generally, are allowable direct costs, less any applicable credits or any allocable indirect cost.

Allowable *direct* costs must be:

Reasonable for the performance of the award. The reasonableness of an expense is determined by assessing whether or not the cost, in its nature or amount, exceeds that which would be spent by a prudent person under the same circumstances. Consideration should be given to whether or not the cost is ordinary and necessary under the terms of the grant; whether the purchase or expense was incurred utilizing sound business practices, at arms-length bargaining, and in accordance with federal and state laws; and whether the expense was incurred under the established practices of the organization.

Allowable allocable *indirect* costs must be:

Allocable to the project or grant in accordance with the relative benefit received. An allocable indirect cost may be charged to a federal grant project so long as (a) it is treated consistently with other costs incurred for the same purpose and is incurred specifically for the award; (b) benefits both the grant project as well as other projects or programs of the organization; and (c) is necessary to the overall operation of the organization, but cannot be directly related to any one program or project. A written cost allocation plan that is reviewed and updated routinely is required in order to allocate indirect costs.

Specifically, *unallowable* costs under Circular A-122 are the following. Those marked with an asterisk may be allowable, but only under limited and pre-approved circumstances; but serious consideration should be given to expensing such items under any government grant without explicit written prior approval from the grantor:

Alcoholic beverages

    Bad debt expense

    Personal use of services or organizational assets (i.e., percentage

of vehicle expense attributed to personal use)

    Donations and contributions to individuals or others

    Entertainment costs

    Fines and penalties*

    Fundraising and investment management costs*

    Lobbying expense*

    Organizational costs*

    Selling and marketing expense*

Indirect cost rate proposals (ICRP) may be submitted to the oversight grantor agency to establish rates for allocating indirect costs to federal awards. These proposals may establish predetermined rates that may be:

A) applied to the current or future periods, based on current costs;

B) applied to current periods and future periods with adjustments made to the computation based on actual costs in future periods

C) approved for temporary rates pending the establishment of a final rate after the actual costs in the period are known; or

D) approved as final to be applied retrospectively based on actual costs.

The method and rules for preparing an ICRP differs between the federal agencies, but those rules and regulations are available by contacting the department or office specified within the grant document.

Audit Standards

The standards that dictate how an audit will be conducted are promulgated by regulatory and/or oversight agencies. There are three types of audit standards, each contain more stringent rules about independence of the auditor and assessments, testing and reporting that must be performed. Each builds on the other, so that an audit under OMB A-133 would also include all of the other standards as well.

➢ *Generally Accepted Auditing Standards* (GAAS) are the first "level" of standards. These standards require that an auditor perform audit planning and testing, as well as assessing accounting principles, estimates, and overall presentation to support an opinion that the financial statements are fairly stated, in all material respects.

➢ *Generally Accepted Government Auditing Standards* (GAGAS) are also known as the "Yellow Book," because the initial standards were bound in a yellow jacket. These standards require that, in addition to the requirements under Generally Accepted Auditing Standards, the auditor consider the organization's internal control system and report any significant deficiencies noted. These standards also require that the auditor assess compliance and to report any noncompliance noted that could have a direct and material effect.

➢ *OMB A-133 Standards* (also known as the Single Audit standards) require that the auditor report on compliance with requirements applicable to certain major federally funded programs and internal controls over compliance with the compliance requirements of those programs and similarly, to report any significant deficiencies or material noncompliance.

Preparing for a Grant Audit

Grantees can benefit by knowing under which standards a grant will be audited. Any organization that receives significant government grants will likely be audited under the Yellow Book. Often grant contracts contain such requirements. Single audits, generally, are required when an organization receives federal funds, whether grant agreements or loan funds, in excess of $500,000. In the case of the Yellow Book audit or the Single Audit, preparation for the audit can reduce the efforts required during the audit by the organization and can benefit the organization by being able to document the requirements that the regulatory agencies and the auditors are attempting to establish.

Under the Yellow Book audit, the auditors are looking to establish that controls exist to limit the organization's exposure to fraud and its ability to promptly detect and correct errors or irregularities.

In assessing an organization's internal control system, there are five elements that the auditor will evaluate, as follows:

➢ *Control Environment*: Is the governing board adequately involved and responsible for performing its fiduciary duties? Does management promote transparency and upward communication? Are policies and procedures formally adopted and updated? Is the board involved in the significant operational areas of the organization? Do the minutes reflect the activities and actions of the governing board?

➢ *Risk Assessment*: Is management and the governing board sufficiently aware of factors that exist within the organization or within its structure for administering and complying grantor regulations to be aware of areas that may increase its exposure to fraud or errors, such as a personnel turnover, new programs or new grants, lack of segregation of duties, cash transactions, or other inherently risky processes within the organization? How is this assessment documented?

➢ *Information and Communication*: Are policies and procedures adequately documented? Do these policies include conflict of interest disclosures, record retention, and whistleblower policies? Are minutes maintained for significant meetings of directors and committees? Are personnel policies updated routinely?

➢ *Monitoring*: Does management and the governing board adequately monitor the organization's activities? Are the policies in place to ensure compliance with rules and regulations? Does oversight of grant-funded activities include ensuring that deadlines and reporting requirements are met and that issues are resolved promptly as they occur? Is the budget monitored routinely as the grant project continues?

➢ *Control Activities*: Activities are in place to limit the risk of financial and compliance activities, such as financial invoicing and receipting, recording liabilities and disbursing payments, and reporting financial activities. Does the structure created to implement and administer grant activities contain controls to identify and correct fraud, irregularities, errors, or noncompliance, were they to occur?

Under the Single Audit standards, auditors will be looking specifically at internal control over compliance with the rules, regulations and terms of the grant award, and will test for certain compliance requirements that are applicable to the federal funds. These compliance requirements consist of the following to the extent that they may apply to any particular grant:

➤ *Activities Allowed and Unallowed*: The auditors will look to the grant agreement to determine the activities that would be included and expected, and the expenditures that match these activities.

➤ *Allowable Costs/Cost Principles*: The allowable costs are discussed earlier in this document and for federal audit purposes in connection with nonprofit awards, Circular A-122 would apply.

➤ *Cash Management*: Often grant advances are allowed, whereby the grantee will either be fully or partially funded in advance of the project, or will be allowed to draw down funds on an "as needed" basis to reimburse costs incurred. The expectation is that these funds will be used quickly, as it would not be the intent of the funding agency that dollars be left to earn interest or be used for other purposes until the grant expenses occur.

➤ *Davis Bacon*: The Davis Bacon Act applies when construction or infrastructure projects are a part of the grant activities in an amount in excess of $2,000. Under this act, wages paid from federal funds are required to be at or above prevailing wage rates, and the grantee must obtain and evaluate certified payroll records from the contractor or engineer overseeing the project.

➤ *Eligibility*: Certain types of funded activities are geared toward a specific population and the funding is to be utilized only or largely to target this group. Often income and/or age are factors in eligibility requirements. These requirements will be found in the grant agreement.

➤ *Equipment and Property Management*: Generally, real property vests with the nonprofit organization when purchased with federal funds, but it would be expected to be utilized for or in connection with the grant program or project for which the funds were provided. Other uses of any equipment or property purchased with these dollars would need to be authorized in writing. Leasing, collateralizing, or disposal should similarly be approved.

➤ *Matching, Level of Effort, and Earmarking*: These criteria would be unique to each grant. Matching generally requires that the grantee contribute a portion of the cost to the project. Matched funds may be in the form of noncash assistance. Use of other federal grant funds to meet matching requirements is prohibited. Level of effort specifies the level of service expected over time. Earmarking refers to a targeted population to benefit from the project or program, or an amount of funds that are allowed to be utilized for certain costs, such as administration or overhead limits.

➤ *Period of Availability*: The grantee would expect that all funds are to be used prior to the end of the grant term, and that expenses incurred before the grant start date not be included in the funded expenses.

➤ *Program Income*: Should the project or program financed with grant funds generate income, the requirement exists that these funds must be used to increase the project budget, deducted from the federal funds expended; or be used to meet any required matched funds by the organization.

➤ *Procurement, Suspension, and Debarment*: This compliance required would apply when funds are used to enter into contracts for services, with the intention of guaranteeing fair and open competition, by advertised bids, estimates, or otherwise.

➤ *Real Property and Relocation Assistance*: These rules apply when a federal project requires homes or businesses and address how land will be acquired and appraised, and what will be paid in the way of compensation or remediation to the owner in the form or purchase price, relocation assistance, or down payment or rent assistance.

➤ *Reporting*: Direct federal awards require using OMB standardized forms; but other forms can be used by pass-through agencies and/or end grantors. The required forms are usually made a part of the grant by inclusion as an appendix.

➤ *Suspension and Debarment*: Are rules that the grantee check to ensure that no contractor has been suspended or debarred from accepting federal funds. Occasionally, this happens when contractors fail to comply with the regulations or grant terms. Before entering into such a contract, the grantee is required to check the database that is maintained by the General Services Administration. Access to this database for this purpose can be obtained at http://epls.arnet.gov/.

➤ *Subrecipient Monitoring*: For the grantees that pass funds through to other agencies, OMB requires that they adequately monitor the use of these funds. They are also required to alert any subrecipients as to the source and amount of such funds. We recommend that this be performed twice a year, as of June 30 and December 31, so that subrecipients are able to properly report, regardless of whether they operate on a fiscal or calendar year.

The various possible auditor's reports as applicable to grant accounting may be as shown in Exhibits 12.1 through 12.4.

EXHIBIT 12.1

Auditor's Report in Accordance with GAAS (only)

INDEPENDENT AUDITORS' REPORT

To the Members of the Board
[Not-for-Profit Organization]

We have audited the accompanying Statements of Financial Position of   [Not-for-Profit Organization, dates]   and the related Statements of Activities, Functional Expenses, and Cash Flows for the years then ended. These financial statements are the responsibility of the Organization's management. Our responsibility is to express an opinion on these financial statements based on our audits.

We conducted our audits in accordance with auditing standards generally accepted in the United States of America. Those standards require that we plan and perform the audits to obtain reasonable assurance about whether the financial statements are free of material misstatement. An audit includes examining, on a test basis, evidence supporting the amounts and disclosures in the financial statements. An audit also includes assessing the accounting principles used and significant estimates made by management, as well as evaluating the overall financial statement presentation. We believe that our audits provide a reasonable basis for our opinion.

In our opinion, the financial statements referred to above present fairly, in all material respects, the financial position of [Not-for-Profit Organization, dates], and the results of its operations and its cash flows for the years then ended in conformity with accounting principles generally accepted in the United States of America.

Our audits were made for the purpose of forming an opinion on the basic financial statements taken as a whole. The supplementary information is presented for the purpose of additional analysis and is not a required part of the basic financial statements. Such information has been subjected to the auditing procedures applied in the audits of the basic financial statements and in our opinion is fairly stated, in all material respects, in relation to the basic financial statements taken as a whole.

_____

CPA Firm Name

_____

City

_____

Date

EXHIBIT 12.2

Auditor's Report in Accordance with GAAS (and in an audit done under GAGAS—Yellow Book): Front Opinion on the Fairness of the Financial Statements

INDEPENDENT AUDITORS' REPORT

To the Board of Directors
[Not-for-Profit Organization]

We have audited the accompanying Statements of Financial Position of ___[Not-for-Profit Organization, dates]___ and the related Statements of Activities, Functional Expenses, and Cash Flows for the years then ended. These financial statements are the responsibility of the Organization's management. Our responsibility is to express an opinion on these financial statements based on our audits.

We conducted our audits in accordance with auditing standards generally accepted in the United States of America and the standards applicable to financial audits contained in Government Auditing Standards, issued by the Comptroller General of the United States. Those standards require that we plan and perform the audits to obtain reasonable assurance about whether the financial statements are free of material misstatement. An audit includes examining, on a test basis, evidence supporting the amounts and disclosures in the financial statements. An audit also includes assessing the accounting principles used and significant estimates made by management, as well as evaluating the overall financial statement presentation. We believe that our audits provide a reasonable basis for our opinion.

In our opinion, the financial statements referred to above present fairly, in all material respects, the financial position of ___[Not-for-Profit Organization, dates]___, and the results of its operations and its cash flows for the years then ended in conformity with accounting principles generally accepted in the United State s of America.

In accordance with Government Auditing Standards, we have also issued our report dated ___[Date]___ on our consideration of ___[Not-for-Profit Organization]___ internal control over financial reporting and on our tests of its compliance with certain provisions of laws, regulations, contracts, grant agreements, and other matters. The purpose of that report is to describe the scope of our testing of internal control over financial reporting and compliance and the results of that testing and not to provide an opinion on the internal control over financial reporting or on compliance. That report is an integral part of an audit performed in accordance with Government Auditing Standards and important in assessing the results of our audits.

_____

CPA Firm Name

_____

City

_____

Date

EXHIBIT 12.3

Auditor's Report in Accordance with OMB A-133 (single audit)
Third report in a single audit

INDEPENDENT AUDITORS' REPORT ON COMPLIANCE WITH REQUIREMENTS APPLICABLE TO EACH MAJOR PROGRAM AND ON INTERNAL CONTROL OVER COMPLIANCE IN ACCORDANCE WITH OMB CIRCULAR A-133

To the Board of Directors
[Not-for-Profit Organization]

We have audited the compliance of _____ with the types of compliance requirements described in the U.S. Office of Management and Budget (OMB) Circular A-133 Compliance Supplement that are applicable to each of its major federal programs for the year ended _____. [Not-for-Profit Organization's]   major federal programs are identified in the summary of auditor's results section of the accompanying Schedules of Findings and Questioned Costs. Compliance with the requirements of laws, regulations, contracts, and grants applicable to each of its major federal programs is the responsibility of the   [The Not-for-Profit Organization's]   management. Our responsibility is to express an opinion on the [Not-for-Profit Organization's]   compliance based on our audit.

We conducted our audit of compliance in accordance with auditing standards generally accepted in the United States of America; the standards applicable to financial audits contained in Government Auditing Standards, issued by the Comptroller General of the United States; and OMB Circular A-133, Audits of States, Local Governments, and Nonprofit Organizations. Those standards and OMB Circular A-133 require that we plan and perform the audit to obtain reasonable assurance about whether noncompliance with the types of compliance requirements referred to above that could have a direct and material effect on a major federal program occurred. An audit includes examining, on a test basis, evidence about the   [Not-for-Profit Organization's]   compliance with those requirements and performing such other procedures as we considered necessary in the circumstances. We believe that our audit provides a reasonable basis for our opinion. Our audit does not provide a legal determination on   [Not-for-Profit Organization's]   compliance with those requirements.

In our opinion, the   [Not-for-Profit Organization's]   has complied, in all material respects, with the requirements referred to above that are applicable to each of its major federal programs for the year ended _____.

A material weakness is a significant deficiency, or combination of significant deficiencies, that results in more than a remote likelihood that a material misstatement of the financial statements will not be prevented or detected by the   [Not-for-Profit Organization's]   internal control.

Our consideration of internal control over financial reporting was for the limited purpose described in the first paragraph of this section and would not necessarily identify all deficiencies in internal control that might be significant deficiencies or material weaknesses. We did not identify any deficiencies in internal control over financial reporting that we consider to be material weaknesses, as defined above.

COMPLIANCE AND OTHER MATTERS

As part of obtaining reasonable assurance about whether the   [Not-for-Profit Organization's]   financial statements are free of material misstatement, we performed tests of its compliance with certain provisions of laws, regulations, contracts, grant agreements, and other matters, noncompliance with which could have a

EXHIBIT 12.3 (*continued*)

direct and material effect on the determination of financial statement amounts. However, providing an opinion on compliance with those provisions was not an objective of our audit and, accordingly, we do not express such an opinion. The results of our tests disclosed no instances of noncompliance or other matters that are required to be reported under Government Auditing Standards.

This report is intended solely for the information and use of the finance committee, management, others within the __[Not-for-Profit Organizations]__, and federal awarding agencies and pass-through entities and is not intended to be and should not be used by anyone other than those specified parties.

_____
CPA Firm Name

_____
City

_____
Date

EXHIBIT 12.4

Auditor's Report in Accordance with GAGAS (Yellow Book): Back Report on Internal Control and Compliance in a Government Audit

INDEPENDENT AUDITORS' REPORT ON INTERNAL CONTROL OVER FINANCIAL REPORTING AND ON COMPLIANCE AND OTHER MATTERS BASED ON AN AUDIT OF FINANCIAL STATEMENTS PERFORMED IN ACCORDANCE WITH GOVERNMENT AUDITING STANDARDS

To the Board of Directors
[Not-for-Profit Organization]

We have audited the financial statements of the ___[Not-for-Profit Organization]___ as of and for the years _____ and have issued our report thereon dated _____. We conducted our audits in accordance with auditing standards generally accepted in the United States of America and the standards applicable to financial audits contained in Government Auditing Standards, issued by the Comptroller General of the United States.

INTERNAL CONTROL OVER FINANCIAL REPORTING
In planning and performing our audit, we considered the ___[Not-for-Profit Organization's]___ internal control over financial reporting as a basis for designing our auditing procedures for the purpose of expressing our opinion on the financial statements, but not for the purpose of expressing an opinion on the effectiveness of the ___[Not-for-Profit Organization's]___ internal control over financial reporting.

A control deficiency exists when the design or operation of a control does not allow management or employees, in the normal course of performing their assigned functions, to prevent or detect misstatements on a timely basis. A significant deficiency is a control deficiency, or combination of control deficiencies, that adversely affects the ___[Not-for-Profit Organization's]___ ability to initiate, authorize, record, process, or report financial data reliably in accordance with generally accepted accounting principles, such that there is more than a remote likelihood that a misstatement of the ___[Not-for-Profit Organization's]___ financial statements that is more than inconsequential will not be prevented or detected by the ___[Not-for-Profit Organization's]___ internal control.

Our audits were made for the purpose of forming an opinion on the basic financial statements taken as a whole. Supplemental information, and the accompanying Schedule of Expenditures presented for purposes of additional analysis as required by the U.S. Office of Management and Budget Circular A-133, Audits of States, Local Governments, and Nonprofit Organizations and is not a required part of the basic financial statements. Such information has been subjected to the auditing procedures applied in the audits of the basic financial statements and in our opinion is fairly stated, in all material respects, in relation to the basic financial statements taken as a whole.

INTERNAL CONTROL OVER COMPLIANCE
The management of ___[Not-for-Profit Organization]___ is responsible for establishing and maintaining effective internal control over compliance with requirements of laws, regulations, contracts, and grants applicable to federal programs. In planning and performing our audit, we considered ___[Not-for-Profit Organization's]___ internal control over compliance with requirements that could have a direct and material effect on a major federal program in order to determine our auditing procedures for the purpose of expressing our opinion

EXHIBIT 12.4 (*continued*)

on compliance, but not for the purpose of expressing an opinion on the effectiveness of internal control over compliance. Accordingly, we do not express an opinion on the effectiveness of the __[Not-for-Profit Organization's]__ internal control over compliance.

A control deficiency in the __[Not-for-Profit Organization's]__ internal control over compliance exists when the design or operation of a control does not allow management or employees, in the normal course of performing their assigned functions, to prevent or detect noncompliance with a type of compliance require-ment of a federal program on a timely basis. A significant deficiency is a control deficiency, or combination of control deficiencies, that adversely affects the __[Not-for-Profit Organization's]__ ability to administer a fed-eral program such that there is more than a remote likelihood that noncompliance with a type of compliance requirement of a federal program that is more than inconsequential will not be prevented or detected by the [Not-for-Profit Organization's]__ internal control. A material weakness is a significant deficiency, or combina-tion of significant deficiencies, that results in more than a remote likelihood that material noncompliance with a type of compliance requirement of a federal program will not be presented or detected by the [Not-for-Profit Organization's]__ internal control.

Our consideration of the internal control over compliance was for the limited purpose described in the first paragraph of this section and would not necessarily identify all deficiencies in internal control that might be significant deficiencies or material weaknesses. We did not identify any deficiencies in internal control over compliance that we consider to be material weaknesses, as defined above.

This report is intended solely for the information and use of the finance committee, management, others within the __[Not-for-Profit Organization]__, and federal awarding agencies and pass-through entities and is not intended to be and should not be used by anyone other than those specified parties.

Summary

The source and use of granted funds varies greatly, from year to year and from agency to agency. Many grantors will continue to fund a program so long as it has produced positive results, or so long as funds are available to do so.

Because organizations often rely heavily on the receipt of grants to fund their programs, it is important that the rules and regulations that are associated with the grant and the granting agency are followed precisely. It is well worth the effort for an agency funded in this manner to be diligent about the administration, recording, reporting, and use of granted dollars.

The first and most important rule is to carefully apply for such funds. Do not promise that which you "hope" to deliver. Be realistic in the budgeting, program description, objectives and out comes proposed in the grant application.

The grant agreement or contract is the source of most of the requirements that are attached to receiving the grant. It is imperative that the requirements therein are clearly understood and are used to guide the actions that are performed with these funds. Pay particular attention to budgets that have been incorporated to the grant agreement and to reporting requirements.

Often grant agreements require an understanding of other regulatory guidance. Many state grants will incorporate federal circulars into the wording in the agreement. Often utilized is the OMB Cost Circulars. This information is readily available on the OMB website.

Grantees often require that the use of their funds be audited by an independent auditor. Depending on the type of audit performed, areas examined and tested will be different. This chapter provides a summary of the types of controls and requirements that will likely be assessed should a government funded grant be audited.

Most importantly, when using grant funds and relying on funding agencies to support programs, an organization must begin with the end in mind, understand the grant agreement, be meticulous in maintaining records and reporting activity, and be timely in meeting project goals and deadlines.

Suggestion: If the prospect of receiving grants is attractive, attend a grant writing seminar the next time one is offered in your area.

13

Implications of Lobbying Expenditures

MOST NOT–FOR–PROFIT ORGANIZATIONS ENGAGE in some sort of lobbying activities such as lobbying pro or con for pending or existing legislate on and lobbying pro or con for the election of an office seeker.

This chapter includes the basic lobbying activities for the following major not-for-profit organizations, sections 501(c)(3, 4, 5, or 6) organizations.

IRC 501(c)(3) Public Charities

In 1934, Congress enacted a lobbying restriction on public charities to require that no substantial part of their activities involve "carrying on propaganda, or otherwise attempting, to influence legislation." Since then, the definition has been expanded, through interpretations and clarifications, but it still remains somewhat ambiguous. The restriction to limit lobbying to keep it from becoming a "substantial" part of a public charity's activities remains in effect today. To date, the issue continues to be the lack of definitive guidance that defines what constitutes "a substantial part of . . . activities." The substantiality issue was deemed to be 5 percent of total activities early on by the Internal Revenue Service (*Seasongood v. Commissioner of Internal Revenue*). This position was later reversed by the Tenth Circuit Court of Appeals in 1972 (*Christian Echoes National Ministry, Inc. v. United States*), stating that "the percentage test . . . obscures the complexity of balancing the organization's activities in relation to its objectives and circumstances."

Further, the 1934 legislation aimed at curtailing the lobbying activities of charitable organizations maintained a broad definition of direct and grassroots lobbying, which could include such activities even if carried on by volunteers with no cost to the organization, and seemed to suggest that a single official position statement could be considered substantial if it had a sufficient impact on the legislative process.

In discussing this issue, it is important to define what is and what is not considered "Lobbying" activity.

Direct lobbying is a communication with any member or any employee of a legislative body when this individual, official, or group is a participant in the legislative process. Lobbying involves the attempt to influence legislation, and can be as simple as a reference to specific legislation and reflects a particular view on that legislation or issue. It can also include any communication that provides support for earlier communication reflecting a view on specific legislation.

Grassroots lobbying involves attempting to influence the general public, or segments thereof, on elections, legislative matters or referendums. Urging members of the public to contact their legislators regarding specific legislation or legislative activity is interpreted as a "call to action" and is considered grassroots lobbying. Advocating, through mass media or otherwise, the adopting or passage of specific legislation by calling the public to action is also grassroots lobbying.

Other activities are not restricted as "lobbying" for public charities:

➤ Attempts to influence an administrative agency. Administrative bodies would include school boards, housing authorities, sewer and water districts, zoning boards or other special purpose boards, whether elected or appointed.

➤ Petitioning the president, the governor, or mayor about executive decisions

➤ Attempting to influence legislators to investigate hearings or to intervene with a governing agency

➤ Testifying on request before a legislative body

➤ Attempting to obtain interpretations of the law from the judicial branch of government

The above definitions will suffice for an initial discussion of lobbying. As will be explained, these definitions change depending upon how the charity decides to report out these expenses.

Political activity can consist of lobbying as above described, but the definition also broadly encompasses advocacy, voter education, and campaign intervention.

Advocacy is the mission of many charitable organizations. To encourage government, the public, and the community to take action and get involved in ways that may affect the change for which the nonprofit was established is common. Often advocacy amounts to attempting to educate others about the cause for which the nonprofit exists, in an effort to foster involvement and support. Since government has the ability to propose and impose legislation that can positively or negatively have an effect on the same areas for which these nonprofits exist, advocacy can involve attempting to influence the legislative process, and in that case, advocacy is lobbying. A charitable organization, established as a 501(c)(3) corporation, must be cautious in this arena because, as such, these organizations are prohibited from political campaign intervention. It is easy to make this connection. The mission for which the nonprofit exists may be severely and negatively impacted by legislative proposals, and there are two candidates for election—one who supports the legislation and one who opposes it. To support a candidate, even indirectly, is illegal, and violation of this prohibition may result in revocation of tax exempt status and the imposition of punitive excise taxes.

Voter education is not prohibited, but is an area of concern for the IRS. Charities are free to perform certain voter education activities, and in fact, some such organizations are established precisely for this purpose. Voter registration drives, voter education, public forums, and debates are all permitted, but caution must be exercised to remain nonpartisan and unbiased, in fact and appearance, in these efforts. Public forums with and formal debate between candidates is commonly conducted by nonprofit organizations without violating the prohibition. In planning and production of these activities, the organizations have clearly provided reasonable amounts of time, equally available to all qualified candidates for election, and fair and impartial treatment that does not promote or advance one candidate over another. There is risk in these types of activities—the preparers of the event or forum could, either inadvertently or intentionally, develop questions that are, or appear to be, biased toward one candidate or one position.

Campaign intervention is prohibited at all levels, federal, state, and local, and what the IRS has determined to be intervention is quite broad. There is no substantiality test like that described below governing lobbying; the prohibition is absolute. Any activity that can appear to favor one candidate or oppose another is considered intervention. Statements of position, whether verbal or written, made directly by a charitable organization or on behalf of a charitable organization in favor or in opposition to any candidate, according to the IRS, clearly violates this prohibition. Offering a candidate a platform to speak on his or her positions, without allowing and providing equal opportunity for all other candidates, is also illegal.

There are exceptions that appear in IRS position papers, but we urge caution in their application:

1. A candidate may speak in a "non-candidate capacity," such as speaking on non-political subjects on that which he or she is considered an expert, but be warned, the constraints of this type of activity far outweigh the practicality of doing so.

   It is of note that the definition of a "candidate for public office" is also murky. Obviously, once an individual has declared his candidacy, his status is evident. However, consider the individual who is widely anticipated to be a candidate, or an incumbent expected to run, but who has not yet officially announced. Obviously, action must be taken to create a candidate, but his action is not always taken by the individual. A committee formed that is promoting a person's record and prospective candidacy, the individual would then be a candidate, though proposed by other than him or herself. The term "candidate for public office" is not restricted to individuals who are associated with or representatives of a political party. Candidates for the local School Board would be "candidate for public office" for purposes of the 501(c)(3) prohibition.

2. Officers, directors, or other leaders of the nonprofit organization may express their personal views, but this expression is limited. The IRS has stated that the prohibition is not intended to restrict free expression on political matters by charity leaders speaking for themselves. However, in attempting to express their personal opinion, individuals closely associated with a charity are warned to be careful not to use the organization's facilities, any of its assets or personnel, and to clearly indicate that their actions or statements are entirely their own, and not that of the charity. It is also recommended that the charity also make a statement to clarify that this individual is not speaking on behalf of or expressing the position of the organization with which he or she is associated.

Another consideration is that a nonprofit organization that links its website to others, risks that they may be intervening, without realizing that they are doing so. Web sites change often, and a link that may have been harmless at one point, may prove to be an expensive and irreversible mistake during an election cycle.

Many 501(c)(3) organizations have created related organizations that are granted status as a 501(c)(4) entity. These organizations have the capacity to legally and extensively perform lobbying activities, but are still not permitted to intervene in political campaigns. However, they are permitted to form a political action committee, under Reg. 1.527–6(f) and (g), which can participate in political campaigns, with very few restrictions. Therefore, the charitable organization can have an indirect political voice, providing proper precautions are taken. Section (c)(4) organizations must be completely separate from the charity; and records must be maintained that no funds from the charity are used in any manner to support the 527 organization. Charities should take care to avoid any financial association with the 527 organization and, in particular, in the use and content of its facilities, website, and links. The exempt organization division of the IRS has created a team of agents whose charge it is to examine the web sites of 501(c)(3) organizations for signs of political activity that is unallowable.

As a part of the Tax Reform Act of 1976, the legislature created Section 501(h) in the Internal Revenue Code that provided an alternative to nonsubstantial activity rules and more clearly defined that which would and would not be included in the definition of lobbying activities. The 501(h) election, once affirmatively elected, provides for a sliding scale to guide organizations in the amount of allowable lobbying expenses before the excise tax is applied.

This election is available to all charitable organizations under 501(c)(3), with the exception of churches, governmental units, and public safety testing organizations. The limit on lobbying expenses is based on a percentage of total expenses. Total expenses, for the purpose of this calculation, do not include capital expenditures, unrelated business income expenses, or fundraising expense if paid to an outside vendor. Once the total expenditures has been calculated, the total allowable lobbying expense can be determined by a simple formula, as follows:

➢ 20 percent of the first $500,000 of total exempt purpose expenditures, plus

➢ 15 percent of the second $500,000 of total exempt purpose expenditures, plus

➢ 10 percent of the third $500,000 of exempt purpose expenditures, plus

➢ 5 percent of the exempt purpose expenditures over $1,500,000

The lobbying limit is capped at $1,000,000. The number is not indexed by the IRS for inflation. The grass-roots lobbying limit is 25 percent of the total lobbying limit, as calculated in this formula. Should an organization exceed these limits, except in extraordinary circumstances, the only penalty is an excise tax of 25 percent of the excess expenditures. Be aware, however, that if these expenditure limits are exceeded by 105 percent over a defined period, tax exempt status may be lost.

Under the 501(h) election, a number of activities have been excluded as being "lobby" expenses, such as using volunteer labor for lobbying purposes, endorsing legislation without spending money to promote the endorsement, public commentary on pending legislation, so long as there is no associated "call to action," and self defense lobbying.

The—perhaps daunting—task is to decide how to identify, track, allocate and calculate those costs that must be reported as lobbying expense. Generally, what is required here is common sense, a reasonable approach applied in good faith, and a competent accountant. All out-of-pocket expenses associated with the activity are to be included, such as the cost of research, development, printing, producing, and mailing. Overhead expenses should be allocated between nonlobbying activities, direct lobbying, and grass-roots lobbying. As with all allocations of indirect costs, it is important that a written cost allocation plan be developed, consistently applied, and reasonable in its approach.

The 501(h) election is made prior to the year end in which the organization wants for this exception to apply. This is an important factor, for after the year ends, the election cannot be then imposed to apply to the amounts already expended. The election is made by filing an IRS Form 5768, which is a one-page, fairly simple application, and the election will then remain in effect until formally revoked (utilizing the same Form 5768). Be sure to keep a copy of the Form 5768, because the IRS does not acknowledge receipt.

501(c)(4), (5), and (6) Organizations

501(c)(4) organizations have been granted exemption under the Internal Revenue Code for the purpose of promoting social welfare, exclusively. Generally types of organizations that are considered social welfare organizations are civic associations and volunteer fire companies, but broadly can include community associations that work to improve the lives for members of the community, preserve the community's traditions, history, architecture or appearance, or encourage industrial development or reduce unemployment. As a part of that mission, lobbying is an expected activity, as a means of supporting or opposing legislation as a means of bringing about civic betterment or social improvement.

501(c)(5) organizations are organizations of labor, agricultural, or horticultural members, and are also allowed to perform lobbying activity. Labor organizations are associations of workers who have formed to protect and promote their interests and secure better working conditions. Agricultural or horticultural organizations promote various cooperative activities to better the conditions of those engaged in these areas, to develop efficiencies or improve products or production.

501(c)(6) are organizations considered to be business leagues, boards of trades, and generally any association of persons with common business interests, for the purpose of promoting such interests. Trade associations and professional associations are business leagues. The 501(c)(6) organization may further its exempt purpose by lobbying, even as its sole activity without jeopardizing its tax exempt status.

Reporting and Notice Requirements under IRC 6033(e)

501(c)(4), (5) and (6) organizations must notify members with a reasonable estimate of the percentage of their dues that will be used to support the cost of lobbying activities—as this percentage is not deductible as a business expense to the individual members. In the alternative, the organization may elect to allow the members to fully deduct their dues, and to pay a proxy tax at the organization level. The proxy tax is assessed at the highest marginal tax rate under the Internal Revenue Code (currently 35 percent). Similarly, if the organization's estimate of the amount of dues that is nondeductible is underestimated, the tax may be paid on the difference, or the organization has the option to increase the percentage in the subsequent year to cover the difference.

There are limited exceptions to the requirements of 6033(e), which include the following:

If at least 90% of the dues paid to the organization by members are nondeductible by the members—such as having 90% of members who are (c)(3) organizations or state or local governments; or

Because the organizations direct lobbying expenditures consist solely of in house expenses that are less than $2,000.

In 1997, the Lobbying Disclosure Act was passed (2 USC 1601 et seq.), requiring that these organizations register and report on their activities and also limits their funding in that they would no longer be eligible to receive federal funds.

Often existing organizations that are exempt under 501(c)(3) will establish a related 501(c)(4) organization to allow it the ability to conduct substantial lobbying activities. However, payments, reimbursements and shared facilities and/or staff must be properly accounted for and these activities must occur at fair market value because this structure could call into question whether or not the 501(c)(3) organization is, by way of such payment or overpayments, subsidizing the lobbying activities of the 501(c)(4) organization. Therefore, any allocation of income or expense between these two organizations must be carefully monitored. A formal cost allocation plan should be in place and should provide for a reasonable, consistent, and documented methodology for any such shared financial activity.

Over the years, and after much legislative debate, a variety of changes and amendments of the Internal Revenue Code, Sections 6033 and 162(e) have provided guidance on how membership organizations must deal with their members in order that the members cannot deduct dues to the extent that their dues are funding lobbying activities. The requirements of the organization, under 6033(e) provide that the organization must provide notice to its members, when they pay dues, a reasonable estimate of the percentage of the members' dues that will be spent on lobbying activities. Section 162(e)(3) denies the deduction of membership dues to the individual, to the same extent. The Code provides enforcement of the requirement by installing "proxy tax" provision. To the extent that an organization provides proper notice, but underestimates the percentage of lobby expense, this proxy tax can be assessed. Currently, the tax is 35 percent of the lobbying expenditures during the tax year, up to the total amount of dues paid. The tax may be waived, however, if the organization is willing to include the excess lobbying expenditures in the calculation of the subsequent year notice to its members. A membership organization does have the option of allowing its members full deductibility of their dues, provided it is willing to pay the proxy tax on its lobbying expenditures. IRC 6033(e) notice requirements do not apply to exempt organizations other than 501(c)(4) social welfare organizations (unless they are veterans' organizations who are exempt); 501(c)(5) (except labor organizations, also exempt) and 501(c)(6) organizations. A further exception applies to in-house expenditures that do not exceed $2,000 during the year and to organizations whose membership consists of at least 90 percent of its dues are not deductible by the members (such as member organizations whose members are 501(c)(3) organizations). For the purposes of these restrictions, the definition of "annual dues" is expanded beyond the payments required for members to be recognized as a member for an annual period, to include similar amounts or voluntary payments or assessments made to an organization to cover basic operating costs and special assessments imposed for the purpose of funding lobbying activities.

Special and complex rules apply when assessing the applicability of these code sections to affiliated organizations, where members at the chapter or local level are joining an organization that is an affiliate paying dues to a state or national organization. Therefore, the code sections should be more closely studied in such situations, as the text of this chapter will not address these types of relationships as they relate to notice and deductibility of member dues.

527 Organizations and Political Action Committees

A political action committee (PAC) is a committee, often established by other organizations (with the exception of 501(c)(3) organizations), be they exempt or nonexempt. They need not be incorporated or otherwise have formal organizational documents, only a separate bank account in which campaign collections funds are deposited and disbursed. The PAC collects nondeductible contributions from members or other groups and makes contributions of up to $5,000 per year in the name of the committee to candidates or political parties. A PAC must register with the Federal Election Commission (FEC) within 10 days of its formation, disclosing its name, address, treasurer, and any affiliations. A PAC can give $5,000 to a candidate per election and up to $15,000 annually to a political party. It is important that the funds contributed to the PAC not be passed to the PAC from the operations of the 501(c)(3) organizations.

The 527 organizations are organized as a separate legal entity and are tax exempt in accordance with Section 527 of the Internal Revenue Code for the specified purpose of raising money for political activities. These activities are unlimited and usually involve voter mobilization, issue advocacy, and the like. Regular disclosure reports must be filed with the FEC if the group engages in activities that advocate the election or defeat of a federal candidate or produce electioneering communications. Otherwise, the group must register with the IRS and the state in which it is located. Donations are not limited to the 527 organizations, as they are with PACs.

Donations to the PAC are nondeductible for tax purposes and the rules are specific and stringent as to how this disclosure must be presented. These rules are applicable to any political organization that has gross receipts in excess of $100,000 during the tax year. Nondeductibility of contributions must be disclosed in an express statement, in a conspicuous and easily recognizable format. These rules apply to printed fundraising materials, telephone solicitations, and television and radio formats.

For the PAC and the 527 organizations, income from investments are taxable, as is any income from nonpolitical fundraising events at the highest corporate income tax rate.

Summary

The Omnibus Budget Reconciliation Act of 1993 (H.R. 2264) significantly affects not-for-profit organizations that incur lobbying expenditures. The general intent of the law, which came into effect January 1, 1994, is to eliminate the deductibility of lobbying expenditures for federal income tax purposes. Not-for-profit organizations classified under Section 501(c)(3) of the Internal Revenue Code are generally exempt from the law as long as the organization does not engage in lobbying that is of direct financial interest to the donor's business and the principal purpose of the donation is not to avoid the non-deductibility rule.

The law applies only to lobbying expenditures related to federal and state legislation. Lobbying expenditures relating to a county, city, or municipality are not subject to the law.

Accounting Calculation

The percentage of dues not deductible by a member for income tax purposes is calculated by dividing the total amount of lobbying expenditures incurred by total dues revenues. For example, if a not-for-profit organization incurs total lobbying expenses of $100,000 and total dues revenues equal $500,000, the nondeductible (disallowable) percentage of dues would be calculated as follows:

Lobbying expenses ÷ Dues revenue = Disallowable percentage

Example:
Lobbying expenses   = $100,000
Dues revenue   = $500,000
Disallowable percentage   =   20%

Communication to Members

It is the responsibility of the not-for-profit organization to report the nondeductible portion of dues payment directly to the member. The statement on nondeductibility of lobbying expenditures *could* read as follows:

The tax deductibility of dues paid to [organization name] as an ordinary and necessary business expense is subject to restrictions imposed as a result of lobbying activities. [Organization name] estimates that the nondeductible portion of your [year] dues is ____%.

In addition, not-for-profit organizations must provide members with a reasonable estimate of the percentage of their dues payment that will be nondeductible for the coming year as part of their dues assessment. The statement *could* read as follows:

As a result of [organization name] lobbying activities, the percentage of dues that may be deducted as an ordinary and necessary business expense is subject to restriction. We *estimate* the nondeductible percentage of your dues payment to be ____%.

Safe Harbor

The law provides for two safe harbors:

1. *The de minimis rule.* If total *in-house* lobbying expenditures are less than $2,000, the organization is exempt from reporting requirements.

2. *Waiver.* If a not-for-profit organization receives 90 percent or more of its dues from individuals or organizations not entitled to deduct their dues as ordinary and necessary business expenses, it is exempt from the nondeductibility rules.

Reporting Requirements

Not-for-profit organizations are required to report total lobbying expenditures and total dues revenues on Form 990.

Optional Proxy Tax

In lieu of the reporting requirements, not-for-profit organizations can opt to pay a proxy tax. The tax is calculated by multiplying total lobbying expenditures by the applicable tax rate. The tax is reported on Form 990-T.

This tax is levied on lobbying expenses up to total dues revenue for the year. The excess is carried forward to the subsequent year.

Hard Money versus Soft Money

Even though "hard money" may also be used to refer to loans that are attached to physical property, real estate, and the like as collateral on real estate loans from non-traditional lenders, the discussion in this book focuses on hard money along with "soft money" in relation to political campaign contributions.

Hard money refers to funds contributed directly to a candidate of a political party. These contributions are regulated, in both source and amount, by law and monitored by the FEC.

Soft money, on the other hand, refers to contributions made directly to the political party as a whole. Prior to 2002, "soft money" referred to funds contributed to political parties that were not directly related to the election of specific candidates; for example, for the purposes of party building, voter registration, campaign office expenses, and the like. Because these contributions were not used for specific candidate advocacy, they were not regulated by the Federal Election Campaign Act of 1971, as the Supreme Court, in the 1975 case of *Buckley v. Valeo*, concluded. Congress made further amends to the FECA in 1976 following the Supreme Court's ruling on the above case, and then passed major amendments in 1979 to streamline the disclosure process and expand the role of political parties.

Soft money also refers to unlimited contributions to organizations and committees other than candidate campaigns and political parties. Exceptions by law would be to state and local parties for use solely in state and local races. Organizations that receive soft money contributions are allowed to legally engage in political activity, but funds from soft money contributions cannot be disbursed for the purpose of promoting the election or defeat of a specific candidate.

How It's Done, the Works, and Prohibition

An advertisement that specifically requests voters to vote for a certain candidate must be paid for by the candidate's campaign funds (hard money) or from special funds of the candidate's respective political party. Federal law regulates contributions to both of these funds. Corporations and labor unions cannot contribute to federal election campaigns but can establish political action committees that can though are limited in the amount of contributions made. Individuals can make contributions directly to all candidates, but again contributions are limited. No organization or individual is exempt from having their political contributions either limited or forbidden by law.

Campaign Contributions

Political campaign contributions are made by individuals, political action committees (PACs), and 527 groups. Corporations and incorporated charitable organizations are prohibited by the FECA of 1971 from making contributions to or spending for a candidate. However, PACs are a good way for these organizations to avoid the long arm of the FEC law.

PACs are private organizations that exist for the purpose of influencing an election. PACs that are corporate or union-based, are restricted to soliciting only union members, their families, shareholders, or executives for money for contributions. PACs are divided into two groups for contribution limits: (1) multicandidate committees are political in nature with more than 50 contributors, registered for a minimum six months, and excluding state party committees, has made contributions to five or more candidates for federal office, and; (2) nonmulticandidate committees that have 50 or less contributors. PACs placing campaign ads on television, radio, or in the print media are required to include a disclaimer that clearly states who paid for the ad.

Contribution limits as mandated by the Federal Election Campaign law for 2009–2010 are shown in Exhibit 13.1 for individuals and PACs. Limits also exist for national party committees; state, district, and local party committees; and authorized campaign committees. These limits can be found on the FEC website.

EXHIBIT 13.1

FEC–Mandated Contribution Limits

	To Each Candidate or Candidate Committee Per Election	To National Party Committee Per Calendar Year	To State, District and Local Party Committee per Calendar Year	To Any Other Political Committee per Calendar Year	Special Limits
Individual may give	$2,400	$30,400	$10,000 (combined limit)	$5,000	$115,500 overall biennial limit $45,600 to all candidates $69,900 to all PACs and parties
PAC (multicandidate) may give	$5,000	$15,000	$5,000 (combined limit)	$5,000	No limit
PAC (non-multicandidate) may give	$2,400	$30,400	$10,000 (combined limit)	$5,000	No limit

For nonprofit organizations with the desire to get involved in political activities, the IRS offers a designation different than tax code section 501(c)(3) that most non-profits are organized under. Nonprofits operating under code section 501(c)(3), are restricted from engaging in any political activities. The new section, 527, allows non-profits to involve themselves in political activities. A 527 group, as they are called, will be engaged to clarify the issues surrounding an individual's candidacy, or to lobby for specific laws or reforms. A 527 group can also elect to be a political action committee, but PACs are subject to more stringent rules in terms of donations.

These organizations, which have become popular and influential, can be a way to avoid some of the campaign financial reform that currently limits the donations a political candidate can take to run for office. A 527 group that is not a PAC is independent of the candidate running for office. 527s, which are similar to PACs, do not contribute funds nor work directly with a candidate's campaign and therefore can operate outside the control of the FEC.

Candidates running for office can have no involvement in raising money for a 527 group, nor can a candidate exercise any control over this group, which can be very effective in influencing voter opinion. But a 527 group must walk a very fine line as to what it can and cannot do. Two such groups from the 2004 presidential campaign, MoveOn and Swift Boat Veterans, were fined by the Federal Election Committee (FEC) for illegal actions committed during the campaign. An FEC investigation discovered that both organizations had actually attacked the candidates and not the issues, and therefore influenced voting for specific candidates. It is a violation of Code Section 527 for an organization operating under it to focus on or advocate for or against a candidate. A 527 group "must" focus on the issues.

Due to the fact that 527 groups are apparently springing up around certain candidacies, Congress is said to be considering changes in the law governing 527s. Currently, there is no campaign reform in process.

Candidates use various forms of advertisings to reach voters: billboards, lawn signs, direct mailings, and leaflets, but the most widely used especially by national candidates and most expensive is the media, specifically, radio and television advertising. In addition, candidates host sit-down dinners for targeted, wealthy donors for a per-plate fee in which large sums of money are raised. These dinners serve a candidate in two ways; they serve not only as a major fundraiser but also as a form of advertising as the candidate speaks about his candidacy, platform, and issues.

Candidates also use other aspects of the public media, newspaper and TV news, which is free advertising for the politician and his platform. In addition, political parties and a candidate's staff will organize rallies, make calls to voters, pass out fliers, and candidates will even take a whistle-stop tour to spread the word about their candidacy and to show that small-town America is important to them.

14

Campaign Contributions, PACs, and 527s

POLITICAL CAMPAIGN CONTRIBUTIONS ARE MADE BY INDIVIDUALS, political action committees (PACs), and 527 groups. Corporations and incorporated charitable organizations are prohibited by the FECA of 1971 from making contributions to or spending for a candidate. However, PACs are a good way for these organizations to avoid the long arm of the FEC law.

PACs are private groups, regardless of size, organized to elect political candidates. State and federal law regulate the organization of "PACs" and, most importantly, what constitutes a "PAC." Under the Federal Election Campaign Act, FECA, an organization that receives contributions or disburses funds in excess of $1,000 in a calendar year for the purpose of influencing a federal election is considered a political action committee for federal purposes. For state purposes, to use the example of Indiana, a PAC is an organization that also attempts to influence the election, but of a state or local candidate, and accepts contributions or disburses funds during the calendar year that in the aggregate exceed $100.

PACs that are corporate or union-based are restricted to soliciting only union members, their families, shareholders, or executives for money for contributions. PACs are divided into two groups for contribution limits: (1) multicandidate committees are political in nature with more than 50 contributors, registered for a minimum six months, and, excluding state party committees, have made contributions to five or more candidates for federal office, and; (2) non-multicandidate committees that have 50 or less contributors. PACs placing campaign ads on television, radio, or in the print media are required to include a disclaimer that clearly states who paid for the ad.

Contribution limits as mandated by the Federal Election Campaign law for 2009–2010 are listed in Exhibit 14.1 for individuals and PACs. Limits also exist for national party committees; state, district, and local party committees; and authorized campaign committees. These limits can be found on the FEC website.

EXHIBIT 14.1

FEC–Mandated Contribution Limits

	To Each Candidate or Candidate Committee Per Election	To National Party Committee Per Calendar Year	To State, District and Local Party Committee per Calendar Year	To Any Other Political Committee per Calendar Year	Special Limits
Individual may give	$2,400	$30,400	$10,000 (combined limit)	$5,000	$115,500 overall biennial limit $45,600 to all candidates $69,900 to all PACs and parties
PAC (multicandidate) may give	$5,000	$15,000	$5,000 (combined limit)	$5,000	No limit
PAC (non-multicandidate) may give	$2,400	$30,400	$10,000 (combined limit)	$5,000	No limit

For not-for-profit organizations with the desire to get involved in political activities, the Internal Revenue Service offered a designation different than tax code section 501(c)(3) that most nonprofits are organized under. Nonprofits operating under code section 501(c)(3) are restricted from engaging in any political activities. The new section, 527, allows nonprofits to involve themselves in political activities. A 527 group, as they are called, will be engaged to clarify the issues surrounding an individual's candidacy, or to lobby for specific laws or reforms. A 527 group can also elect to be a political action committee (PAC), but PACs are subject to more stringent rules in terms of donations.

These organizations, which have become popular and influential, can be a way to avoid some of the campaign financial reform that currently limits the donations a political candidate can take to run for office. A 527 group that is not a PAC is independent of the candidate running for office. 527s, which are similar to PACs, do not contribute funds nor work directly with a candidate's campaign and therefore can operate outside the control of the FEC.

Candidates running for office can have no involvement in raising money for a 527 group, nor can a candidate exercise any control over this group, which can be very effective in influencing voter opinion. But a 527 group must walk a very fine line as to what it can and cannot do. Two such groups from the 2004 presidential campaign, MoveOn and Swift Boat Veterans, were fined by the FEC for illegal actions committed during the campaign. An FEC investigation discovered that both organizations had actually attacked the candidates and not the issues, and therefore influenced voting for specific candidates. It is a violation of Code Section 527 for an organization operating under it to focus on or advocate for or against a candidate. A 527 group "must" focus on the issues.

Due to the fact that 527 groups are apparently springing up around certain candidacies, Congress is said to be considering changes in the law governing 527s. Currently there is no campaign reform in process.

PACs and Regular, Legislative Caucus, and Candidate Party Committees

States have different regulations for the operation of PACs. Failure to adhere to campaign finance requirements by filing reports on a timely basis may result in fines of $50 per day with a maximum fine of $1,000. Failure to file penalties can also subject a person to criminal prosecution. Other campaign finance violations may also result in even more severe civil penalties.

With federal filing requirements being enforced at the federal level, federal PACs and federal candidates file campaign finance reports with the FEC. The federally required reports consist of the following: federal equivalent of statement of organization; federal campaign finance reports, and; reports of independent expenditures.

A political action committee that accepts contributions or disburses funds for a federal office election must file reports with the FEC and, depending on the state, may not need to file at the state level, such as the example of Indiana. However, if that same PAC accepts contributions or disburses funds for candidates at both the federal and state level, then it must file reports with both the FEC and applicable state election division.

PACs also refer to all campaign finance committees that are not candidates committees, regular or legislative caucuses committees, or auxiliary party organizations.

Contributions received by PACs include cash, checks, gifts of property or services, loans, in-kind contributions, and any item of value. However, donations of rent, office expenses, management fees, solicitation or contribution costs, or administrative costs are not considered "contributions."

PACs may only make contributions to campaigns of an elected official. The funds cannot be used for other purposes such as lobbying or fees for lobbyists.

Though federal law prohibits corporations, federal government contractors, unions, and foreign nationals from making contributions or expenditures to influence federal elections, some states—to use the example of Indiana again—allow corporations and unions to make contributions to candidates for state elections. It is also unlawful for federal candidates to accept contributions from state and local PACs. Only federal PACs, those registered with the Federal Election Commission, may contribute to candidates seeking federal office.

Based on the state an organization operates and organizes in, foreign nationals may form a PAC, however, they cannot conduct any business in that particular state, which would render it useless.

In addition to the restrictions already listed, "foreign nationals, national banks, and other federally chartered corporations are prohibited under the Federal Election Campaign Act from making contributions or expenditures related to state and local elections."

As stated in the Federal Election Campaign Act and found on the FEC website, "a domestic subsidiary of a foreign corporation may not establish a federal political action committee (PAC) to make federal contributions if":

1. The foreign parent corporation finances the PAC's establishment, administration, or solicitation costs; or
2. Individual foreign nationals:
   a. participate in the operation of the PAC;
   b. serve as officers of the PAC;
   c. participated in the selection of persons who operate the PAC; or
   d. make decisions regarding PAC contributions or expenditures.

In the latter part of 2004, the FEC publicized a new rule that required some 527 organizations engaged in federal campaigns "to use 50% hard money" to pay their expenses. But the rule stopped short of regulating when a 527 organization must register as a political committee. Hard money refers to contributions regulated by the Federal Election Campaign Act. The FEC settled three cases in December 2006 and one in February 2007 against 527 organizations for various violations of federal campaign law during the 2004 election cycle. The violations included failing to register as a political committee, abide by contribution limits, source prohibitions, and disclosure requirements, as well as failure to abide by federal campaign finance laws. The total fines paid by these four organizations amounted to $139,500.

The explosion of advertising spending by both parties and candidates highlights the continuous battle over hard or soft money and the extent to which political campaigns have gone to buy as much advertising as possible. During the 2008 presidential and senate campaigns, the amount spent on advertising by the Democratic and Republican parties to get candidates elected grew to exceed $1.5 billion, making advertising the single highest expenditure in campaign politics. These advertising expenditures covering both 2007 and 2008 do not include the amount spent by the candidates themselves. This information, from a 2009 edition of *USA Today*, was derived from a report of the Federal Election Commission.

In addition, the FEC also reported the following information related to 2008 campaigns: The Republican National Committee spent approximately $54 million to oppose the candidacy of President Barack Obama; the Democratic Party, in turn, spent $51 million to oppose various Republican Senate candidates.

John McCain and Barack Obama took different avenues of funding their campaigns. McCain registered for matching funds from the government's election campaign funds and abided by state-by-state restrictions and an overall spending limit of $54 million for the primary campaign. Obama on the other hand, opted out of the federal public presidential campaign financing plan. This federal plan is funded by taxpayers who check the box on their tax returns: "Do you wish to contribute $3 to the presidential campaign fund?" The president would have been limited to $84.1 million in campaign spending for the general election if he chose to use federal matching funds. It was reported he would have been able to raise $200 million. If a candidate opts out of the federal matching funds program, he or she is free to raise as much money as possible but still must abide by all federal campaign finance laws and FEC reporting requirements.

An advertisement that specifically requests voters to vote for a certain candidate must be paid for by the candidate's campaign funds (hard money) or from special funds of the candidate's respective political party. Federal law regulates contributions to both of these funds.

Corporations and labor unions cannot contribute to federal election campaigns but can establish an election committee that can, though these committees are limited in the amount of contributions made.

Hard Money versus Soft Money

Even though "hard money" may also be used to refer to loans that are attached to physical property, real estate, and the like, as collateral on real estate loans from non-traditional lenders, the discussion in this book focuses on hard money along with "soft money" in relation to political campaign contributions.

When we speak of political contributions in the United States, we divide the discussion between the terms hard and soft money.

Hard money refers to funds contributed directly to a candidate of a political party. These contributions are regulated, in both source and amount, by law and monitored by the FEC.

Soft money, on the other hand, are contributions made directly to the political party as a whole. Prior to 2002, "soft money" referred to funds contributed to political parties that were not directly related to the election of specific candidates—for example, for the purposes of party building, voter registration, campaign office expenses, and the like. Because these contributions were not used for specific candidate advocacy, they were not regulated by the Federal Election Campaign Act of 1971, as the Supreme Court, in the 1975 case of *Buckley v. Valeo,* concluded. Congress made further amendments to the FECA in 1976 following the Supreme Court's ruling on the above case, and then passed major amendments in 1979 to streamline the disclosure process and expand the role of political parties.

The Bipartisan Campaign Reform Act of 2002 (also known as BCRA, McCain–Feingold Act) prohibits unregulated contributions to national party committees. The key provisions of the act are

> 1) a ban on unrestricted ("soft money") donations made directly to political parties (often by corporations, unions, or wealthy individuals) and on the solicitation of those donations by elected officials; 2) limits on the advertising that unions, corporations, and nonprofit organizations can engage in up to 60 days prior to an election; and 3) restrictions on political parties' use of their funds for advertising on behalf of candidates (in the form of "issue ads" or "coordinated expenditures").

Soft money also refers to unlimited contributions to organizations and committees other than candidate campaigns and political parties. Exceptions by law would be to state and local parties for use solely in state and local races. Organizations that receive soft money contributions are allowed to legally engage in political activity, but funds from soft money contributions cannot be disbursed for the purpose of promoting the election or defeat of a specific candidate.

The BCRA, McCain–Feingold Act, was challenged in 2003 in a Supreme Court case, by the California Democratic Party, National Rifle Association, and various individuals, including U.S. Senator, Mitch McConnell, Republican, Kentucky. It became known as *McConnell vs. Federal Election Commission.* The plaintiffs argued that the provisions of the Act were an infringement on their First Amendment rights.

In addition to the previously mentioned prohibitions related to foreign nationals, one should also review FEC information, including its website, related to additional foreign national prohibitions concerning the following: assisting foreign national contributions or donations; and soliciting, accepting, or receiving contributions and donations from foreign nationals.

Information that is provided on the Web and via other media, including this book, outside the Federal Election Commission or any of the 50 states, should only be used as a guide and not in lieu of federal, state, or local election laws.

CHAPTER 15

Internal Audit Committees

MANY NOT–FOR–PROFIT ORGANIZATIONS HAVE ESTABLISHED or intend to establish an Internal Audit Committee. This chapter addresses important aspects of Audit Committee responsibilities, but it is intended as a starting point and does not note all possible responsibilities. There is also the suggestion that the not-for-profit organization *draft* Audit Committee charges and thoroughly review the draft with the organization's independent CPA.

Committee Members

Members of the Audit Committee should be *independent* of management of the organization. As such, members should not be on the board, nor should they be employees. This independence should result in impartial judgments made under the committee's scope of work. Also, the committee should be headed by a qualified chairperson.

Training

Unless the not-for-profit organization represents accountants, adequate training is absolutely necessary.

It is suggested that the committee's responsibilities be reviewed by the organization's independent CPA firm so that they can plan the training geared to the particular nuances of the committee members.

Responsibilities

At a *minimum,* the training should educate the committee's members on the proper way to:

➤ Review cash transactions

➤ Review check transactions

➤ Review credit card transactions

➤ Check accuracy of compensation to employees and consultants

➤ Assure that there are no "ghosts" on the payroll

➤ Assure that the organization does not do business with "ghost" vendors

➤ Review the reasonableness of employee credit card transactions

➤ Review the Accounting and Financial Policies to assure the policies are in accordance with accounting procedures as applicable to not-for-profit organizations and that they are followed

➤ Review the Risk Management Policies to assure completeness and reasonableness

➤ Review the adequacy of all insurance policies, such as the Fidelity Bond and Officers and Directors' Errors and Omissions Policies

➤ Review the Disclosure of Records to assure that they are in accordance with prevailing federal and state requirements

➤ Assure the completeness of Office Administration Policies

➤ Assure that the individuals with accounting responsibilities are competent

➤ Assure that controls are adequate regarding safeguarding confidential information such as customer credit card detail, employee personnel records, etc.

➤ Assure the organization has a complete Fraud Action Plan if a defalcation has been discovered

And . . . *important,*

➤ Review the existing Internal Control Policies to assure they are adequate and followed!

Reports

The committee should prepare a report noting areas audited, deficiencies noted, and possible recommendations for improvement.

The report should be presented to the board of directors by the chairperson or that person's designee.

Visits

The frequency of Internal Audit Committee visits would, of course, depend on the organization itself. At a minimum, the committee should conduct visits at least once per year.

Surprise Visit

It is arguable, but the committee should consider having their visit unannounced and preferably on a pay day. The committee should have employees sign for their checks or direct deposit receipts and have adequate follow-up for employees not present to assure their existence.

Relationship with Independent CPAs

In addition to adequate training, the Internal Audit Committee should have an on-site meeting with the organization's independent CPA.

Items to be discussed with the independent CPA include, but are not limited to, the following:

➤ The organization's audit, review or compilation reports

And . . . *important,*

➤ Review and discuss of the organization's Management Letter and follow up to see that problems and recommendations for improvement were followed

➤ Review of issues that may have resulted in Qualified Opinions, Adverse Opinions, or Disclaimers of Opinion

➤ Review of the "brainstorming session" items conducted by the CPA's staff assigned to the organization's audit

Outside Assistance

Dependent on the nature of the organization, the Internal Audit Committee may require assistance from outside professionals.

Such competent outside assistance may be needed by:

➤ Independent CPAs

➤ Independent counsel

➤ Independent information technology

➤ Independent financial analysts

➤ Independent insurance professional

Summary

Once again, this chapter has been constructed to serve as a starting point for establishing an Internal Audit Committee and not as a final document to be adopted.

For further information please consider contacting AICPA, the American Institute of CPAs.

Also, with regard to an in-depth discussion on internal controls, please refer to the appropriate chapter in this manual and consider reviewing *Establishing Policies and Procedures to Prevent Fraud and Embezzlement in Not-for-Profit Organizations,* also published by John Wiley & Sons.

CHAPTER 16

The Accounting Policies and Procedures Manual

A NOT-FOR-PROFIT ORGANIZATION'S ACCOUNTING SYSTEM should be designed to be efficient and to meet the organization's needs. Assuming that an organization has effective budget, accounting, and financial management systems in operation, these systems should be backed up by an official organization manual of accounting and financial policies and procedures.

The manual should describe the accounting operation and related policies and procedures in clear, simple, easy-to-understand language. This manual should be presented to the organization's board of directors for approval and adoption as the official accounting method of the organization.

This official manual has several advantages for those involved in any aspect of the organization's financial management, including the board of directors, the chief executive officer, and the accounting staff. The manual signifies to the board of directors that the accounting department has formal directions regarding exactly how the accounting and financial affairs of the organization are to be handled and how the financial statements are to be presented. The manual should clearly state that the organization's staff has no authority to deviate from established organization policy in financial matters. It should state that any deviation from established policy without approval is a serious offense, with possible consequences ranging from inconsistent and misleading accounting statements to fraud and other ramifications that would place the organization's assets at risk.

The chief executive officer is somewhat protected from board criticism on the handling of the financial affairs of the organization. The chief executive officer, generally speaking, rarely has a formal accounting or financial background, yet is usually held primarily responsible for fiscal problems. An official manual of accounting and financial policies and procedures allows the chief executive officer to manage the organization with the comfort of knowing its financial affairs are operating in accordance with official board direction. Assuming that the chief executive officer is an effective manager and the accounting staff is competent, the possibility of typical organization financial management problems is diminished.

The official organization manual of accounting and financial policies and procedures assures the financial staff that the financial statements and underlying accounting policies meet with board approval and that the accounting staff will not be held responsible for financial problems if they are operating effectively and carrying out the directions of the board and the chief executive officer. [For additional information, see *Model Policies and Procedures for Not-for-Profit Organizations* by Edward J. McMillan, John Wiley & Sons, Inc., 2003.]

Preparing the Manual

Review of the manual should prepare a person who is unfamiliar with the organization to run the financial operation. The manual first should describe the method of accounting, illustrate the financial statement formats, detail the chart of accounts and the logic of how it was set up, and then describe and define how every account is to be handled from the accounting and policy perspective.

Every account, including balance sheet accounts, should be listed and described in detail.

Accounting Descriptions—Examples

Account Number: 100-00075
Account Name: Depreciation
Policy: It is the policy of the organization to depreciate fixed assets, other than real property and electronic equipment, by the straight-line method over a 10-year period.

Real property will be depreciated by the straight-line method over a 30-year period.

Electronic equipment will be depreciated by the straight-line method over a 4-year period.

Assets will be capitalized in accordance with the organization's capitalization cutoff point policy.

Account Number: 10-00076
Account Name: Capitalization Cutoff Points
Policy: It is the policy of the organization to expense assets in the period purchased if these assets cost $250 or less individually.

Assets costing in excess of $250 individually will be capitalized and depreciated in accordance with the organization's depreciation policies.

The manual does not end at this point. It also should describe operational policies that affect the accounting operation. The manual should cover many areas of policy, including the following:

➢ Purchase orders

➢ Public access to records

➢ Use of logo on forms

➢ Resale merchandise inventory valuations

➢ Lockbox procedure

➢ Bank reconciliations

➢ Controls over incoming cash/checks

➢ Check disbursements

➢ Petty cash fund disbursements

➢ Investment policies

➢ Prepaid expenses

➢ Accounts payable accounts

➢ Deferred revenues

➢ Travel expenses

➢ Travel advances

➢ Collection procedures

➢ Accounts receivable write-off procedures

➢ Use of time sheets

➢ Discounts on accounts payable

➢ Discounts on accounts receivable

➢ Depreciation

➢ Capitalization cutoff points

➢ Amortization

A few areas may be addressed in separate manuals or at a minimum should be included in the manual of accounting and financial policies and procedures. These areas include the following:

➢ A forms manual, which describes all the forms used by the organization, describes how to complete them, and gives other useful information on forms.

➢ A retired forms manual, which contains forms that are no longer used by the organization and the logic and approval process used to change or eliminate the forms.

➤ A manual on records retention and destruction, which should formally address well-thought-out policies for records retention and destruction. (Old records that are rarely, if ever, used take up valuable space, yet premature destruction of records can be a costly and sometimes embarrassing mistake.)

➤ A year-end manual, which describes in detail what tasks must be completed to ensure that procedures are followed in conjunction with the end of the fiscal year. (Examples include inventory counts, contacting the independent CPA firm, and preparing audit verification letters.)

➤ A data processing manual, which describes data processing procedures, requests for service, maintenance calls, and so forth.

Policy Descriptions—Examples

Subject: Petty Cash Fund Disbursements

Discussion: To reduce check disbursement volume, most organizations maintain a petty cash fund, sometimes called an imprest fund, to pay for small expenditures.

The larger the organization, the larger the petty cash fund can be. Typically, petty cash funds range from $250 to $2,000.

The procedures for safeguarding, access to, disbursing from, and replenishing of petty cash funds should be straightforward and clear.

Policy: It is the policy of the organization to maintain a petty cash fund of $500.

It is the responsibility of the controller and that person's designee to ensure that the petty cash fund is under lock and key at all times.

Disbursement from the petty cash fund may be only for approved expenditures of $25 or less. A receipt must accompany every disbursement. The receipt must be signed by the person receiving the cash and the person disbursing the cash.

The petty cash fund will be replenished as needed and at the end of every month. The replenishment check for the petty cash fund will be made out to the person primarily responsible for maintenance of the fund, with the word *agent* following his or her name. The expenses will be reviewed and the resulting check will be signed by other responsible parties.

Subject: Discounts on Accounts Receivable

Discussion: It is common for organizations to offer discounts to customers if the customer pays before the debt is due.

Typically, the discount is 2 percent if the bill is paid within 10 days.

Effective use of a discount policy can improve cash flow, because many organizations are mandated to take advantage of all discounts.

Policy: It is the policy of the organization to offer customers a 2 percent discount if the invoice is paid within 10 days.

An account titled Discounts Taken, a contra-revenue account, will account for these discounts on the financial statements.

Example:

Merchandise Sales	$XXX
Less Discounts Taken	($XXX)
Less Cost of Goods Sold	($XXX)
Net Merchandise Sales	$XXX

CHAPTER 17

Restricted–Fund Transactions

FOR NOT–FOR–PROFIT ORGANIZATIONS the accounting treatment and financial statement presentation of restricted funds can be confusing. Restricted-fund accounting is unique to not-for-profit organizations and government, and there are material differences between the two. In fact, there are differences among trade associations, professional associations, charities, hospitals, and educational institutions regarding the accounting treatment of restricted funds. This chapter concentrates on restricted-fund accounting as it applies primarily to professional and trade associations, chambers of commerce, and foundations.

Why the Confusion?

The confusion surrounding the accounting treatment and financial statement presentation of restricted funds stems from the fact that before 1994 not-for-profit organizations, unlike commercial businesses, were not bound by required language and reporting requirements promulgated by the American Institute of Certified Public Accountants (AICPA) as necessary for formal financial statement presentations.

In response to this confusion, AICPA released Statement of Financial Accounting Standards #117 (SFAS #117), *Financial Statements of Not-for-Profit Organizations*; SFAS #116, *Accounting for Contributions Received and Contributions Made*; and SFAS #136, *Transfer of Assets to a Not-for-Profit Organization Charitable Trust*. See the appendixes for a more detailed discussion of these standards.

The Old Way

The following comparison explores the differences between the old and current methods. Before AICPA issued the new standards, restricted funds were included in the fund balances or members' equity liability section of not-for-profit organizations' balance sheets. Four basic funds were used:

- The general fund (including board-designated funds)
- Current restricted funds
- Endowment funds
- Fixed-assets funds

The General Fund (Including Board–Designated Funds)

The general fund was known by several names, which added to the confusion. It was known as the current unrestricted fund, the current fund, and the current general fund. The term *general fund* will be used in this discussion.

The general fund was used to finance general activities of the not-for-profit organization and was unrestricted in that purpose. The general fund had a subcategory of board-designated funds; these funds were *internally* restricted to any activity the board saw fit. These internal restrictions had no legal restrictions, and the board was free to terminate or reallocate these funds at any time. The general fund was not protected from creditor action.

As a result of the lack of legal restrictions surrounding board-designated funds, and the confusion it caused readers of financial statements, AICPA took the position that these funds should be included in the general fund for financial statement presentation.

Current Restricted Funds

As with the general fund, the current restricted fund was also known by other names, including restricted fund, donor-restricted fund, and special-purpose fund. Contributions to current restricted funds were for specific purposes. These were *external* restrictions imposed by the donor(s) and were *legally* restricted. In other words, monies expended from these funds could be used only for the specific and express purposes of the fund. To divert these funds to any other activity would have required permission of the donor(s) or legal recourse.

Endowment Funds

Endowment funds were also *externally* restricted, but differed greatly from current restricted funds. Endowment funds generally were assets contributed to not-for-profit organizations on either a term or a permanent basis. The earnings could be used to help offset operating expenses of the association, or restrictions could be made on the earnings, according to the donor's wishes.

When an endowment was a term endowment, the asset either would revert to the donor or the donor's designee at a certain time, such as death of the donor, or would remain with the organization. If the asset remained with the organization, restrictions regarding use of the principal were removed at the end of the term by transferring the principal from the endowment fund to the general fund.

When the endowment was permanent, the asset remained with the organization in perpetuity. The principal of perpetual endowments remained whole, and the earnings were used according to the donor's wishes.

Fixed-Assets Funds

As with the general fund and the current restricted fund, fixed-assets funds were known by several names, including building fund, land fund, and equipment fund. Once traditional, the popularity of fixed-assets funds has steadily decreased, for good reasons. These funds confused readers of financial statements, created difficult bookkeeping procedures, and generally served no purpose. They implied that certain assets were available for designated activities only and were not available for the use of the organization as a whole, which was rarely the case.

Financial Statement Presentation

The old way of presenting the four restricted funds in the financial statements is shown in Exhibit 17.1.

EXHIBIT 17.1

Not-for-Profit Organization's Balance Sheet (Old Way)

[Date]

Liabilities and Fund Balance

Fund Balances:

General fund	$XXX
Current restricted funds	XXX
Endowment funds	XXX
Fixed-assets funds	XXX
	$XXX

It was conceivable for not-for-profit organizations to have several different and distinct funds within each of the four funds. When this occurred, the funds within each fund category were added together and presented in summary on the balance sheet, for a financial statement presentation that was easier to understand and less cumbersome. The detail might have appeared as supplemental information.

The New Way

Restricted funds are now accounted for in a net assets section of the Statement of Financial Position (balance sheet). The net assets section has three types of funds:

> ➢ Unrestricted net assets

> ➢ Temporarily restricted net assets

> ➢ Permanently restricted net assets

Unrestricted Net Assets

The new unrestricted net assets account is essentially the same as the old general fund account. The account is used to finance the general activities of the not-for-profit organization, which is unrestricted in that purpose. The account is subject to creditor action.

Unrestricted net assets can be considered a not-for-profit organization's net worth (total assets minus total liabilities). In other words, if a not-for-profit organization converted all its assets to cash at book value and paid off all its debts, the remaining funds would be the organization's net worth, called unrestricted net assets.

Another way to view unrestricted net assets is to compare them with retained earnings in the financial statements of commercial organizations. If a not-for-profit organization totaled all the revenues it had received since it was in existence and subtracted from this figure the total expenses for the same period, the resulting profit or loss would be the organization's unrestricted net assets.

The unrestricted net assets account balance changes only once a year, at year-end. At the end of a fiscal year the profit or loss for the year (the increase or decrease in unrestricted net assets) is added to or deducted from the unrestricted net assets carried forward at the beginning of the year. The new unrestricted net assets balance will remain unchanged until the end of the new fiscal year.

As in the case of the general fund, unrestricted net assets *include* board-designated funds. Board-designated funds are internal restrictions only. They are not separately classified on the Statement of Financial Position, and they are not protected from creditor action. Board-designated funds have no accounting significance.

Unrestricted net assets are classified as a liability on the financial records because the IRS requires that not-for-profit organizations have a dissolution clause in their bylaws. There are no owners in a not-for-profit organization; if the organization dissolves, its net worth is not distributed to individuals. In the event of a dissolution, the assets and liabilities of the organization are absorbed by the not-for-profit organization named in the bylaws. A genuine liability does exist, although the probability of a transfer is remote.

Temporarily Restricted Net Assets

The new temporarily restricted net assets account is similar to the old current restricted funds. To be considered a temporarily restricted net asset, external restrictions on the use of contributions are imposed by the donors. It is important to classify temporarily restricted net assets correctly, because proper classification and accounting could protect contributions to such accounts from creditor action.

An example of temporarily restricted net assets is contributions to a scholarship fund. Donors voluntarily contribute to the fund with the understanding that the monies contributed will be used only to fund scholarships. The donations are not included among the revenues of the organization, but instead are classified as a temporary liability on the Statement of Financial Position until the scholarship is awarded. When the scholarship is awarded, it simply reduces the liability and is not considered an expense of the organization.

All temporarily restricted net assets, whatever the number, are added together and presented in summary on the Statement of Financial Position as one figure. It is acceptable to provide detail of the individual funds as a supplemental statement or in the footnotes to the financial statements.

Permanently Restricted Net Assets

The best examples of permanently restricted net assets are term or perpetual endowments. An endowment is established when the donor transfers cash (the corpus) or other assets for use by a not-for-profit organization, but the use is restricted to the donor's wishes. The not-for-profit organization is prohibited from diverting these assets to activities other than those specified by the donor.

Although a perpetual endowment remains with the not-for-profit organization in perpetuity, assets transferred to a not-for-profit organization via a term endowment revert to the donor or the donor's designee at a certain time, such as the death of the donor. It is permissible and common for a term endowment to be transferred to the not-for-profit organization, at which time it is often reclassified as unrestricted.

As in the case of temporarily restricted net assets, all permanently restricted net assets are added together and presented in summary on the Statement of Financial Position. Detail usually is provided in a supplemental statement or in the footnotes to the financial statements.

Financial Statement Presentation

The new way of presenting restricted funds in the financial statements is shown in Exhibit 17.2.

EXHIBIT 17.2

Not-for-Profit Organization's Statement of Financial Position (New Way)

Statement of Financial Position

[Date]
Liabilities and Net Assets

Net Assets:

Unrestricted net assets	$XXX
Temporarily restricted net assets	XXX
Permanently restricted net assets	XXX
	$XXX

CHAPTER 18

The Basics of Intermediate Sanctions

INTERMEDIATE SANCTIONS LEGISLATION became law as part of the Taxpayer Bill of Rights 2, passed on July 31, 1996. The legislation was prompted by high-profile cases of not-for-profit organization insiders benefiting from unfair and excessive economic advantages as a result of their influential positions. Until the passage of the intermediate sanctions, the IRS's only recourse when faced with such abuses was to punish the *organization* by revoking its tax-exempt status. The IRS did not want to do this because it was patently unfair to the innocent beneficiaries of the organization's noble goals. For example, if the chief staff executive of a worthwhile charity cheated the charity, it would be absurd to revoke the tax-exempt status of the charity, yet the IRS was essentially powerless to punish the individual.

All of that has changed with intermediate sanctions. Under the new rules, *individuals* participating in "excess benefit transactions" are held personally responsible for severe penalties in the form of excise taxes.

Excess Benefits

An excess benefit is the excess of the value of services or property received by an individual over the value of the services or property provided by the individual. General examples include the following:

➢ Receiving compensation disproportionate to services provided

➢ Benefiting from loans where the interest rate is below current market

➢ Taking business trips to exotic locations where no business is conducted and expenses are not reimbursed to the organization

➢ Receiving free professional advice and services

➢ Taking part in illegal deferred compensation agreements

➢ Purchasing property when the value is significantly higher than the selling price

Specific examples include the following:

> ➤ The board members all have full-time jobs separate from the organization. The board meets only four times a year. The board members decide to compensate themselves for their involvement in the amount of $200,000 each at the end of the year.

> ➤ The chief staff executive purchases a home and mortgages the home through the organization at an interest rate of 2 percent when the prevailing interest rate on settlement date was 8 percent.

> ➤ The chairman of the board is reimbursed by the organization for expenses incurred for his "business trip" to Tahiti. The chairman traveled first class, stayed in a five-star hotel, and had all expenses, including souvenirs, charged to the organization. No business was conducted.

> ➤ The treasurer found herself the object of a lawsuit, the circumstances of which had nothing at all to do with the organization's purpose. She retained an expensive law firm to represent her, and the legal bills were paid by the organization.

> ➤ The executive vice president benefited from a deferred compensation agreement, deferring monies well in excess of legal limitations. Additionally, the money was "hidden" and not shown as an asset of the organization and not at risk as required for nonqualified plans.

> ➤ The board approves the purchase of company cars for board members' personal use. At the end of the year they bought the cars from the organization for $1,000 each, although the actual value of each car was $20,000.

Individuals Affected

Two types of individuals are affected by the intermediate sanctions: a disqualified person or an organization manager.

A disqualified person is:

1. An individual in a position to exercise substantial influence on the affairs of the organization

2. Family members of the above

3. Business entities over which the person has 35 percent or more control

4. Individuals listed in Part V of the organization's Form 990 (officers, directors, trustees, and key employees)

5. Independent contractors possessing such influence

6. Certain influential members and donors

An organization manager is an officer, director, or trustee of the organization or other individuals having similar powers.

Computation of the Excise Tax

Three types of excise taxes fall under intermediate sanctions: initial, secondary, and a tax on organization managers. The following is an example of how the initial excise tax works:

> A board member purchases an automobile worth $21,000 from the organization for $1,000. The excise benefit would be $20,000 ($21,000 value less $1,000 paid). The individual will be assessed an initial excise tax equal to 25 percent of the excess benefit, or $5,000 on this car (25 percent × $20,000).
>
> Additionally, the organization must be made whole. Not only does the individual have to pay the $5,000 excise tax, he or she also must reimburse the organization the entire $20,000 excess benefit.

The following is an example of how the secondary excise tax works:

> If the individual did not make the organization whole, that individual will be taxed at 200 percent of the value of the excess benefit. In this case, the individual would be assessed an excise tax of $40,000 ($20,000 × 200 percent).

The following is an example of how the tax on organization managers works:

> If organization managers willfully and knowingly do nothing to prevent an excess benefit transaction, knowing it was improper, even if they did not benefit personally, they will be assessed an excise tax of 10 percent of the excess benefit. In this case, they would be assessed $2,000 ($20,000 × 10 percent), limited to $10,000 per transaction.

Organizations Affected

Two types of tax-exempt organizations are affected by the intermediate sanctions legislation: 501(c)(3) organizations, with the exception of private foundations, and 501(c)(4) organizations. It is likely that intermediate sanctions will be extended to other not-for-profits, such as 501(c)(6) organizations, although now they are not technically covered.

Conclusion

This chapter covers the *basics* of intermediate sanctions and provides general guidelines. The actual statute and regulations are very complex and should be discussed with the organization's attorney and CPA.

The Basics of Not-for-Profit Accounting and Financial Statements

ALTHOUGH NOT-FOR-PROFIT ORGANIZATIONS may prepare their financial statements under Generally Accepted Accounting Principles (GAAP), these statements differ from comparable financial statements prepared for commercial entities. Financial statements prepared by a not-for-profit organization and audited by an independent certified public accountant must be prepared in accordance with the provisions of the accounting standards issued by the Financial Accounting Standards Board (FASB) and distributed by the American Institute of Certified Public Accountants (AICPA). They are:

> Statement of Financial Accounting Standards #116 (See Appendix B)

> Statement of Financial Accounting Standards #117 (See Appendix A)

> Statement of Financial Accounting Standards #124 (See Appendix C)

> Statement of Financial Accounting Standards #136 (See Appendix D)

Although some of the provisions included in the standards reflect only terminology differences, there are substantive accounting differences.

Key Definitions

Nonprofit—This term can cause confusion; a nonprofit organization *can* make a profit. The term *nonprofit* is used because when a nonprofit organization operates at a profit, the profit *cannot* be distributed to the board, influential committee chairs, or members. However, when a commercial organization, a sole proprietorship, a partnership, or a stock corporation operates at a profit, the profit is distributed to the owners, partners, and stockholders accordingly. (*Note:* To minimize confusion, the term *not-for-profit* is used in this book.)

Tax-exempt—This term also may lead to confusion because it implies that a tax-exempt organization doesn't pay taxes, when in actuality it does. A typical tax-exempt organization may pay some or all of the following taxes:

➢ Social Security (FICA) tax

➢ Medicare tax

➢ Federal Unemployment (FUTA) tax (*Note:* 501(c)(3) organizations are exempt from this tax.)

➢ Lobby tax

➢ State sales tax

➢ State unemployment tax

➢ State personal property tax

➢ State real estate tax

➢ Various county and local taxes

Tax-exempt means that a not-for-profit organization is exempt from an *income tax* on its profit if it has one. However, not-for-profit organizations may be required to pay an income tax (unrestricted business income tax) if profit was derived from a source of revenue unrelated to the purpose of the not-for-profit organization.

Typical Financial Statements

A not-for-profit organization is responsible for completing its own financial statements monthly. These statements are different from audited financial statements issued by certified public accountants (CPAs), because the CPA-issued statements are subject to the rigorous auditing standards and would include a Statement of Cash Flows and footnotes to the financial statements that are rarely included as a part of internal statements.

A not-for-profit organization should prepare the following internal statements:

➢ Statement of Financial Position (balance sheet)

➢ Statement of Activity (income statement)

Statement of Financial Position

The following sample and discussion illustrate the various elements of a Statement of Financial Position.

Not-for-Profit Organization
1.   ## Statement of Financial Position
2.   ## March 31, 20XX

Assets

3. Current Assets:		
4. Cash and Cash Equivalents	$500,000	
5. Accounts Receivable	50,000	
6. Inventory	60,000	
7. Prepaid Expenses	20,000	
8. Total Current Assets		$630,000
9. Plant, Property, and Equipment:		
Land	$100,000	
Building	500,000	
Equipment	300,000	
Subtotal	$900,000	
Less Accumulated Depreciation	(300,000)	
Net Plant, Property, and Equipment		$600,000
10. Other Assets:		
11. Investments	$400,000	
12. Cash, Temporarily Restricted	10,000	
13. Cash, Permanently Restricted	$100,000	510,000
14. Total Assets		$1,740,000

Liabilities and Net Assets

15. Current Liabilities:		
16. Accounts Payable	$140,000	
17. Accrued Payroll and Payroll Taxes	120,000	
18. Total Current Liabilities		$260,000
19. Long-Term Liabilities:		
20. Note Payable	$125,000	
Total Long-Term Liabilities		125,000
21. Other Liabilities:		
22. Deferred Income, Dues	$175,000	
23. Deferred Income, Conferences	140,000	
Total Other Liabilities		315,000

24.	Net Assets:		
25.	Unrestricted Net Assets	$930,000	
26.	Temporarily Restricted Net Assets	10,000	
27.	Permanently Restricted Net Assets	100,000	1,040,000
	Total Liabilities and Net Assets		$1,740,000

Discussion of Accounts and Terminology: Statement of Financial Position

1. **Statement of Financial Position:** Unique to not-for-profit organizations. This is simply another term for a balance sheet, a term used by commercial entities. This statement shows the organization's assets and liabilities against those assets. Assets must always equal liabilities.

2. **Date:** Date on which data were captured. The Statement of Financial Position continually changes, so it is important to note the date on which the data were captured. In this example, the statement represents a snapshot of the assets and liabilities of the organization at midnight on March 31, 20XX.

3. **Current Assets:** Includes cash, items that will be converted to cash, and other accounts that the organization benefits from in the current period.

4. **Cash and Cash Equivalents:** Cash on hand, certificates of deposit, etc.

5. **Accounts Receivable:** Monies owed to the organization by customers, members, etc.

6. **Inventory:** Items, such as books, owned by the organization and held for eventual sale. Inventories are recorded in the financial statements at cost to the organization, not at the selling price.

7. **Prepaid Expenses:** Expenditures made in a current period that the organization will benefit from in some future period. For example, a hotel requires a deposit in March for an event that won't be held until August.

8. **Total Current Assets:** The subtotal of the four accounts (cash and cash equivalents, accounts receivable, inventory, and prepaid expenses). It is important to classify any amount properly because this information will be used to compute financial ratios.

9. **Plant, Property, and Equipment:** Includes cost, accumulated depreciation, and resulting book value of land, buildings, furniture, office equipment, and so forth. All such assets are recorded at original cost, even if the items have appreciated in value, and reduced in value by accumulated depreciation recorded corresponding to those assets.

10. **Other Assets:** Assets not classified in the other accounts.

11. **Investments:** Recorded at market value in accordance with Statement of Financial Accounting Standards #124.

12. **Cash, Temporarily Restricted:** Cash contributions held in trust by the not-for-profit organization for a temporary period of time. This money eventually will be spent in accordance with the donor's directions.

13. **Cash, Permanently Restricted:** Cash contributions held in trust by the not-for-profit organization in perpetuity. The earnings attributed to permanently restricted funds can be either unrestricted or temporarily restricted. This type of asset used to be called an endowment fund.

14. **Total Assets:** The aggregate net value of all assets held by the organization.

15. **Current Liabilities:** Amounts owed by the organization and due to be paid within 12 months of the date of the Statement of Financial Position.

16. **Accounts Payable:** Amounts owed to creditors and vendors, and the current-year portion of long-term debt.

17. **Accrued Payroll and Payroll Taxes:** Unpaid wages owed to employees and payroll taxes withheld.

18. **Total Current Liabilities:** Total of all amounts owed and due within 12 months of the date of the Statement of Financial Position.

19. **Long-Term Liabilities:** Monies owed by the organization not due to be paid in the current year.

20. **Note Payable:** Usually secured debt.

21. **Other Liabilities:** Any liability not classified as current or long-term debt.

22. **Deferred Income, Dues:** Liability for monies received for dues not yet taken into income.

23. **Deferred Income, Conferences:** Monies received by exhibitors and others for a future event. This is considered a liability because these amounts would have to be paid back if the conference were not held.

24. **Net Assets:** The equity portion of the Statement of Financial Position.

25. **Unrestricted Net Assets:** The net profit or loss the organization has experienced since it has been in existence. Could also be compared to net worth.

26. **Temporarily Restricted Net Assets:** See #12.

27. **Permanently Restricted Net Assets:** See #13.

Statement of Activity

The following sample and discussion illustrate various elements of a statement of activity.

1.   **Statement of Activity**
2.   **For the Three–Month Period Ended 3/31/XX**

3. Revenues:

	Dues	$150,000
	Advertising	100,500
	Book Sales	30,000
4.	Less Cost of Goods Sold	(20,000)
	Seminars	20,000
	Magazine Sales	15,000
	Rent	30,000
	Miscellaneous	10,000
	Total Revenue	$335,500

5. Expenses:

	Salaries	$120,000
	Fringe Benefits	40,000
	Printing	100,000
	Postage	25,000
	Travel	15,000
	Depreciation	5,000
	Total Expenses	$305,000

6. Increase (Decrease) in Unrestricted Net Assets — $30,500

Discussion of Accounts and Terminology: Statement of Activity

1. **Statement of Activity:** Unique to not-for-profit organizations. It is similar to income statement or statement of profit and loss, terms used by commercial organizations. It simply states the not-for-profit organization's revenues, expenses, and results of operations.

2. **Date:** A specific period of time. The Statement of Activity shows the not-for-profit organization's revenues and expenses for a period of time—in this case, year-to-date figures for three months. After a year is completed, the result of operations for the year is added to or deducted from unrestricted net assets on the Statement of Financial Condition.

3. **Revenues:** Also called income. In accordance with the Statement of Financial Accounting Standards #117, revenues for not-for-profit organizations are always presented as gross, not net.

4. **Cost of Goods Sold:** Actual cost to the organization for items sold. This account is not included with expenses.

5. **Expenses:** All expenditures not capitalized, used to pay off debts that apply to the current period.

6. **Increase (Decrease) in Unrestricted Net Assets:** Not-for-profit terminology for profit or loss.

Accounting Methods

Cash Accounting. The cash accounting method is relatively simple and is generally used by new or very small not-for-profit organizations. In cash accounting, revenues are recorded in the Statement of Activity only if the actual cash has been received. Expenses are shown only if the expense actually has been paid.

Although cash accounting is easy, the resulting profit or loss shown in the financial statements is often misleading.

Note: There is an important exception in cash accounting. Purchases of assets that exceed certain value, and that the organization will use for a period of time, must be capitalized on the Statement of Financial Position and depreciated accordingly.

Accrual Accounting. While somewhat more difficult than cash accounting, accrual accounting is more accurate and reliable. In accrual accounting, revenues are shown on the Statement of Activity if they have been *earned,* even if they haven't been received. Expenses are shown if the expense has been *incurred,* even if the expense hasn't been paid.

CHAPTER 20

Private Foundations

THERE ARE MANY NONPROFIT ORGANIZATIONS whose names may include the term "foundation." This term, in and of itself, has no legal meaning. It is the IRS's designation that defines whether a nonprofit will fall under the public charity or private foundation rules.

Definition

The IRS considers any and all nonprofit organizations described in Section 501(c)(3) to be private foundations, unless the organization meets certain criteria that could exclude it from being considered a private foundation. Basically, the designation of a private foundation is the default. Private foundations are legal entities that are established by a group or a family or even an individual, for the purpose of philanthropy.

Nonprivate foundation status can be established by an organization that is:

1. A church or association of churches

2. An educational organization that maintains a regular faculty and has an enrolled student body (i.e., a school or college)

3. An organization whose function is to provide medical care, or medical education or research

4. An organization whose support is substantially from the government or from direct or indirect contributions from the general public, which is organization for the purpose of receiving, holding, investing, or administering property and making expenditures for a college or university, commonly known as an educational endowment fund

5. A governmental unit

6. An organization that usually receives its support from a governmental unit or from contributions from the general public

7. An organization that receives more than 33 percent of its support from gifts, grants, contributions, and receipts from activities related to its except purpose and receives less than 33 percent of its income from investments and unrelated business

8. An organization that is operated for the benefit of or to further the purposes of one of the organizations operating under 1–7 above (a supporting organization)

9. An organization that exists exclusively for the testing of public safety

These organizations typically have the following distinguishing features:

1. They are supported by a single source of funding, usually gifts from one donor, a family or a corporation, rather than the general public at large

2. Payments of distributions and expenses come from investment income rather than from the proceeds of fundraising or from contributions

3. Generally, they make grants to achieve their charitable purposes, rather than to directly operate programs

Private foundations are, by definition, one of two types, *operating* and *nonoperating*. *Private operating foundations* are actively involved in charitable, religious, educational, or similar activities. They are subject generally to the same tax on net investment income and to most other requirements and restrictions, with the exception that they are not subject to the excise or penalty tax for failure to distribute income in accordance with IRS rules. Operating foundations often are museums, libraries, or historic landmarks.

Taxation and Private Foundations

The main reason that an organization is established under and maintains its structure as a private foundation is that this structure allows for more control. The control to determine the areas that the foundation funds through grants and distributions and the focus of its contributions is important to many donors. This structure allows for that control by the foundation board or managers, but with significant oversight. Any benefits derived by substantial contributors or disqualified persons trigger significant penalty taxes. These taxes can be assessed not only to the foundation, but in some cases, also to the managers of the foundation and/or the disqualified persons. Specifically, taxes associated with private foundations are as follows.

The net investment income tax of 2 percent of the investment income is unavoidable to private foundations, but it can be reduced to 1 percent if the organization meets the criteria for making qualifying distributions. The formula for reducing the tax is that the organization must make annual distributions that are equal to or exceed an amount formulated by the Internal Revenue Service, that is,

Assets × Average percentage payout) + (1% × Net investment income for the year)

More detail on this calculation can be found on the IRS website and in a variety of IRS publications. This tax must be reported on Form 990-PF and be paid annually at the time for filing that return or in quarterly estimated tax payments if the total tax for the year is $500 or more.

Excise taxes on self-dealing are assessed when a private foundation engages in what the IRS deems to be prohibited transactions with disqualified persons. Disqualified persons can include substantial contributors or their relatives or any corporation, trust, or partnership in which the donor directly or indirectly owns a significant portion (greater than 35 percent). Prohibited transactions include (but are not limited to) furnishing goods as a vendor, use of facilities, selling or leasing of property or payment of compensation that may be considered to be unreasonable when compared to persons in similar positions in other organizations of approximately the same size.

Basically, the designation of a private foundation is the default. Private foundations are legal entities that are established by a group or a family or even an individual, for the purpose of philanthropy.

Excise taxes are charged when a foundation fails to distribute at least 5 percent of the market value of its assets. These grants or distributions do not include grants that are paid to other private foundations or organizations that are "supporting organizations" as defined in the Internal Revenue Code.

Excise taxes are assessed on "excess" business holdings. Business holdings involve ownership of the stock or other securities issued by a business enterprise, and excessive generally is defined as 20 percent of the corporation's voting stock, less the amount of voting stock owned by the foundations officers, directors, or substantial contributors and their families.

Excise taxes may be charged if the foundation invests its funds in a less than prudent manner, such as trading on margin, trading future contracts, trading in option agreements, or short selling, as this may jeopardize the foundation's ability to continue with its charitable purpose.

Certain types of expenses by a private foundation may generate penalty excise taxes. These taxable expenditures would include supporting political candidates or campaigns, grants to individuals or supporting organizations or foreign charities. Though political expenditures and lobbying is clearly prohibited, other grants may be allowable with significant monitoring and, in some cases, advance written approval from the IRS.

Contributions to operating foundations are usually deductible up to 50 percent of the donor's adjusted gross income. (Contributions to nonoperating foundations are limited to 30 percent of the donor's adjusted gross income.)

Nonoperating foundations are grant makers that primarily make distributions to other 501(c)(3) organizations. Nonoperating foundations are subject to income distribution requirements that they pay out a minimum (at present, 5 percent) of the market value of their assets, and are subject to excise taxes should they not meet the minimum distributions as prescribed by the IRS. These foundations would include organizations that are family foundations. Family foundations are used by families to work toward common goals or to install the value of philanthropy to future generations in the family. Corporations or members of a certain sector may establish foundations, such as the Milton S. Hershey Foundation or the North American Railway Foundation, the purposes of which may or may not be specific to a particular cause. Foundations can support one particular area of interest, such as preserving the history of a certain effort, promoting a variety of likeminded goals, or improving social or cultural areas, such as food banks and shelters, or preserving the arts, or they may support a variety of organizations and the focus or targeted grantees may change from year to year.

Often, these organizations attempt to build their endowments through investments and expend only the minimum amount necessary to a variety of grant programs.

Summary

In summary, if an organization cannot establish that it is not a private foundation, then the next step would be to determine if it functions as an operating or nonoperating foundation. The benefits of qualifying as a private *operating* include the following:

1. Operating foundations are not subject to the income distribution requirements.

2. Donors to operating foundations are subject to a charitable contribution deduction limitation of 50 percent of adjusted gross income, whereas donors to nonoperating foundations are restricted to a charitable contribution deduction limitation of 30 percent of adjusted gross income.

3. Private operating foundations, if they are able to meet the criteria as "exempt foundations," do not pay tax on investment income.

# of Financial
Standards #117
ments
it Organizations

SFAS #117, general-purpose external financial statements pro-
organizations were often confusing. This confusion stemmed
accounting terminology regarding individual accounts and
financial statement presentation formats for the old balance
ements of not-for-profit organizations.

ganizations, specifically universities, hospitals, museums, and
present financial statements that focused on the organization
ganizations included a cash flow statement with the external
Some organizations prepared their income statements on the
ording expenses, while others completed their income state-
al method.

organizations must comply with the new provisions in SFAS
nsistency will benefit everyone connected with the statement,
rs of the statement such as banks and lending institutions, as
have fiduciary financial responsibilities.

SFAS #117 addresses the following three important areas:

➢ Terminology changes

➢ Complete set of financial statements and important changes therein

➢ The new net assets section on the Statement of Financial Position

---

Reprinted with permission from *Not-for-Profit Organization's Guide to the New Accounting Ruling*. Copyright U.S. Chamber of Commerce, September 1996.

The following chart compares previous SFAS #117 terminology and financial statements with the changes in the new standard.

Terminology Changes

Pre-SFAS #117	Post-SFAS #117
Balance Sheet	Statement of Financial Position
Income Statement	Statement of Activity
Profit (Loss)	Increase (Decrease) in Unrestricted Net Assets
Fund Balances	Net Assets
General Fund Balance	Unrestricted Net Assets
Endowment Funds	Permanently Restricted Net Assets
Current Restricted Funds	Temporarily Restricted Net Assets
Plant Fund	(none)
Board-Restricted Funds	(none)

Changes Under the Complete Set of Financial Statements

Balance Sheet	Statement of Financial Position
Income Statement	Statement of Activity
(Not Required)	Statement of Cash Flows
Accompanying Notes	Accompanying Notes

Effective Dates

A not-for-profit organization with $5 million in assets and $1 million in expenses is required to comply with the new standards for the organization's fiscal year that begins after December 15, 1994. An organization with less than $5 million in assets and $1 million in expenses is required to comply with the new standards for the organization's fiscal year that begins after December 15, 1995.

Scope

SFAS #117 applies to the not-for-profit organizations that are addressed in Chapter 1 of this manual. Not-for-profit organizations include, but are not limited to, trade associations, professional associations, charities, foundations, chambers of commerce, boards of trade, hospitals, universities, and museums.

Inconsistencies

If an inconsistency arises concerning the provisions of SFAS #117 and prior AICPA pronouncements, including SOP 78-10, the provisions of SFAS #117 will apply and other provisions and prior pronouncements no longer will be acceptable.

SFAS #117

Financial Statements

The financial statements of a not-for-profit organization can be broken down into either internal financial statements or external financial statements.

Internal financial statements of a not-for-profit organization can be constructed in any manner that meets the needs of the organization. These statements are not required to meet the provisions of SFAS #117 and should instead focus on the managerial needs of the board and upper management. Therefore, SFAS #117 does not address internal financial statements of not-for-profit organizations.

External financial statements of a not-for-profit organization must comply with the provisions of SFAS #117 in all respects. External financial statements must be constructed to meet the needs of both management and other parties who have an interest in the organization. The financial statements, including the notes to the financial statements, should provide the following information:

➢ The organization's assets, liabilities, and net assets included in the Statement of Financial Position

➢ An accounting of changes in the new classes of net assets, including unrestricted net assets, temporarily restricted net assets, and permanently restricted net assets

➢ The Statement of Cash Flows

➢ The Statement of Financial Position that should be constructed to provide equity information

➢ The Statement of Activity that should provide for the service efforts of the organization

Scope of External Financial Statements

SFAS #117 requires that a complete set of financial statements for all not-for-profit organizations include the Statement of Financial Position, the Statement of Activity, the Statement of Cash Flows, and accompanying notes.

While Generally Accepted Accounting Principles now require not-for-profit organizations to provide information concerning loss contingencies, accounting changes, and so forth, the requirements for not-for-profit external financial statements are generally no more stringent than requirements for commercial activities.

SFAS #117 does not specify when or how to measure revenues, expenses, gains, losses, assets, liabilities, and net assets. However, it does discuss how to report these items.

The Statement of Financial Position

In the past it was common for not-for-profit organizations not to report on the organization as a whole. The Statement of Financial Position now must focus on the organization as a whole regarding its total assets and liabilities and net assets. Reporting on segments of organizations alone is no longer permitted.

While the Statement of Activity reports activities for a period of time, the Statement of Financial Position will continue to report activities for a moment of time. The statements will provide information that will enable the reader of the financial statements to:

➤ Assess the organization's ability to continue to provide services, and

➤ Assess the organization's liquidity.

Aggregating Assets and Liabilities

The Statement of Financial Position provisions of SFAS #117 provide that assets and liabilities be organized into reasonably homogeneous groups. Typical homogeneous groups include the following:

➤ Cash and cash equivalents

➤ Marketable securities

➤ Fixed assets and depreciation allowances

➤ Prepaid expenses

➤ Accounts payable

➤ Notes payable

However, contrary to commercial organizations, cash or assets that have been received with donor-imposed restrictions on the use of the assets should not be listed with cash or other current assets that are unrestricted. They should instead be recorded near fixed assets on the Statement of Financial Position. Including restricted cash with cash and cash equivalents would distort the organization's financial ratios, such as the current ratio or the acid test ratio.

Liquidity information should be recorded on the Statement of Financial Position by classifying assets according to their proximity to cash and classifying liabilities in accordance with their maturity dates. Assets and liabilities also can be classified as either current or noncurrent. Additionally, the notes of the financial statement should provide more detailed information concerning specific maturity dates, restrictions, or other information that would be useful to the reader of the statements.

The New Net Assets Section

The new net assets section in the Statement of Financial Position of a not-for-profit organization now has three classes of accounts:

➤ Unrestricted net assets

➤ Temporarily restricted net assets

➤ Permanently restricted net assets

It is important to emphasize that these are classes of accounts, since a not-for-profit organization could have several types of temporarily and permanently restricted net assets. If a not-for-profit organization has more than one temporarily or permanently restricted net asset activity, the total of all temporarily restricted activities is reported on the Statement of Financial Position as one figure, as is the total of all permanently restricted activities.

Information regarding temporarily and permanently restricted net assets, including both the time and the purpose of the restrictions, should be detailed in notes to the financial statements.

Permanently restricted net assets are typically broken down into the following two types:

➤ Assets, such as works of art, that were donated with the understanding that they must be preserved and never sold.

➤ Assets donated with the stipulation that they be invested as a source of income. This income could be either temporarily restricted or unrestricted, depending upon the donor's wishes.

Assets that were permanently donated as a source of income are permanent endowment funds.

Temporarily restricted net assets typically have one of the following restrictions:

➤ Time restrictions, meaning that the resource could be used only at a particular moment of time or at the passage of time

➤ Purpose restrictions, meaning that the resource could be used only for a specific activity

It also is possible to have both time and purpose restrictions. Assets with both time and purpose restrictions are term endowments.

Unrestricted net assets are the result of operations of the not-for-profit organization. Such assets are simply revenues earned less expenses incurred since the organization's inception, and can be compared in some respects to retained earnings of commercial organizations. It is also helpful to consider a not-for-profit organization's unrestricted net assets as the organization's net worth, excluding temporarily and permanently restricted net assets.

Often a not-for-profit organization has board-designated voluntary restrictions. Board-designated voluntary restrictions—for example, voluntarily earmarking assets for a particular purpose—are included among the unrestricted net assets of the organization. A board is free to designate portions of its funds for certain activities;

however, these are included among unrestricted net assets since they are not bound by purpose or time restrictions by a voluntary donor.

The following exhibits illustrate the new Statement of Financial Position format and are presented on a comparable basis. Exhibit A.1 illustrates an organization with no temporarily or permanently restricted net assets. Exhibit A.2 expands the statement to include restricted net assets. When reviewing this statement, please note where cash relating to restricted activities has been placed in proximity to fixed assets.

Not-for-Profit Organization's Statement of Financial Position December 31, 20XX

Assets

	Year 2	Year 1
Cash and Cash Equivalents	$151,500	$92,000
Accounts Receivable	9,000	8,000
Inventories	12,000	70,000
Prepaid Expenses	4,000	5,000
Contributions Receivable	11,000	10,000
Less Allowance for Uncollectables	(2,500)	(2,000)
Fixed Assets	95,000	90,000
Less Accumulated Depreciation	(25,000)	(20,000)
Total Assets	$255,000	$193,000

Liabilities and Net Assets

	Year 2	Year 1
Liabilities:		
Accounts Payable	$15,000	$13,000
Notes Payable	65,000	70,000
Deferred Grant Revenues	40,000	50,000
Total Liabilities	$120,000	$133,000
Net Assets:		
Unrestricted Net Assets	$135,000	$60,000
Total Liabilities and Net Assets	$255,000	$193,000

EXHIBIT A.2

Not-for-Profit Organization's
Statement of Financial Position
December 31, Year 2 and Year 1

Assets

	Year 2	Year 1
Cash and Cash Equivalents	$50,000	$35,000
Accounts Receivable	9,000	8,000
Inventories	12,000	10,000
Prepaid Expenses	4,000	5,000
Contributions Receivable	11,000	10,000
Less Allowance for Uncollectables	(2,500)	(2,000)
Assets Restricted to Future Investment in Equipment	13,000	13,000
Fixed Assets	95,000	95,000
Less Accumulated Depreciation	(25,000)	(20,000)
Assets with Permanent Restrictions	25,000	25,000
Total assets	$191,500	$174,000

Liabilities and Net Assets

	Year 2	Year 1
Accounts Payable	$15,000	$13,000
Notes Payable	65,000	70,000
Deferred Grant Revenues	40,000	50,000
Total Liabilities	$120,000	$133,000
Net Assets:		
Unrestricted	$33,500	$16,000
Temporarily Restricted	13,000	
Permanently Restricted	25,000	25,000
Total Net Assets	$71,500	$41,000
Total Liabilities and Net Assets:	$191,500	$174,000

The Statement of Activities

It is important to remember that the new Statement of Activities for not-for-profit organizations must focus on the organization as a whole.

The statement should be designed to provide readers information concerning:

➤ The effects of transactions on the three classes of net assets

➤ Any relationships that exist between or among these transactions and how they affect each other

➤ How the organization uses its resources to provide and continue programs and services for its constituencies

The Statement of Activities and accompanying notes should enable the reader of the financial statement to:

➤ Evaluate the organization's performance during the period

➤ Assess the organization's service efforts and its ability to continue services

➤ Assess how the organization's management has discharged its responsibilities accordingly

Reporting Changes in the Three Classes of Net Assets

The new Statement of Activities should be designed to report on all the changes for all three of the new classes of net assets: unrestricted, temporarily restricted, and permanently restricted net assets. Revenues, expenses, gains, losses, and reclassification information also should be aggregated into items that possess similar characteristics, since they are reasonably homogeneous groups.

Reporting Revenues, Expenses, Gains, and Losses among the New Classes of Net Assets in the Statement of Activity

A controversial aspect of SFAS #117 is the requirement that the Statement of Activities report all expenses as expenses relating to unrestricted net assets. This requirement can best be explained by using an example of a not-for-profit organization that receives contributions to a scholarship fund.

A scholarship fund would clearly be included among temporarily restricted net assets. Contributions received from donors for the purpose of awarding scholarships would increase this particular temporarily restricted net asset class of account. When the scholarship is subsequently awarded, the expense would be recorded among the unrestricted activities of the organization on its Statement of Activity. To offset this expense, monies may be transferred or reclassified from temporarily restricted net assets to unrestricted net assets accordingly to balance the financial statements. This reclassification revenue account would typically be called "net assets released from restrictions."

Income or gains credited to temporarily restricted net assets or permanently restricted net assets will typically increase the value of that particular class of net assets. When a corresponding expenditure is made that relates to the particular class of asset, the expenditure will be listed among the expenses of the unrestricted class. Again, revenues must be reclassified from a temporarily or permanently restricted account to the unrestricted accounts accordingly.

Typically, the recording of contributions to temporarily or permanently restricted net asset classes of accounts is very clear, as is the use of earnings or gains on the account. Donor-restricted contributions are reported as restricted revenues or gains; the contributions will increase temporarily or permanently restricted net assets accordingly.

Gains and losses on investments, and other assets included in temporarily or permanently restricted net assets, will be recorded as increases in unrestricted net assets, unless it is clear that the use of the gain or loss is restricted for that specific asset and/or for a specific period of time.

Reporting revenues, expenses, gains, and losses among the three new classes of net assets does not preclude operating revenues versus nonoperating revenues, or earned revenues versus unearned revenues, and so forth. SFAS #117 neither encourages nor discourages this type of reporting.

Reporting at Gross

SFAS #117 also requires that the not-for-profit organization report revenues and expenses at gross rather than at net. For example, an organization is not permitted to report net publication sales. In this case, gross publication sales and associated cost of goods sold must be reported.

However, fees such as custodial and advisor services can, in fact, be deducted from the gross before they are reported.

Gains and losses from incidental transactions also can be reported at net, as these transactions are typically beyond the control of the organization. For example, if an organization sells an asset that is not replaced, the net gain or loss from the sale or transaction can be reported, and gross reporting is not required.

Natural and Functional Reporting Requirements

To enable a not-for-profit organization to assess its use of its resources, SFAS #117 requires all not-for-profit organizations to report their activities on a functional basis that includes program services and supporting activities. Only voluntary health and welfare organizations must use the natural method of reporting information. Voluntary health and welfare organizations must report on both the functional and the natural basis of reporting. Natural-presentation financial statements provide information concerning salaries, rent, and other line items, instead of grouping them into program services and the like.

Not-for-profit organizations other than health and welfare organizations are encouraged, but not required, to report information on both the functional and the natural basis in a matrix format.

Program Services and Supporting Activities

Program services are those activities that fulfill the organization's mission. For example, membership organizations provide benefits to its members such as producing magazines and newsletters, and the like. Other program services may include providing public educational services or medical research. Typical supporting activities would include administrative functions of which the recipient of the program services is only incidentally aware, such as the running of a warehouse operation or the accounting function of an organization.

The following three examples illustrate how a not-for-profit organization that has no temporary or permanently restricted net asset classes of accounts may present a Statement of Activities and changes in unrestricted net assets by using each of the following:

1. Functional basis (Exhibit A.4)

2. Natural basis (Exhibit A.5)

3. Functional and natural matrix (Exhibit A.6)

When reviewing the three Statements of Activity in the exhibits, note how the change in unrestricted net assets relates to the final unrestricted net assets balance in the Statement of Financial Position (Exhibit A.3).

EXHIBIT A.3

Not-for-Profit Organization's Statement of Financial Position December 31, 20XX

Assets

	Year 2	Year 1
Cash and Cash Equivalents	$151,500	$92,000
Accounts Receivable	9,000	8,000
Inventories	12,000	70,000
Prepaid Expenses	4,000	5,000
Contributions Receivable	11,000	10,000
Less Allowance for Uncollectables	(2,500)	(2,000)
Fixed Assets	95,000	90,000
Less Accumulated Depreciation	(25,000)	(20,000)
Total Assets	**$255,000**	**$193,000**

Liabilities and Net Assets

	Year 2	Year 1
Liabilities:		
Accounts Payable	$15,000	$13,000
Notes Payable	65,000	70,000
Deferred Grant Revenues	40,000	50,000
Total Liabilities	$120,000	$133,000
Net Assets:		
Unrestricted Net Assets	$135,000	$60,000
Total Liabilities and Net Assets	**$255,000**	**$193,000**

Functional Method (Exhibit A.4)

This method is in accordance with SFAS #117 in the following ways:

➤ Revenues are presented at gross.

➤ Expenses are classified as either program or supporting activities on a functional basis.

➤ Changes in unrestricted net assets are clearly presented.

The disadvantage of this method is that expense detail by line item (salaries, rent, etc.) is not presented on the statements.

EXHIBIT A.4

Not-for-Profit Organization's
Statement of Activities and Changes in
Unrestricted Net Assets (Functional Basis)
Year Ended December 31, 20XX

Unrestricted Revenues:	
Dues	$500,000
Contributions	200,000
Interest	50,000
Total Unrestricted Revenues	$750,000
Expenses:	
Program A	$125,000
Program B	150,000
Program C	250,000
Management & General	150,000
Total Expenses	$675,000
Increase in Unrestricted Net Assets	$75,000
Unrestricted Net Assets, Beginning of Year	60,000
Unrestricted Net Assets, End of Year	**$135,000**

Natural Basis (Exhibit A.5)

This method alone is not in accordance with SFAS #117, in that not-for-profit organizations have the options to present the Statement of Activities on a *functional* basis. The natural method does not break down revenues into program and supporting activities.

Voluntary health and welfare organizations now must present their Statement of Activity on both the functional and the natural basis. Considering this, a voluntary health and welfare organization's financial statements could include a Statement of Activity combining Exhibits A.4 and A.5, or as a functional and natural matrix as illustrated on Exhibit A.6.

EXHIBIT A.5

Not-for-Profit Organization's Statement of Activities and Changes in Unrestricted Net Assets (Natural Basis) Year Ended December 31, 20XX

Unrestricted Revenues:	
Dues	$500,000
Contributions	200,000
Interest	50,000
Total Unrestricted Revenues	$750,000
Expenses:	
Salaries	$200,000
Fringe Benefits	40,000
Printing	150,000
Postage	75,000
Rent	125,000
Travel	85,000
Total Expenses	$675,000
Increase in Unrestricted Net Assets	$75,000
Unrestricted Net Assets, Beginning of Year	$60,000
Unrestricted Net Assets, End of Year	$135,000

Functional and Natural Matrix (Exhibit A.6)

This method is in accordance with SFAS #117 standards for all not-for-profit organizations in the following ways:

➤ Revenues are presented at gross.

➤ Expenses are classified as either program or supporting activities.

➤ Changes in unrestricted net assets are clearly presented.

After a review of this statement, the reader should realize why SFAS #117 encourages all not-for-profit organizations to prepare their Statement of Activity using both the natural and the functional methods. This method has the advantage of presenting more detailed information in an easy-to-understand matrix format that meets the standards of SFAS #117.

Remember, while all not-for-profit organizations must present their Statement of Activities on a functional basis, only voluntary health and welfare organizations are required to present both the functional and natural methods. Not-for-profit organizations, however, are encouraged to use both methods.

Not-for-Profit Organization's
Statement of Activities and Changes in Unrestricted Net Assets
(Functional and Natural Matrix)
Year Ended December 31, 20XX

	Program A	Program B	Program C	Management & General	Total
Unrestricted Revenues:					
Dues	$90,000	$175,000	$125,000	$110,000	$500,000
Contributions		200,000			200,000
Interest				50,000	50,000
Total Unrestricted Revenues	$90,000	$375,000	$125,000	$160,000	$750,000
Expenses:					
Salaries	$36,000	$70,000	$50,000	$44,000	$200,000
Fringe Benefits	7,000	14,000	10,000	9,000	40,000
Printing	28,000	20,000	60,000	42,000	150,000
Postage	15,000	14,000	36,000	10,000	75,000
Rent	20,000	20,000	50,000	35,000	125,000
Travel	19,000	12,000	44,000	10,000	85,000
Total Expenses	$125,000	$150,000	$250,000	$150,000	$675,000
Increase (Decrease) in Unrestricted Net Assets	$(35,000)	$225,000	$(125,000)	$10,000	$75,000
Unrestricted Net Assets, Beginning of Year					$60,000
Unrestricted Net Assets, End of Year					$135,000

Now, expand the statements to include activity in temporarily and permanently restricted net assets classes of accounts in addition to the information already presented.

Remember, as part of SFAS #117, all expenses are recorded in the unrestricted net assets class of accounts. This will require transferring revenues from the temporarily and permanently restricted classes of accounts to the unrestricted class to offset the associated expenses. Note how changes in the various net assets accounts relate to the final balances of these accounts on the Statement of Financial Position (Exhibit A.7).

The Statement of Activity (Exhibit A.8, Format 1) has reported unrestricted activity on a functional basis, and it includes activity for both restricted classes of net assets by representing increases or decreases in the three new assets classes of accounts. Only the total of all three classes of net assets balances are presented, and the detail of the individual account balance appears only on the Statement of Financial Position (Exhibit A.7).

EXHIBIT A.7

Not-for-Profit Organization's
Statement of Financial Position
December 31, 20XX

Assets

	Year 2	Year 1
Cash and Cash Equivalents	$151,500	$92,000
Accounts Receivable	9,000	8,000
Inventories	12,000	10,000
Prepaid Expenses	4,000	5,000
Contributions Receivable	11,000	10,000
Less Allowance for Uncollectables	(2,500)	(2,000)
Assets restricted to investment in equipment and corpus of permanently restricted net assets	235,000	210,000
Fixed Assets	95,000	90,000
Less Accumulated Depreciation	(25,000)	(20,000)
Total Assets	**$490,000**	**$403,000**

Liabilities and Net Assets

	Year 2	Year 1
Accounts Payable	$15,000	$13,000
Notes Payable	65,000	70,000
Deferred Grant Revenues	40,000	50,000
Total Liabilities	$120,000	$133,000
Net Assets:		
Unrestricted	$135,000	$60,000
Temporarily Restricted	130,000	110,000
Permanently Restricted	105,000	100,000
Total Net Assets	$370,000	$270,000
Total Liabilities and Net Assets	**$490,000**	**$403,000**

Not-for-Profit Organization's
Statement of Activities
Year Ended December 31, 20XX

Change in Unrestricted Net Assets:	
Revenues:	
Dues	$500,000
Contributions	200,000
Interest	50,000
Total Unrestricted Revenues	$750,000
Net Assets Released from Restrictions:	
Expiration of Time Restrictions	$40,000
Satisfaction of Program Restrictions	50,000
Total Net Assets Released from Restrictions	$90,000
Total Unrestricted Revenues and Other Support	$840,000
Expenses:	
Program A	$125,000
Program B	150,000
Program C	250,000
Program D	40,000
Program E	50,000
Management & General	150,000
Total Expenses	$765,000
Increase in Unrestricted Net Assets	$75,000
Changes in Temporarily Restricted Net Assets:	
Contributions	$60,000
Net Assets Released from Restrictions	(40,000)
Increase in Temporarily Restricted Net Assets	$20,000
Changes in Permanently Restricted Net Assets:	
Increase from Long-Term Investments	$55,000
Net Assets Released from Restrictions	(50,000)
Increase in Permanently Restricted Net Assets	$5,000
Total Increase in Net Assets	$100,000
Net Assets, Beginning of Year	270,000
Net Assets, End of Year	**$370,000**

The Statement of Activity (Exhibit A.9, Format 2) presents the same information in a matrix rather than a columnar format. Note that the final balances for each class of account are illustrated with the final balances noted on the Statement of Financial Position (Exhibit A.7).

EXHIBIT A.9, FORMAT 2

Not-for-Profit Organization's
Statement of Activities
(with Activity in the Unrestricted, Temporarily Restricted, and Permanently Restricted Classes of Accounts)
Year Ended December 31, 20XX

	Unrestricted	Temporarily Restricted	Permanently Restricted	Total
Revenues:				
Dues	$500,000			$500,000
Contributions	200,000	$60,000		260,000
Interest	50,000		$55,000	105,000
Income from Long-Term Investments				
Net Assets Released from Restrictions:				
Expiration of Time Restrictions	40,000	(40,000)		
Satisfaction of Program Restrictions	50,000		(50,000)	
Total Revenues	$840,000	$20,000	$5,000	$865,000
Expenses:				
Program A	$125,000			$125,000
Program B	150,000			150,000
Program C	250,000			250,000
Program D	40,000			40,000
Program E	50,000			50,000
Management & General	150,000			150,000
Total Expenses	$765,000			$765,000
Changes in Net Assets	$75,000	$20,000	$5,000	$100,000
Net Assets, Beginning of Year	$60,000	$110,000	$100,000	$270,000
Net Assets, End of Year	$135,000	$130,000	$105,000	$370,000

Another material change in SFAS #117 that affects the audited statements of a not-for-profit organization is the requirement that a full set of audited financial statements now include a Statement of Cash Flows. Essentially, SFAS #117 amended SFAS #95 to extend its provisions to include not-for-profit organizations.

As in the case for a commercial organization, the Statement of Cash Flows for a not-for-profit organization will consist of the following three categories, which will be on the face of the statement, if applicable:

➢ Net cash used by operating activities

➢ Net cash used by investing activities

➢ Net cash used by financing activities

The Statement of Cash Flows can be prepared by using the direct or the indirect method.

The Direct Method

The direct method for preparing a Statement of Cash Flows reports gross receipts and gross expenses by category and nets them out to arrive at the net cash flow from operations. The direct method is preferred but not required. The direct method is illustrated in Exhibit A.10.

EXHIBIT A.10

Not-for-Profit Organization's
Statement of Cash Flows (Direct Method)
Year Ended December 31, 20XX

Cash flows from operations:	
Cash received for services	$500,000
Cash received from contributions	50,000
Cash collected on receivables	40,000
Interest received	40,000
Other receipts	30,000
Cash expenses paid	(700,000)
Net cash used by operations	(40,000)
Cash flows from investing activities:	
Purchase of equipment	(150,000)
Purchase of investments	(75,000)
Net cash used by investing activities	(225,000)
Cash flows from financing activities:	
Restricted contributions:	
Investment in endowment	110,000
Other financial activities:	
Payments on long-term debt	(75,000)
Net cash used by financing activities	35,000
Net decrease in cash and equivalents	(230,000)
Cash and equivalents, beginning of year	365,000
Cash and equivalents, end of year	**$135,000**
Reconciliation of changes in net assets to net cash:	
Operating activities:	
Change in net assets	$90,000
Adjustments to reconcile:	
Depreciation	25,000
Increase in accounts receivable	(125,000)
Restricted contributions for long-term investments	(80,000)
Decrease in inventories	20,000
Increase in accounts payable	30,000
Net cash used by operations	**$(40,000)**

(*Note:* This statement is unrelated to financial statements previously presented.)

The Indirect Method

The indirect method for preparing a Statement of Cash Flows starts with the total change in net assets from the Statement of Activities. Adjustments are then made for items that do not have an effect on cash, such as depreciation, changes in related asset and liability accounts, and reversal of year-end actuals. The indirect method is illustrated in Exhibit A.11.

EXHIBIT A.11	

Not-for-Profit Organization's
Statement of Cash Flows (Indirect Method)
Year Ended December 31, 20XX

Cash flows from operations:

Change in net assets	$90,000
Adjustments to reconcile:	
Depreciation	25,000
Increase in accounts receivable	(125,000)
Restricted contributions for	
long-term investments	(80,000)
Decrease in inventories	20,000
Increase in accounts payable	30,000
Net cash used by operations	(40,000)
Cash flows from investing activities:	
Purchase of equipment	(150,000)
Purchase of investments	(75,000)
Net cash used by investing activities	(225,000)
Cash flows from financing activities	
Restricted contributions:	
Investment in endowment	110,000
Other financial activities:	
Payments on long-term debt	(75,000)
Net cash used by financing activities	35,000
Net decrease in cash and equivalents	(230,000)
Cash and equivalents, beginning of year	365,000
Cash and equivalents, end of year	**$135,000**

(*Note:* This statement is unrelated to financial statements previously presented.)

The Statement of Cash Flows

While not preferred, use of the indirect method is acceptable.

Comparative Financial Statements

SFAS #117 does not require that a complete set of audited financial statements include prior-year comparative information; however, including this information is encouraged.

The Statement of Changes in Net Assets

As previously noted, a complete set of financial statements for not-for-profit organizations includes the following:

➤ The Statement of Financial Position

➤ The Statement of Activities

➤ The Statement of Cash Flows

➤ Accompanying notes

While not required, a set of financial statements of not-for-profit organizations often includes a statement of changes in fund balance. Many organizations may want to include the replacement for the statement of changes in fund balance, now called the Statement of Changes in Net Assets. While encouraged, the inclusion of this statement is not required.

This statement may be presented in either a vertical format or a matrix format, illustrated in Exhibits A.12 and A.13, respectively.

EXHIBIT A.12

Not-for-Profit Organization's
Statement of Changes in Net Assets
(Vertical Method)
Year Ended December 31, 20XX

Unrestricted Net Assets:

Total Unrestricted Revenues	$750,000
Net Assets Released from Restrictions	90,000
Total Unrestricted Expenses	(765,000)
Increase in Unrestricted Net Assets	$75,000

Temporarily Restricted Net Assets:

Contributions	$65,000
Net Assets Released from Restrictions	(40,000)
Increase in Temporarily Restricted Net Assets	$20,000

Permanently Restricted Net Assets:

Income from Long-Term Investments	$55,000
Net Assets Released from Restrictions	(50,000)
Increase in Permanently Restricted Net Assets	$5,000

Total Increase in Net Assets	$100,000
Net Assets, Beginning of Year	270,000
Net Assets, End of Year	$370,000

EXHIBIT A.13

Not-for-Profit Organization's
Statement of Changes in Net Assets
(Matrix Method)
Year Ended December 31, 20XX

	Unrestricted	Temporarily Restricted	Permanently Restricted	Total
Revenues:				
Total Unrestricted Revenues	$750,000			$750,000
Contributions		$60,000		60,000
Income from Long-Term Investments			$55,000	55,000
Net Assets Released from Restrictions	90,000	(40,000)	(50,000)	
Total Revenues	$840,000	$20,000	$5,000	$865,000
Expenses:				
Total Unrestricted Expenses	765,000			765,000
Change in Net Assets	$75,000	$20,000	$5,000	$100,000
Net Assets at Beginning of Year	60,000	110,000	100,000	270,000
Net Assets at End of Year	$135,000	$130,000	$105,000	$370,000

Notes to Financial Statements

SFAS #117 requires that the notes to the financial statements disclose relevant information in the following four areas:

➤ Policy disclosures (Note A)

➤ Purposes and amounts included in the temporarily restricted net assets class of accounts (Note B)

➤ Purposes and amounts included in the permanently restricted net assets class of accounts (Note C)

➤ Statement of functional expenses (voluntary health and welfare organizations) (Note D)

Note A

Contributions of cash or other assets, the uses of which are restricted by donors and limited by the organization, are treated as restricted support, are included in the temporarily restricted net assets or permanently restricted net assets classes of accounts, are reclassified to the unrestricted net assets class, and are reported as net assets released from restrictions.

All of the organization's expenses, including expenses relating to assets previously included among the temporarily restricted net assets or permanently restricted net assets classes of accounts, are decreases in unrestricted net assets.

Note B

Temporarily restricted net assets are to be used for the following purposes:

Program D:

Equipment purchases	$100,000
Seminars	30,000
	$130,000

Note C

Permanently restricted net assets are to be used for the following purposes:

Investments in perpetuity, earnings from which are to be used to support

Program E:

Scholarships	$105,000

Note D

Expenses of the organization for program and support activities were as follows:

Program

	1	2	3	Management & General	Fund-Raising	Total
Salaries	$20,000	$25,000	$30,000	$15,000	$20,000	$110,000
Fringe benefits	2,000	2,500	3,000	1,500	2,000	11,000
Supplies	3,000	2,000	5,000	6,000	3,000	19,000
Travel	7,000		3,000	6,000		16,000
Rent	2,000	2,000	2,000	3,000	3,000	12,000
Depreciation				10,000		10,000
Printing	6,000	7,000	4,000		16,000	33,000
Total expenses	**$40,000**	**$38,500**	**$47,000**	**$41,500**	**$44,000**	**$211,000**

(*Note:* This note is unrelated to the financial statements previously presented.)

Other notes to the financial statements that are encouraged, but not required, include:

➤ A detail of assets reclassified to the unrestricted net asset class due to the expiration of time restrictions or the accomplishment of purpose restrictions

➤ Investment gain or loss detail

Statement of Financial Accounting Standards #116
Accounting for Contributions Received and Contributions Made

Background

The purpose of SFAS #116 is to eliminate the confusion surrounding contributions of cash and other items, including contributed collections and contributed services. The provisions of SFAS #116 that concern when contributions are recognized in the organization's respective financial statements extend to both commercial and not-for-profit organizations.

While the provisions of SFAS #116 extend to both not-for-profit and commercial organizations, it is important to remember that Section 501(c)(3) organizations are particularly affected because only contributions to 501(c)(3) organizations are deductible by the donor.

Please note, however, that the standard does not address the tax ramifications of making contributions to not-for-profit organizations.

Highlights

SFAS #116 addresses the following three important areas:

➤ When and how to recognize contributions in the financial statements

➤ Rules for classifying contributions as unrestricted support, temporarily restricted support, or permanently restricted support

➤ Rules for the recognition of contributed services into the financial statements of not-for-profit organizations

---

Reprinted with permission from *Not-for-Profit Organization's Guide to the New Accounting Ruling.* Copyright U.S. Chamber of Commerce, September 1996.

Effective Dates

A not-for-profit organization with $5 million in assets and $1 million in expenses must comply with the new standards for the organization's fiscal year that begins after December 15, 1994. An organization with less than $5 million in assets and $1 million in expenses is required to comply with the new standards for the organization's fiscal year that begins after December 15, 1995.

Scope

SFAS #116 applies to all not-for-profit organizations addressed in Chapter 1 of this manual. Not-for-profit organizations include, but are not limited to, trade associations, professional associations, charities, foundations, chambers of commerce, boards of trade, hospitals, universities, and museums.

The provisions of SFAS #116 concerning when and how to report donations in financial statements also apply to commercial organizations.

Provisions of SFAS #116 apply to voluntary contributions of cash or other assets and now include promises to give. This statement does not apply to transactions in which both the receiving organization and the donating organization essentially receive value. This statement also does not apply when the receiving organization is merely acting as an agent, trustee, or intermediary instead of as the ultimate receiving organization.

It is acceptable to use terms such as *donation* or *gift* instead of the word *contribution,* but terminology such as *grant, award, appropriation,* and so forth, is to be avoided because these terms imply that the receiving organization will give value.

Inconsistencies

If an inconsistency arises concerning the provisions of SFAS #116 and prior AICPA pronouncements, including SOP 78-10, the provisions of SFAS #116 will apply, and other provisions and prior pronouncements are no longer acceptable.

Definitions

A **contribution** is an unconditional transfer of cash or other assets to an entity, or a settlement or cancellation of the entity's liabilities in a voluntary nonreciprocal manner by another entity acting other than as an owner. Other assets may include securities, land, buildings, use of facilities, materials, supplies, intangible assets, services, and unconditional promises to give at some point in the future.

A **donor-imposed condition** is a transfer of assets or a promise to give that specifies that a future and uncertain event whose occurrence or failure to occur gives the promisor the right of return of the assets transferred or releases the promisor from its obligations to transfer the asset.

A **donor-imposed restriction** is a limitation on the use of contributed assets. It specifies a use that is more specific than the broad limits resulting from the nature of the organization, the environment in which it operates, and the purpose specified in its articles of incorporation, bylaws, or comparable documents.

A **promise to give** is a written or oral agreement to contribute cash or other assets to another entity. For the contribution to be recognized in the financial statement, there must be sufficient evidence in the form of verifiable documentation that a promise was made and received. A communication that does not clearly indicate that it is a promise and that indicates an unconditional intention to give that is legally enforceable is considered an unconditional promise to give.

We will now discuss the important details included in SFAS #116.

Recognition of Contributions

Contributions will now be recognized as revenue in the period received or as an asset, a decrease of liabilities, or an expense, depending on the form of the benefit received. Contributions will also be measured at their fair values.

Additionally, contributions received by a not-for-profit organization will now be reported as either restricted support or unrestricted support, and will be appropriately classified in the new net assets section of the Statement of Financial Position.

Recognition of Contributed Services

One of the more controversial aspects of SFAS #116 is the requirement that the contribution of services be recognized in the financial statements of a not-for-profit organization if one of two circumstances is recognized:

1. The contributed services create or enhance a nonfinancial asset, or
2. The contributed services would have required skills that the organization would have had to pay for if the services had not been donated.

The statement provides that these services include but not be limited to services provided by accountants, architects, carpenters, doctors, electricians, lawyers, nurses, plumbers, teachers, or other professionals or craftsmen.

Example 1

A not-for-profit organization embarks upon an accreditation program to accredit its member institutions. Accountants, attorneys, and other professionals volunteered their time to accomplish the accreditation program, and the value of their time must be included in the financial statements. Typically, these professionals would provide the organization with a statement concerning the value of their time, and that statement would be the basis for the inclusion of the contributed services. In this case, that aggregate value of the contributed labor will result in an amortizable asset, in this case, an accreditation program, and a corresponding revenue in the financial statements. This nonfinancial asset will be amortized in accordance with the organization's amortization policies.

Example 2

A church wants to build a new church hall and appeals to its congregation for support. In this case, architects, carpenters, electricians, plumbers, bricklayers, and other craftsmen volunteer their time and help to erect the church hall. Each of these individuals provides a statement to the church concerning the value of their time, and the aggregate value increases the value of the church hall and results in a corresponding revenue. While not-for-profit organizations often rely heavily on contributed labor in the ordinary and necessary performance of the organizations' activities, it would be impractical to recognize all contributed labors as revenue. Not-for-profit organizations in such situations are encouraged, but not required, to disclose in the footnotes of their financial statement the fair value of these contributed services.

Contributed Collections Items

A not-for-profit organization can either capitalize or not capitalize its collections in its financial statements. Capitalization of selected collections is precluded. If the not-for-profit organization has elected to capitalize its collection, the donation of new collection items would be recognized as revenues in the financial statements. Conversely, a not-for-profit organization that has elected not to capitalize its collection would not recognize current contributions as revenues or gains in the financial statements. An entity that has chosen not to capitalize its collections would disclose this and additional information in the footnotes of the financial statements.

Finally, SFAS #116 indicates that it is unnecessary for entities to recognize the contributions of works of arts, historical treasures, and other similar assets if these donated items are added to collections that meet all of the following conditions:

➤ The items are held for public exhibition, education, research, or furtherance of a public service, rather than for financial gain.

➤ The items are protected, kept unencumbered, cared for, and preserved.

➤ The items are subject to an organizational policy that requires the proceeds from sales of collection items to be used to acquire other collection items for future collections.

Recognition of Contributions in the Financial Statements of Not-for-Profit Organizations

Contributions to not-for-profit organizations will now be classified in the new net assets section of the Statement of Activities, and will now be regarded as either unrestricted support, temporarily restricted support, or permanently restricted support. Classification into one of these accounts will depend on the donor's wishes. Contributions without any donor-imposed restrictions will be reported as unrestricted support and will increase unrestricted net assets, while donations with restricted support will increase either temporarily restricted or permanently restricted net assets, depending on the nature of the contribution.

Another somewhat controversial aspect of SFAS #116 is the recognition of unconditional promises to give in the financial statements of a not-for-profit organization. Unconditional promises to give will now be recognized in the financial statements of a not-for-profit organization if substantial documentation exists that support the promises. The receipt of an unconditional promise to give will result in revenue in the current period, and the organization will set up a sufficient allowance account on the Statement of Financial Position. An unconditional promise to give can be either restricted support or unrestricted support, depending on the circumstances of the donation.

The recognition of long-lived assets received will also be recorded in the not-for-profit organization's financial statements as either restricted or unrestricted support, depending on the nature of the gifts. Also, the not-for-profit organizations must now disclose in the footnotes of its financial statement its accounting policy concerning recognition of and classification of long-lived assets.

Expiration of Donor-Imposed Restrictions

A donor-imposed restriction on a contribution can have either time restrictions or purpose restrictions, or both. In either case, a not-for-profit organization will recognize the contribution in its financial statements for the period in which the restriction expires. When a restriction does expire, the organization will make a reclassification entry increasing the value of one class of net assets while decreasing the value of another class of net asset account. Reclassifications are recorded separately from other transactions in the financial statements.

Contributions Made

Again, the provisions of SFAS #116 extend to both commercial organizations and not-for-profit organizations. Regardless, a contribution made will be recognized as an expense in the period in which the contribution is made. Contributions made shall be recognized as a decrease of assets, as in the example of a cash contribution, or as an increase of a liability account, as in the case of a promise to give. Contributions can take the form of a decrease in cash and, of course, a corresponding contribution expense, a reduction in inventory and a resulting contribution expense, or an increase in the liability account and a corresponding contribution expense.

Fair-Value Measurement

The value of a noncash type of donation, such as a contribution received in the form of a service, is to be measured according to its fair value and recorded in the organization's financial statement accordingly. Quoted market prices, if available, are regarded as the best evidence of the fair value of both monetary and nonmonetary assets.

Regarding the recognition of the fair value of an unconditional promise to give cash in future periods, it is appropriate to determine the present value of these estimated future cash flows by using an appropriate discount rate. Finally, unconditional promises to give that are expected to be paid in less than one year may be measured at net realizable value.

Conditional Promises to Give

A conditional promise to give that depends on the occurrence of a specified future of an uncertain event to bind the giver will be recognized in the financial statements when the condition is substantially met. When the condition is substantially met, the conditional promise becomes unconditional, and it is recorded in the financial statements accordingly.

When a not-for-profit organization receives assets with conditions, the assets will be accounted for as a liability account in the Statement of Financial Position, rather than included among unrestricted, temporarily restricted, or permanently restricted net assets when the condition is met. The asset will be reclassified accordingly once the conditions placed on it are met.

Finally, a conditional promise to give will be considered unconditional if it is highly likely that the condition will be met. For example, a stipulation that the donee provide an annual report to receive a subsequent annual payment is not considered a conditional promise to give, since the possibility of not meeting that administrative requirement is remote.

Disclosure of Promises to Give

Disclosure of promises to give in the not-for-profit organization's financial statements will depend on whether the promise is conditional or unconditional.

For an unconditional promise to give, the financial statements of the organization would disclose the following:

➢ The amount of promises receivable in less than one year, in one to five years, and in more than five years

➢ The amount of allowance for uncollectible promises receivable

For a conditional promise to give, the financial statements of the organization would disclose the following:

➢ The amount of the amounts promised

➢ A description and amount for each group of promises having similar characteristics such as amounts of promises conditioned on establishing new programs, completing a new building, and raising matching gifts by a specified date

Financial Statement Presentation and Disclosure for Collections

Again, a not-for-profit organization that holds a collection can either capitalize the collection or not capitalize the collection. A not-for-profit organization that does not recognize and capitalize its collections will report the following on the face of its Statement of Activities separately from revenues, expenses, gains, and losses:

➢ Cost of collection items purchased as a decrease in the appropriate class of net assets

➢ Proceeds from sales of collection items and an increase in the appropriate class of net assets

➢ Proceeds from insurance recoveries of lost or destroyed collection items as an increase in the appropriate class of net assets

Examples

When classifying contributions in the financial statements, the following four areas must be addressed before deciding on the correct classification:

1. Are there any donor-imposed conditions (i.e., is the contribution conditional or unconditional)?

2. Should the contribution be recognized currently, sometime in the future, or not at all?

3. What is the amount of the contribution?

4. Will the contributions be recorded in the unrestricted, temporarily restricted, or permanently restricted net assets classes of accounts?

Example 1

A donor contributed $20,000 to a medical society to study a disease and to educate the public.

1. Is the contribution conditional or unconditional?
A. This is an unconditional contribution.

2. Should the contribution be recognized currently, sometime in the future, or not at all?
A. This contribution should be recognized currently.

3. What is the amount of the contribution?
A. The amount of the contribution is $20,000.

4. Will the contributions be recorded in the unrestricted, temporarily restricted, or permanently restricted net assets class of accounts?
A. This contribution would be recorded in the temporarily restricted net asset class of accounts.

Journal Entry:

Debit		Cash	$20,000
	Credit	Temporarily Restricted Net Assets Class Revenue	$20,000

Example 2

A donor donated a building to a foundation. The building cost the donor $100,000. The building had two appraisals on the date of donation, one at $120,000 and one at $124,000.

1. Is the contribution conditional or unconditional?
A. This is an unconditional contribution.

2. Should the contribution be recognized currently, sometime in the future, or not at all?
A. This contribution should be recognized currently.

3. What is the amount of the contribution?
A. The amount of the contribution is $122,000.

4. Will the contributions be recorded in the unrestricted, temporarily restricted, or permanently restricted net assets class of accounts?

A. This donation would be recorded in the unrestricted net assets class of accounts, as there are no donor restrictions on its use.

Journal Entry:

Debit	Building	$122,000	
	Credit	Unrestricted Net Assets	
		Class Revenue	$122,000

Example 3

A museum appealed for contributions to build a wing. Donors sent in $200,000.

1. Are the contributions conditional or unconditional?
A. These are unconditional contributions.

2. Should the contributions be recognized currently, sometime in the future, or not at all?
A. These contributions should be recognized currently.

3. What is the amount of the contributions?
A. The amount of the contributions is $200,000.

4. Will the contributions be recorded in the unrestricted, temporarily restricted, or permanently restricted net assets class of accounts?
A. These contributions would be recorded in the temporarily restricted net assets class of accounts.

Journal Entry:

Debit	Cash	$200,000	
	Credit	Temporarily Restricted Net Assets	
		Class Revenue	$200,000

Example 4

An estate gifted $750,000 to a hospital. The gift is to be invested in perpetuity but the earnings can be used to offset operating costs.

Treatment of the corpus:

1. Is the contribution conditional or unconditional?
A. This is an unconditional gift.

2. Should the contribution be recognized currently, sometime in the future, or not at all?
A. This gift should be recognized currently.

3. What is the amount of the contribution?
A. The amount of the gift is $750,000.

4. Will the contributions be recorded in the unrestricted, temporarily restricted, or permanently restricted net assets class of accounts?

A. This gift will be recorded in the permanently restricted net assets class of accounts.

Journal Entry:

Debit	Cash	$750,000	
	Credit	Permanently Restricted Net Assets	
		Class Revenue	$750,000

Treatment of the earnings:

1. Is the contribution conditional or unconditional?
A. The earnings are unconditional.

2. Should the contribution be recognized currently, sometime in the future, or not at all?
A. The earnings will be recognized currently.

3. What is the amount of the contribution?
A. The amount to be recognized would be the actual earnings.

4. Will the contributions be recorded in the unrestricted, temporarily restricted, or permanently restricted net assets class of accounts?
A. The earnings will be recorded in the unrestricted net assets class of accounts.

Journal Entry:

Debit	Cash	$XXX	
	Credit	Unrestricted Net Assets Class	
		Revenues	$XXX

Example 5

A high school alumna said she would contribute $100,000 from her estate to the school if she did not survive a serious forthcoming operation.

1. Is the contribution conditional or unconditional?
A. This is a conditional contribution in that the only way the school would receive the gift would be if she did not survive.

2. Should the contribution be recognized currently, sometime in the future, or not at all?
A. Since no money changed hands, this contribution may be recognized in the future or may not be recognized at all.

3. What is the amount of the contribution?

A. No amount of this contribution is recorded at this time.

4. Will the contributions be recorded in the unrestricted, temporarily restricted, or permanently restricted net assets class of accounts?

A. The contribution will not be recorded unless the condition is met.

Journal Entry:

None at this time.

If she does not survive the operation:

1. Is the contribution conditional or unconditional?

A. The condition has been met, making this an unconditional contribution. It will be necessary to record the transaction.

2. Should the contribution be recognized currently, sometime in the future, or not at all?

A. The contribution will be recognized currently.

3. What is the amount of the contribution?

A. The amount of the contribution would be $100,000.

4. Will the contributions be recorded in the unrestricted, temporarily restricted, or permanently restricted net assets class of accounts?

A. The contribution would be recorded in the unrestricted net assets class of accounts since the donor did not stipulate any purpose restrictions.

Journal Entry:

Debit		Unconditional Promises to Give	$100,000
	Credit	Unrestricted Net Assets Class	
		Revenues	$100,000

Example 6

A donor donated 500 shares of stock to a foundation. On the date of the gift, the stock traded at a high of $32 and at a low of $28.

1. Is the contribution conditional or unconditional?

A. This is an unconditional contribution.

2. Should the contribution be recognized currently, sometime in the future, or not at all?

A. This contribution should be recognized currently.

3. What is the amount of the contribution?

A. The amount of the contribution is $15,000 (500 shares times the average prior per-share value of $30).

4. Will the contributions be recorded in the unrestricted, temporarily restricted, or permanently restricted net assets class of accounts?

A. This contribution would be recorded in the unrestricted net assets class of accounts, as there are no donor restrictions on its use.

Journal Entry:

Debit		Investments	$15,000
	Credit	Unrestricted Net Assets Class	
		Revenues	$15,000

Example 7

The board of directors of a not-for-profit organization designated $50,000 of the current year's increase in unrestricted net assets to be set aside for future legal contingencies.

1. Is the contribution conditional or unconditional?

A. There are no donors, so there is no contribution.

2. Should the contribution be recognized currently, sometime in the future, or not at all?

A. Since this is not a contribution, it will not be recognized in the financial statements at all.

3. What is the amount of the contribution?

A. There is no contribution.

4. Will the contributions be recorded in the unrestricted, temporarily restricted, or permanently restricted net assets class of accounts?

A. The transaction has effectively already been recorded as activity in the unrestricted net assets class, and reclassification to a restricted class is prohibited.

Journal Entry:

None.

Example 8

A church appealed to its congregation for assistance in building a church hall. An architect contributed his time and donated the drawings. He sent a statement that his time was worth $50,000. An attorney donated her time and sent a statement that her time was worth $20,000. Bricklayers donated their time and sent in statements that the value of their time was $30,000.

1. Is the contribution conditional or unconditional?
A. This is an unconditional contribution of services.

2. Should the contribution be recognized currently, sometime in the future, or not at all?
A. These contributed services should be recognized currently.

3. What is the amount of the contribution?
A. The amount of the contributed services totals $100,000.

4. Will the contributions be recorded in the unrestricted, temporarily restricted, or permanently restricted net assets class of accounts?
A. This contributed labor should be included in the unrestricted net assets class of accounts.

Journal Entry:

Debit		Church Hall	$100,000
	Credit	Unrestricted Net Assets	
		Class Revenues	$100,000

(*Note:* The $100,000 will be added to other costs associated with building the hall and will be depreciated accordingly.)

Example 9

A commercial member of a not-for-profit organization allows the organization to use, at no charge, one of his conference rooms for the organization's monthly board of directors meetings, as long as space is available. The member rents out the conference room to the other parties at $500 per meeting.

1. Is the contribution conditional or unconditional?
A. This is conditional on the availability of the room.

2. Should the contribution be recognized currently, sometime in the future, or not at all?
A. This contribution will be recognized currently if the space is used.

3. What is the amount of the contribution?
A. The amount of the contribution is $500 per meeting.

4. Will the contributions be recorded in the unrestricted, temporarily restricted, or permanently restricted net assets class of accounts?
A. This contribution would be recorded in the unrestricted net assets class of accounts, as there are no donor restrictions on its use.

Journal Entry:

Debit		Conference Room Rental Expense	$500
	Credit	Unrestricted Net Assets Class	
		Revenues	$500

Example 10

A citizen acting as the executor of her grandfather's estate was left a journal that he kept, detailing his experiences in World War II. She gave the journal to the local historical museum.

1. Is the contribution conditional or unconditional?
A. This is an unconditional contribution.

2. Should the contribution be recognized currently, sometime in the future, or not at all?
A. This contribution should be recognized currently.

3. What is the amount of the contribution?
A. This contribution has no apparent value.

4. Will the contributions be recorded in the unrestricted, temporarily restricted, or permanently restricted net assets class of accounts?
A. Since the contribution has no value, it will not be recorded in any of the net assets class of accounts.

Journal Entry:

None.

Example 11

A renowned explorer sent a $50,000 check to a hospital. The accompanying letter said that the hospital was to hold the money until the donor returned from a solo exploration of the South Pole. The letter indicated that if he did not survive the journey, the hospital could keep the funds for whatever use it desired. If he returned from the trip, he wanted the money back.

1. Is the contribution conditional or unconditional?
A. This is a conditional contribution, in that the hospital could keep the money only if the explorer did not survive.

2. Should the contribution be recognized currently, sometime in the future, or not at all?
A. This contribution may be recognized in the future or not at all.

3. What is the amount of the contribution?
A. The amount of the contribution is $50,000 if the condition is met.

4. Will the contributions be recorded in the unrestricted, temporarily restricted, or permanently restricted net assets class of accounts?
A. If the contribution is met, it will be recorded in the unrestricted net assets class of accounts.

Journal Entry:

Upon the hospital's receipt of the check and letter:

Debit		Cash	$50,000	
	Credit	A Liability Account		$50,000

If the explorer returned safely and the money was returned:

Debit		The Liability Account	$50,000	
	Credit	Cash		$50,000

If the explorer did not return:

Debit		The Liability Account	$50,000	
	Credit	Unrestricted Net Assets		
		Class Revenues		$50,000

Example 12

An art museum's policy is to capitalize its collection. An heir of a world-famous artist donated an original painting to the museum with the stipulation that the painting could never be sold. The painting had an average appraised value of $2 million.

1. Is the contribution conditional or unconditional?
A. This is an unconditional contribution.

2. Should the contribution be recognized currently, sometime in the future, or not at all?
A. This contribution will be recognized currently.

3. What is the amount of the contribution?
A. The amount of the contribution is $2 million.

4. Will the contributions be recorded in the unrestricted, temporarily restricted, or permanently restricted net assets class of accounts?
A. This contribution will be recorded in the permanently restricted net assets class of accounts.

Journal Entry:

Debit		Capitalized Collection	$2,000,000	
	Credit	Permanently Restricted Net Assets		
		Class of Accounts		$2,000,000

Example 13

> Q. What would the journal entry have been if the same museum in Example 12 had a policy of not capitalizing its collection?
>
> A. None, since the museum had a policy not to capitalize its collection. Rather, this information would be disclosed in the footnotes of the financial statements.

Example 14

On its dues invoice, a not-for-profit organization solicited contributions from its members, and informed them that their donations would be sent to a local charity, which is another not-for-profit organization. The organization received a voluntary contribution of $5,000.

> 1. Is the contribution conditional or unconditional?
> A. This is an unconditional contribution.
>
> 2. Should the contribution be recognized currently, sometime in the future, or not at all?
> A. The contribution would be recognized currently.
>
> 3. What is the amount of the contribution?
> A. The amount of the contribution is $5,000.
>
> 4. Will the contributions be recorded in the unrestricted, temporarily restricted, or permanently restricted net assets class of accounts?
> A. The contribution will be recorded in the unrestricted net assets class of accounts of the charity, not the original organization, which is acting as an intermediary.

Journal Entry:

On receipt of the contributions:

Debit		Cash	$5,000	
	Credit	A Liability Account to the Charity		$5,000

On remittance of the funds to the charity:

Debit		The Liability Account to the Charity	$5,000	
	Credit	Cash		$5,000

On the charity's books on receipt of the funds:

Debit		Cash	$5,000	
	Credit	Unrestricted Net Assets		
		Class of Accounts		$5,000

Example 15

A not-for-profit organization has a liability of $15,000 on its books for money owed to a CPA firm for auditing services. The CPA firm advised the not-for-profit organization that the debt had been cancelled because the work had been considered pro bono.

1. Is the contribution conditional or unconditional?
A. This is an unconditional contribution.

2. Should the contribution be recognized currently, sometime in the future, or not at all?
A. The contribution will be recognized currently.

3. What is the amount of the contribution?
A. The amount of the contribution is $15,000.

4. Will the contributions be recorded in the unrestricted, temporarily restricted, or permanently restricted net assets class of accounts?
A. This contribution will be recorded in the unrestricted net assets class of accounts.

Journal Entry:

Debit		Accounts Payable	$15,000	
	Credit	Unrestricted Net Assets		
		Class of Accounts		$15,000

Example 16

A charity embarked on a fund-raising event and included pledge cards in its promotional materials. The charity received pledges totaling $17,000.

1. Is the contribution conditional or unconditional?
A. These are unconditional contributions.

2. Should the contribution be recognized currently, sometime in the future, or not at all?
A. These contributions will be recognized currently.

3. What is the amount of the contribution?
A. The amount of the contributions is $17,000.

4. Will the contributions be recorded in the unrestricted, temporarily restricted, or permanently restricted net assets class of accounts?
A. These contributions will be recorded in the unrestricted net assets class of accounts.

Journal Entry:

Debit		Pledges Receivable	$17,000	
	Credit	Unrestricted Net Assets		
		Class of Accounts		$17,000

Example 17

A not-for-profit chamber of commerce was awarded a $30,000 grant from a county government to conduct an economic impact study for the county. The results of the study are to be included in a report sent to the county at the conclusion of the grant.

Q. Will the transaction be recorded in the chamber of commerce's records?

A. Since this is a grant, it will not qualify as a contribution in the chamber's records. Instead, this transaction would be handled in accordance with the chamber's accounting policies concerning grant accounting.

Statement of Financial Accounting Standards #124

Accounting for Certain Investments Held by Not-for-Profit Organizations

Background

Prior to the adoption of SFAS #124, the accounting treatment of investments held by not-for-profit organizations was generally inconsistent. The lack of required accounting treatment of investments resulted in some not-for-profit organizations reporting investments in their financial statements at cost, some at the lower of cost or market, and some at market valuation.

All not-for-profit organizations must now comply with the new provisions of SFAS #124. As in the case of SFAS #116 and #117, the resulting consistency will benefit everyone connected with the statement.

Highlights

SFAS #124 addresses investments in the following:

➢ Equity securities with determinable fair value.

➢ All debt securities with determinable fair value.

➢ The statement does *not* apply to equity securities accounted for under the equity method or to investments in consolidated subsidiaries.

The fair value of equity securities is determinable if any of these three conditions are met:

1. Values are available via a recognized U.S. stock exchange.

2. Foreign securities are traded in a foreign market similar to U.S. stock exchanges.

3. The value of mutual funds is published currently.

Reprinted with permission from *Not-for-Profit Organization's Guide to the New Accounting Ruling*. Copyright U.S. Chamber of Commerce, September 1996.

Effective Date

The statement is effective for fiscal years beginning after December 15, 1995.

Scope

SFAS #124 applies to all not-for-profit organizations, including, but not limited to, trade organizations, professional associations, charities, foundations, chambers of commerce, boards of trade, hospitals, universities, and museums.

Inconsistencies

If an inconsistency arises concerning the provisions of SFAS #124 and prior AICPA pronouncements, including FASB Statement No. 115, *Accounting for Certain Investments in Debt and Equity Securities*, the provisions of SFAS #124 will apply and other provisions and prior announcements no longer will be acceptable.

SFAS #124

Reporting Revenues

In accordance with SFAS #117, *Financial Statements of Not-for-Profit Organizations*, all revenues are to be reported in the Statements of Activities as increases or decreases in unrestricted net assets, unless their use is temporarily or permanently restricted by the donor.

Example 1

A donor makes a cash gift of $50,000 to a not-for-profit organization. The donor stipulates that the corpus is permanently restricted and the earnings are restricted for the use of Program A. The gift earned interest of $3,000 in year one.

Journal Entry:

On award of the gift:

Debit	Restricted Cash	$50,000	
Credit	Permanently Restricted Net Assets		$50,000

On receipt of $3,000 interest revenue:

Debit	Restricted Cash	$3,000	
Credit	Program A Revenues		$3,000

Example 2

A donor makes a gift of $20,000 in stock to a not-for-profit organization. The donor stipulates that the gift is permanently restricted and the dividends are unrestricted. Dividends in the amount of $1,000 were received in year one.

Journal Entry:
On award of the gift:

Debit		Permanently Restricted Investment	$20,000
	Credit	Permanently Restricted Net Assets		$20,000

On receipt of $1,000 dividend income:

Debit		Unrestricted Cash	$1,000
	Credit	Unrestricted Net Assets Revenue		$1,000

Example 3

A donor made a $25,000 gift of stock to a not-for-profit organization. The gift and all earnings related to the gift are restricted for the use of Program B. Earnings for year one were $2,000.

Journal Entry:
On receipt of $25,000 gift of stock:

Debit		Temporarily Restricted Investment	$25,000
	Credit	Temporarily Restricted Net Assets		$25,000

On receipt of $2,000 earnings:

Debit		Temporarily Restricted Cash	$2,000
	Credit	Temporarily Restricted Net Assets Revenue		$2,000

Reporting Investment Gains and Losses

Again, in accordance with SFAS #117, gains and losses will be recorded in the Statement of Activity as increases or decreases in *unrestricted* net assets unless their use is permanently or temporarily restricted by the donor.

Example 1

A donor makes a gift of $75,000 in stock, stipulating that the corpus is permanently restricted and earnings and gains are unrestricted. The gift earned $6,000 in dividends at year-end, and the fair value of the original gift was $85,000 at year-end.

Journal Entry:
On receipt of the gift:

Debit		Permanently Restricted Investment	$75,000
	Credit	Permanently Restricted Net Assets		$75,000

On receipt of $6,000 in dividends:

Debit		Unrestricted Cash	$6,000
	Credit	Unrestricted Net Assets Revenue		$6,000

Recording the $85,000 fair value at year-end:

Debit		Permanently Restricted Investment	$10,000
	Credit	Unrestricted Net Assets Revenue		$10,000

Example 2

A donor made a gift of $50,000 in stock, stipulating that both the corpus and the earnings are to be used for Program C. The gift earned $2,500 in dividends. At year-end the fair value of the gift was $40,000.

Journal Entry:

On receipt of the gift:

Debit		Temporarily Restricted Investment	$50,000
	Credit	Temporarily Restricted Net Assets		$50,000

On receipt of $2,500 in dividends:

Debit		Temporarily Restricted Cash	$2,500
	Credit	Temporarily Restricted Net Assets Revenue		$2,500

Recording the $40,000 fair value at year-end:

Debit		Temporarily Restricted Net Assets Revenue	$10,000
	Credit	Temporarily Restricted Investments		$10,000

Example 3

A donor made a $2 million gift in stock and stipulates that the corpus is permanently restricted but the earnings are unrestricted. The gift earned $150,000 in dividends. At the end of year one the fair value was $2 million.

Journal Entry:

On receipt of the gift:

Debit		Permanently Restricted Investment	$2,000,000
	Credit	Permanently Restricted Net Assets		$2,000,000

On receipt of $150,000 in dividends:

Debit		Unrestricted Cash	$150,000
	Credit	Unrestricted Net Assets Revenue		$150,000

Recording the $2 million fair value at year-end:

Debit		Permanently Restricted Investment	$100,000
	Credit	Unrestricted Net Assets Revenue		$100,000

Note: Gains and losses on investments increase or reduce the value of the *asset* in the financial statements and appear as a gain or loss in the *unrestricted* net assets class of accounts unless gains and losses are temporarily or permanently restricted by the donor.

Disclosures

Statement of Activity

➢ Investment income composition and net gains or losses on investments at fair value

➢ A reconciliation of investment return and description of accounting policy

Statement of Financial Position

➤ Segregation of investments by type—equity securities, real estate, U.S. obligations, and so forth

➤ The basis for computing values for other than equity securities with determinable fair value and all debt securities

➤ Accounting policy used to estimate fair value of other than financial instruments

➤ Deficiencies on donor-restricted endowments

APPENDIX D

Statement of Financial Accounting Standards #136

Transfer of Assets to a Not-for-Profit Organization or Charitable Trust that Raises or Holds Contributions for Others

Background

The provisions of SFAS #116, *Accounting for Contributions Received and Contributions Made*, does not address "transfers of assets in which the reporting entity acts as an agent, trustee, or intermediary, rather than as a donor or donee" (paragraph 4). This standard is applicable to such organizations.

Highlights

SFAS #136 addresses the following areas:

➢ Accounting of transactions between a not-for-profit organization or charitable trust (the recipient organization) and another entity eventually receiving all or part of the donated assets (the beneficiary)

➢ Transactions that are not technically contributions

➢ Disclosure of fund-raising expenses

➢ Guidance on situations where one organization has "variance power" over another

Effective Dates

SFAS #136 affects financial statements issued after December 15, 1999.

Scope

SFAS #136 applies to any not-for-profit organization receiving assets, all or part of which will be distributed to another organization.

Inconsistencies

SFAS #136 supersedes FASB Interpretation #42, *Accounting for Transfers of Assets in Which a Not-for-Profit Organization Is Granted Variance Power.*

Discussion

SFAS #136 establishes standards for transactions in which a donor makes a contribution by transferring assets to a not-for-profit organization or charitable trust (the recipient organization) that accepts the assets from the donor and agrees to (a) use those assets on behalf of or (b) transfer those assets, the return on investment of those assets, or both, to a beneficiary specified by the donor. It also establishes standards for transactions that take place in a similar manner but are not contributions because the transfers are revocable, repayable, or reciprocal.

The Recipient

SFAS #136 requires a recipient organization that accepts cash or other financial assets from a donor and agrees to (a) use those assets on behalf of or (b) transfer those assets, the return on investment of those assets, or both, to a specified unaffiliated beneficiary, to recognize the fair value of those assets as a liability to the specified beneficiary concurrent with recognition of the assets received from the donor. However, if the donor explicitly grants the recipient organization variance power or if the recipient organization and the specified beneficiary are financially interrelated organizations, the recipient organization is required to recognize the fair value of any assets it receives as a contribution received.

Variance power may be defined as having the authority to redirect the funds. Not-for-profit organizations are financially interrelated if (a) one organization has the ability to influence the operating and financial decisions of the other and (b) one organization has an ongoing economic interest in the net assets of the other. With this guidance, FASB is clearly saying that in most cases federated fund-raising organizations such as the United Way should not record contributions for the amounts they receive that are designated by the donor for a specified beneficiary.

The Beneficiary

The specified beneficiary recognizes its rights to the assets held by a recipient organization as an asset of its own, unless the donor has explicitly granted the recipient organization variance power. Those rights are either an interest in the net assets of the recipient organization, a beneficial interest, or a contribution receivable. If the beneficiary and the recipient organization are financially interrelated organizations, the beneficiary is required to recognize its interest in the net assets of the recipient organization and adjust that interest for its share of the change in net assets of the recipient organization (equity method). If the beneficiary has an unconditional right to receive all or a portion of the specified cash flows from a charitable trust or other identifiable pool of assets, the beneficiary is required to recognize that beneficial interest, measuring and subsequently remeasuring it at fair value, using a valuation technique such as the present value of the estimated expected future cash flows. If the recipient organization is explicitly granted variance power, the specified beneficiary does not recognize its potential for future distributions from the assets held by the recipient organization. In all other cases, a beneficiary recognizes its rights as a contribution receivable.

SFAS #136 also details four circumstances in which a transfer of assets to a recipient organization is accounted for as a liability by the recipient organization and as an asset by the resource provider because the transfer is revocable or reciprocal. Those four circumstances are:

1. The transfer is subject to the resource provider's unilateral right to redirect the use of the assets to another beneficiary.

2. The transfer is accompanied by the resource provider's conditional promise to give or is otherwise revocable or repayable.

3. The resource provider controls the recipient organization and specifies an unaffiliated beneficiary.

4. The resource provider specifies itself or its affiliate as the beneficiary, and the transfer is not an equity transaction.

If the transfer is an equity transaction and the resource provider specifies itself as beneficiary, it records an interest in the net assets of the recipient organization (or an increase in a previously recognized interest). If the resource provider specifies an affiliate as beneficiary, the resource provider records an equity transaction as a separate line item in its Statement of Activities, and the affiliate named as beneficiary records an interest in the net assets of the recipient organization. The recipient organization records an equity transaction as a separate line item in its Statement of Activities.

Disclosure

SFAS #136 also includes two new disclosure requirements. First, if an organization chooses to disclose a ratio of fund-raising expenses to funds raised, it must disclose how it computes that ratio. Second, an organization that transfers assets to a recipient organization and names itself as the beneficiary must disclose the recipient organization receiving the transfer, whether variance power was granted, the terms under which the recipient organization will distribute the assets, and the aggregate amount recognized in the Statement of Financial Position and whether the amount is reflected as an interest in the net assets of the recipient organization or as another asset.

Examples

Scenario

A not-for-profit organization allows potential donors three choices in its annual fund-raising campaign: donors can give without restrictions, direct their donations to one of three activities conducted by the not-for-profit organization, or specify that the donation be transferred to another not-for-profit organization.

Example 1

A donor makes an unrestricted gift to the not-for-profit organization.

Journal Entry:

Debit		An Asset Account at the		
		Fair Market Value of the Gift	$XXX	
	Credit	Contributions Revenue		$XXX

Example 2

A donor makes an unrestricted gift but specifies that it be used to fund one of the activities monitored by the not-for-profit organization.

Journal Entry:

Debit		An Asset Account at the		
		Fair Market Value of the Gift	$XXX	
	Credit	Temporarily Restricted Net Assets		$XXX

Example 3

A donor makes an unrestricted gift but directs that the gift be transferred to another not-for-profit organization.

Journal Entry (on the books of the recipient organization):

Debit		An Asset Account at the		
		Fair Market Value of the Gift	$XXX	
	Credit	A Liability Account		$XXX

Journal Entry (on the books of the beneficiary organization):

Debit		Accounts Receivable at Net	$XXX	
	Credit	Contributions Revenue at Net		$XXX

(*Note:* Recipient organizations would record the gift under the provisions of SFAS #116, #117, and #124.)

Scenario

Instead of the situation described earlier and the first three examples, the not-for-profit organization retained the right to redirect gifts if the organization made the decision that other needs are greater. In this situation, the not-for-profit organization has exercised variance power.

Example 4

A donor makes a gift under the previously noted scenario.

Journal Entry (on the books of the recipient organization):

Debit	An Asset Account at the		
	Fair Market Value of the Gift	$XXX	
Credit	Contributions Revenue		$XXX

Journal Entry (on the books of the beneficiary organization):

None.

Scenario

A church solicits contributions to fund a scholarship for an individual at a seminary.

Example 5

The church receives contributions.

Journal Entry:

Debit	An Asset Account at the		
	Fair Market Value	$XXX	
Credit	A Liability Account		$XXX

The church transfers the asset to the seminary.

Journal Entry:

Debit	The Liability Account	$XXX	
Credit	A Liability Account to the Individual		$XXX

Scenario

An individual creates an account at a bank (a trustee) that will distribute assets in accordance with the individual's directions to a not-for-profit organization. The bank and the not-for-profit organization are not financially interrelated. (*Note:* SFAS #136 does not establish standards for commercial organizations, i.e., the trustee bank.)

Journal Entry (on the books of the not-for-profit organization):

There are a few possible journal entries, depending on whether the account held by the bank is irrevocable, whether just the earnings will be remitted to the not-for-profit organization, and so on. The not-for-profit organization will record journal entries in accordance with the provisions of SFAS #116, #117, and #124.

Financially Interrelated Organizations

There will be occasions when donations are received by one not-for-profit organization that is financially interrelated to another not-for-profit organization. An example of two financially interrelated organizations would be a not-for-profit hospital and the hospital's foundation.

The basis for determining whether two not-for-profits are financially interrelated is a thorough examination of the relationship between the two organizations via analysis of their respective board representation, studying both organization's bylaws, and so forth.

If it is determined that the two not-for-profit organizations are, in fact, financially interrelated, the standard directs that it is probable the equity method of accounting should be employed and accounting for contributions is complex, and the statement of SFAS #136 should be studied in its entirety very carefully.

Glossary

Accrual Accounting.   Accounting method by which revenue is recognized when earned and expenses are recognized when incurred. It attempts to match revenue and expenses independently of cash receipts and disbursements.

Aged Statements.   A report breaking down the accounts receivable and accounts payable schedules into monthly categories based on the original date of the invoice.

Amortization.   Expensing an intangible asset or leasehold improvement over its useful life.

Assets.   Economic resources, including cash, receivables, property, and intangibles.

Audits.   A service offered by independent CPAs that ensures "full assurance' on the accuracy of information contained in an audit. The information is considered to be "presented fairly."

Audit Exceptions.   Problems incurred during the course of an audit by the independent CPA or the IRS.

Audit Opinions.   There are four types of audit opinions offered by independent CPAs:
Unqualified. The organization's information has "no qualifications" that the reader should be aware of.
Qualified. An audit opinion that states important negative issue(s) were uncovered during an audit and noted on the opinion letter.

Adverse. The audit information has been interpreted as substantially misstated.
Disclaimer. The CPA has withdrawn from offering an audit opinion and issues a no opinion statement.

Audited Financial Statement. Financial statement audited by an independent CPA who has issued an accompanying opinion letter.

Balance Sheet. See *Statement of Financial Position.*

Board-Designated Funds. Amounts designated by a board of directors for specific internal restrictions. Board-designated funds are included among unrestricted net assets and have no legal or accounting significance because the restriction has not been placed by a donor.

Board of Directors Responsibilities. Nonprofit boards have three basic duties with regard to their service (see Chapter 2 for full explanation):
Duty of Loyalty
Duty of Obedience
Duty of Care

Book Value. The carrying value of an asset or liability, regardless of actual or market value. It is computed at cost less accumulated depreciation.

Capital Budget. Budget that projects cash required to purchase fixed assets and the resulting depreciation calculations.

Capital Lease. A lease that is recorded as an asset and depreciated rather than expensed on the financial records as payments are made.

Capitalization. Recording the cost of assets purchased on the organization's Statement of Financial Position rather than expensing them in the period purchased. Capitalized assets are depreciated.

Cash Accounting. Accounting method by which revenue is recognized as cash is received and expenses are recognized as cash is disbursed.

Cash Flow Budget. Budget that projects cash available balances at the end of each month to ensure that sufficient cash is available to meet ongoing obligations and to maximize investment opportunities.

Check 21. A law that permits banks to forward *images* of check detail to account holders rather than the original checks.

Collections. Assets that meet the following three criteria:
1. It must be held for public exhibition as a service rather than for financial gain.
2. It must be kept protected, unencumbered, preserved, and cared for.
3. If sold, proceeds must be used to acquire other collection items.

Not-for-profit organizations are not required to capitalize collections of works of art, historical items, and the like, and donations of such items are not recorded as contributions in the financial statements unless the collection is capitalized. Rather, these contributions will be disclosed in the footnotes of the financial statements.

Compilation. A service provided by CPAs that results in "no assurance" on the financial data. The data represent the management of the client.

Conditions of Employment Agreement. A document that advises approving prospective employees of the organization's right to conduct background checks, recover intellectual property termination of employment policy as well as several other important areas (see Chapter 7 for full explanation).

Conditional Promise to Give. The donor is not bound to keep the promise of a donation unless a specific future event occurs (a condition). Conditional promises to give are not recorded in the financial statement until and unless the condition is met.

Continuous Budgeting. A process whereby monthly budgets are projected a year in advance every month after the current period's financial statements are prepared.

Contribution. A voluntary, nonreciprocal transfer of labor, cash, or other assets from one entity to another. A contribution may also be a cancellation of debt.

Cost of Goods Sold. The actual cost of items sold to the organization that the organization intends to resell.

Credit. An entry in an account that will result in a reduction in an asset account, an increase in a liability account, or a decrease in an expense account.

Current Assets. Cash and cash equivalents plus assets that are expected to be converted to cash or consumed during the next 12 months.

Current Liabilities.   Obligations due to be paid during the next 12 months.

Current Restricted Funds.   See *Temporarily Restricted Net Assets.*

Current-Year Budget.   Also called tactical plan. Organization's financial goals for the current year.

Debit.   An entry in an account that results in an increase in an asset account, a reduction in a liability account, or an increase in an expense account.

Debt Security.   A security indicating a creditor relationship with an organization. Debt securities include applicable preferred stock, applicable mortgage obligations, U.S. government securities, municipal securities, corporate bonds, commercial paper, convertible debt, and all securitized debt investments. Trade accounts receivable usually do not meet the definition of debt security.

Deferred Charges.   Also known as prepaid expenses. An expenditure incurred in one period, the benefits of which are not realized until a later accounting period. It is recorded as an asset on the balance sheet.

Deferred Revenue.   Revenue received before it is earned. It is recorded as a liability on the balance sheet.

Depreciation.   Expensing a tangible asset over its economic life.

Disclosure of Information.   Federal and state requirements that certain forms be provided to requesters (see Chapter 6 for full explanation).

Direct Lobbying.   Communication with a member or employee of a group that participants in the legislative process.

Donor-Imposed Condition.   Prevents the receiving organization from recording a contribution in the financial statements until a future condition specified by the donor has been met. If the condition has not been met, the organization must either return the asset or forgive the promisor of any obligation.

Donor-Restricted Endowment Fund.   See *Permanently Restricted Net Assets.*

Endowment Fund.   See *Permanently Restricted Net Assets.*

Engagement Letter.   Written agreement between a CPA and their client concerning an audit.

Equity Security.   Represents an ownership interest, such as common stock or preferred stock. Also includes the rights to acquire, such as warrants, rights, and call options.

Expensing a Disbursement.   Recording a disbursement of cash as an expense in the financial records rather than capitalizing the disbursement and recording it as an asset in the financial records.

Fair Value.   The amount at which an asset could be bought or sold by willing parties, including quoted prices on a domestic or foreign stock exchange. Does not include forced sales.

Financial Ratio.   Computation to assess an organization's ability to pay debt, earning power, return on investment, and so forth.

Form 990.   Federal information return required to be filed by nonprofits meeting certain budget and assets financial thresholds. This form is open for public inspection.

Form 990-EZ. Federal information return required for smaller nonprofits with budget and asset financial thresholds lower than those organizations required to file Form 990. Required for nonprofits that regularly experience gross receipts of over $25,000 per year.

Form 990-N.   Electronic information required for very small nonprofits with gross receipts routinely under $ 25,000 per year.

Form 990-PF. Information return required to be filed by Private Foundations.

Form 990-T.   Unrelated Business Income Tax Return.   A tax return required for nonprofits having gross revenues of $ 1,000 or more per year from revenue sources that are considered not unrelated to the organization's tax-exempt purpose. Form 990-DT must be filed even if the organization experienced a loss. If the organization experienced a profit, the tax is based on prevailing corporate tax rates.

Fraud Action Plan.   A well-thought-out strategy of action to be taken if the organization experiences or is suspicious of fraud or embezzlement.

Functional Accounting. Method of accounting that classifies revenues and expenses according to specific goals, departments, functions, and so forth.

Functional Classification. Assigning revenues and expenses to specific supporting or program activities of a not-for-profit organization.

General Fund. See *Unrestricted Net Assets.*

Generally Accepted Accounting Principles (GAAP). A technical term encompassing conventions, rules, and procedures governing acceptable accounting practice.

Generally Accepted Auditing Standards (GAAS). Assumptions and rules that govern the CPA's ability to accept an auditing engagement and procedure that must be undertaken during the course of the audit.

Grassroots Lobbying. An attempt to influence the general public or portion thereof on elections, legislative matters, or referendums.

Gross Revenues. The grand total of revenues received before deducting associated costs of goods sold and discounts taken.

Hard Money. Funds contributed directly to candidates for political parties.

Imprest Fund. Also known as petty cash fund. Cash kept on hand to pay for minor expenditures.

Income Statement. See *Statement of Activity.*

Intangible Asset. A nonfinancial asset to an organization with economic value. Examples include purchased copyrights with future royalty benefits, and so forth.

Internal Audit Committees. Committees formed by nonprofits to review the organizations financial operation, policies, etc. They are typically staffed by nonboard members, nonstaff, and the like to improve independence.

Internal Controls. A system of policies that employees of nonprofits must follow to reduce the possibility of fraud or embezzlement.

Internal Financial Statement. Unaudited financial statement used for management purposes only.

IRS Form 990.   Information return required to be filed by not-for-profit organizations.

IRS Form 990-T.   Tax return required to be filed by not-for-profit organizations for tax on unrelated business income.

Leasehold Improvement.   An expenditure that improves leased property, such as the purchase of office carpeting. The value of the improvement transfers to the owner of the property after the lease terminates.

Liability.   Obligation to pay an amount or render services as a result of a past transaction.

Lobbying.   Action concerning legislation or election of office seekers.

Long-Range Plan.   Organization goals projected five or more years into the future.

Natural Classification.   Classifying revenues and expenses as line items in the financial statements rather than by functions.

Net Assets.   Section of the Statement of Financial Position that includes unrestricted net assets, temporarily restricted net assets, and permanently restricted net assets.

Net Revenues.   Gross revenues less associated cost of goods sold and discounts taken.

Net Worth.   See *Unrestricted Net Assets.*

Nonreciprocal Transfer.   A contribution of labor, cash, or other assets from one entity to another. The donating entity must not receive anything of value in return and does not retain any right to have the contribution returned under any circumstances.

Not-for-Profit Organization.   An organization exempt from federal income taxes under Internal Revenue Code Section 501(c), and which possesses the following characteristics:
- ➢ There is no owner equity interest.
- ➢ Earnings must not enure to individuals.

Office of Management Budget (OMB) Circulars.   Circulars issued by the executive branch of the U.S. government. The three specifically affecting nonprofits are:
    A-21: Cost principals for educational institutions

A-87: Cost principals for state, local or Indian tribal government

A-133: Cost principals for nonprofit organizations

Operating Lease.   An expense line-item lease. Operating lease expense is recognized on the financial statements as payments are made.

Optional Proxy Tax.   A tax paid on Form 990-T based on current lobbying expenses multiplied by the applicable tax rate. This tax is paid if the organization has *not* passed on a nondeductable dues percentage to dues paying members.

Permanent Restriction.   A restriction placed on assets contributed to a not-for-profit organization that the not-for-profit organization must hold in perpetuity. Earnings may be either temporarily restricted or unrestricted.

Permanently Restricted Net Assets.   Formally called endowment funds. Permanently restricted net assets can be in the form of cash, securities, collection items, buildings, and so forth, and must be held by the not-for-profit organization in perpetuity. Earnings from permanently restricted net assets can be either temporarily restricted or unrestricted.

Plant Fund.   An obsolete not-for-profit organization account.

Political Action Committees (PACs).   Committees (other than 501(c)(3) organizations) that collects nondeductible contributions and makes contributions to candidates of political parties. PAC funds may not be commingled with operating funds.

Prepaid Expenses.   Also known as deferred charges. An expenditure incurred in one accounting period, the benefits from which are not realized until a later accounting period. It is recorded as an asset on the balance sheet.

Promise to Give.   An unconditional or conditional written or oral agreement to make a contribution of labor, cash, or other assets from one entity to another.

Quid Pro Quo Contribution.   Contribution for which the donor receives some value in return.

Requests for Proposals (RFPs) for CPA Services. An application forwarded to potential CPA firms that requires important data be addressed.

Restricted Support.   Revenues or gains from contributions that are restricted by the donor and not included in the unrestricted class of accounts.

Retirement of Assets.   Removing the cost and accumulated depreciation of an asset from the financial statements and records.

Revenue Ruling 87–41. An IRS questionnaire consisting of 20 questions that all employers should address when deciding if an individual should be classified as an employee or independent contractor.

Review.   A service provided by a CPA firm that results in "limited assurance" on the financial data.

Soft Money.   Contributions made directly to a political party.

Statement of Activity.   Revenues, expenses, and results of activities of not-for-profit organizations. In commercial organizations, this statement is called the income statement or profit and loss statement.

Statement of Changes in Net Assets.   Financial statement of a not-for-profit organization indicating how results of operations have affected unrestricted net assets (net worth of the organization), temporarily restricted net assets, and permanently restricted net assets.

Statement of Financial Position.   Assets, liabilities, and net assets of a not-for-profit organization. In commercial organizations, this statement is called the balance sheet.

Temporarily Restricted Net Assets.   Assets held by a not-for-profit organization, the use of which is for a purpose specified by the donor.

Temporary Restriction.   A donor-imposed restriction requiring a not-for-profit organization holding the asset to use the asset for a specific purpose or an asset that reverts to the unrestricted class of accounts upon the passage of time.

Unconditional Promise to Give.   A contribution binding on the promisor.

Unrelated Business Income Tax (UBIT).   Taxes paid by a nonprofit on Form 990-T if the organization experienced a profit from revenues unrelated to their mission.

Unrestricted Net Assets.   The cumulative excess of revenues over expenses (deficit) of a not-for-profit organization that is not restricted by donors to the permanently restricted or temporarily restricted net assets classes of account.

Unrestricted Support.   Contributions not restricted by donors for a specific purpose.

Voluntary Health and Welfare Organizations.   Not-for-profit organizations organized to address health and welfare problems and funded by voluntary contributions. Their Statement of Activity must be presented using both the functional and the natural method.

Wholly Owned Taxable Subsidiaries.   A commercial organization primarily owned by a nonprofit to reduce taxes and protect tax-exempt status.

Index

Accounting. *See* Accrual accounting;
    Functional accounting
  calculation, 135
  descriptions, examples, 154
  methods, 177
  policies, 12–13
    descriptions, examples, 157
  policies/procedures manual, 153
    preparation, 154–156
    separation, 155–156
  services, RFP (example), 101e
  statements, basics, 171
Accounting for Contributions Received
    and Contributions Made (SFAS #116),
    19, 159
Accounting for Transfers of Assets in Which
    a Not-for-Profit Organization Is
    Granted Variance Power (FASB
    Interpretation #42), 240
Accounts, temporarily restricted/
    permanently restricted classes,
    205e
Accounts payable, 175
Accounts receivable, 174
Accrual accounting, 245
  method, 177
Accrued payroll, 175
Activity
  allowance/nonallowance, 118
  restraint, 55
  statement, 253

Administrative costs, increase,
    55
Adverse audit opinions, 88, 92, 246
  example, 93e
Advertising
  forms, 139
  income, IRS consideration, 29
  limits, 146
Advocacy, 128–129
Aged statements, 245
American Institute of Certified Public
    Accountants (AICPA) standards,
    issuance, 159–160, 171
American Society of Association Executives,
    100
Amortization, 245
Annual distributions, 181
Annual dues, definition, 133
Annuities, exclusion, 29
Application for Automatic Extension of Time
    to File Corporation Income Tax
    Return (Form 7004), 25
Assets, 245. *See also* Current assets;
    Intangible asset; Net assets
  dual use, 30
  liabilities, aggregation, 186
  misappropriation, 106
  retirement, 253
Audited financial statements, issuance, 103,
    109
Auditing standards, application, 98

Audits, 87–95, 245
  committees. *See* Internal audit committees
  components, 106
  conducting, CPA office (impact), 61
  delay, 60–61
  design, 106
  exceptions, 245
  fees, control, 104
  fieldwork, 103, 109
    completion, 87–88
  informal handling, 61
  objective, 106
  opinions, 245–246
  preparedness, 61–63
  procedures, 106–107
  requirement, absence, 96
  standards, 116
Authorized signers, change (approval),
    74–75
Average acquisition indebtedness, 29
Average adjusted basis, 29

Background check, form, 52e
Balance Sheet (Statement of Financial
    Position), 10, 23, 246
  accounts, 154
  presentation, 162e
Bank account signers, financial personnel
    prohibition, 71
Bank reconciliation copy, attachment, 71
Bank statement copies, off-site forwarding, 70
Beneficiary, assets rights, 240–241
Binding arbitration, 53–54
Bipartisan Campaign Reform Act (BCRA),
    146, 147
Board-approved accounting policies/
    procedures manual, usage, 66
Board-designated funds, 160, 246
Board of directors
  internal financial statements, forwarding,
    11
  records examination, 45
  responsibilities, 246
Book value, 246
Buckley v. Valeo, 136, 146
Budget. *See* Capital budget; Cash flow
    budget; Current-year budget
Budgeting process, 103
Business, consideration, 27

Campaign contributions, 137, 141
Campaign financial reform, avoidance, 139
Campaign intervention, 128, 129
Campaign politics, expenditures, 145
Candidate party committees, PACs
    (relationship), 143–146
Capital budget, 246
Capitalization, 246
Capital lease, 246
Care, duty, 9–13, 246
Cash accounting, 246
  method, 177
Cash flow
  budget, 246
  statement, 88
Cash management, 118
Cash transactions, organizational
    investigation, 75
Certified Public Accountants (CPA)
  advice, 110
  contact, 81
  copies, usage, 81
  management letter, review, 12
  management responsibilities, 107–108
  notekeeping, 81–82
  opinion letter, 88
  organization office visit, 74
  services, 100
    RFPs, 252
    types, 87
Certified Public Accountants (CPA) firm
  auditing standards, 96
  audit objective, 106
  audit procedures, 106–107
  deadline date, 103
  disclaimer of opinion, 94, 95e
  engagement administration, 108–109
  fees, 108–109
  functions, understanding, 87
  independence, reputation, 100
  information, requirement, 102
  interview, 103
    notification date, 102
  retention, 11
  selection, 100–109
    criteria, 102
  usage, 87
Charges. *See* Deferred charges

Charitable contributions, deductions (restrictions), 33, 37–38
Charitable organizations
    501(c)(3) corporation establishment, 128–129
    501(c)(3) election, 131
    lobbying activities, curtailment, 127
Charities
    activities, risk, 129
    voter education activities, 129
Check 21, 85, 247
Checks
    payment, organizational prohibition, 75
    scanners, organizational research, 77–78
    transactions, organizational investigation, 75
Chief executive officer, criticism protection, 153–154
Child care benefits, damages, 37
Christian Echoes National Ministry, Inc. v. United States, 127
COGS. *See* Cost of Goods Sold
Collections, 247
    disclosure, 221
    items. *See* Contributed collections items
Communication, organization element, 117
Comparative financial statements, 210
Compensation Information (Schedule J), 23
Compilation, 98, 247
    example, 99e
Computer passwords, change, 83
Conditional promise to give, 220, 247
Conditions of employment agreement, 47, 247
    binding arbitration, 53
    customer information, surrender, 49
    elements, 47–53
    erroneous statements, termination, 47
    form, 50e-52e
    gifts, offers/acceptance, 47
    involuntary terminations, 48–49
    leaves of absence, 48–49
    management day, 48
    office, immediate removal, 49
    organization intellectual property, surrender, 49
    organization usage, 73
    prosecution, 49
    review, 82

sick days, 48
    uninterrupted vacation, 48
Conferences, deferred income, 175
Confidential information, sharing, 107
Conflict of Interest Agreement, organization usage, 74
Continuous budgeting, 247
Contractual documents, components, 62–63
Contributed collections items, 218–219
Contributed services. *See* Recognition of contributed services
Contributions, 247
    considerations, 144
    limits, 137
        list, 138e, 142e
    made, 220
    recognition, 217
    term, usage, 216
Control activities, 117–118
Control environment, organization element, 117
Controlled organizations, income, 29
Coordinated expenditures, 146
Corporate Estimated Tax (Form 1120-W), 26
Cost allocation plan, 133
Cost circulars, 114–116
Cost of Goods Sold (COGS), 177, 247
Cost principles, allowance, 118
Costs, allowance, 118
CPAs. *See* Certified Public Accountants
Credit, 247
Credit card transactions, organizational investigation, 75
Current assets, 174, 247
Current liabilities, 175, 248
Current restricted funds, 160, 248
    external restrictions, 160
Current-year budget, 248
Customer information, surrender, 49
    form, 51d

Davis Bacon Act, 118
Debates, permission, 129
Debit, 248
Debit memorandums (DMs), investigation, 70
Debt-financed property, gross revenue taxability, 29
Debt-financed property, term (usage), 29

Debt security, 248
Deferred charges, 248
Deferred income, 175
Deferred revenue, 248
De *minimis rule*, 136
Dental insurance benefits, damages, 37
Depreciation, 248
Direct costs, allowance, 115
Direct lobbying, 128, 248
Direct method, 206
    example, 207e
Disability insurance benefits, damages, 37
Disbursement, expensing, 249
Disclaimer of opinion, 94
    example, 95e
Disclosure for collections, 221
Disclosure of information, 39–43, 248
    exemptions, 43
    group returns, 41
    issues, 40
    policies, 39–40
        sample, 43
    records
        board of directors examination, 45
        disclosure, 43–44
    records, inspection
        availability, 40–41
        exclusion, 41
        IRS, impact, 42
        location, 41
        right, 40
    reimbursement, 42
    requests, 42–44
    state requirements, 42–43
Disqualified person, definition, 18
Dividends, 56–57
Domestic subsidiary, PAC nonestablishment,
    144
Donor-imposed condition, 248
    term, usage, 217
Donor-imposed restriction
    expiration, 219
    term, usage, 217
Donor-restricted endowment fund, 248
Dues
    deferred income, 175
    receipt, 136
    revenue, calculation, 135
    tax deductibility, 135

Duty of care (board of directors responsi-
    bility), 10–13, 246
Duty of loyalty (board of directors responsi-
    bility), 9, 246
Duty of obedience (board of directors
    responsibility), 9, 246

Earmarking, 118–119
Embezzlement
    impact. *See* Not-for-profit organizations
    window of opportunity, 74
Employees
    background checks, organizational
        requirement, 76
    benefits, damages, 37
    bonding, 72
    coworker interaction, 83
    credit cards, organizational elimination, 76
    dismissal, circumstances, 84
    information, surrender, 51e
    office escort, 83
    protection, 83
    status, IRS issues, 33–34
    termination, 75
        notetaking, 84
        witness, presence, 82
Employment agreement, conditions, 47, 247.
    See also Conditions of employment
    agreement
Employment law attorney, contact, 81
End grantee, 113
Endowment funds, 160–161, 248. *See also*
    Donor-restricted endowment fund
    external restriction, 160
Engagement administration, 108–109
Engagement letter, 103, 249
    example, 105e
    usage, 104–109
e-Postcard (990–N), 16, 249
Equipment, management, 118
Equity security, 249
    fair value, 233
Erroneous statements, termination, 47
    form, 50e
Estimated taxes
    computation, 26
    underpayment, penalty, 27
Estimated tax payments
    due date, 26

process, 26
requirement, 26
Excess benefits, examples, 167–168
Excess business holdings, excise tax
    assessment, 181
Excise tax, 181
    application, 130
    assessment, 181
    charge, 181
    computation, 169
Executives, notetaking, 84
Executive Summary, inclusion, 11
Exempt activities, exploitation, 30
Exempt Organization Income Tax Return
    (Form 990–T), 41
Exempt Organizations Divisions, 42
Exit interview, requirement, 75
Expenses, 177. *See also* Prepaid expenses
    allocation, monitoring, 133
    reporting, 191–192
External financial statements, scope, 185

Facilities, dual use, 30
Fair value, 249
    measurement, 220
Federal Election Campaign Act (FECA), 136
    impact, 141
Federal election campaigns,
        corporation/labor union contribu-
        tions (ineligibility), 137
Federal Election Commission (FEC)
    contribution limit mandate, 137
    FEC-mandated contribution limits, 138e,
        142e
    fines, 139
    PAC registration, 134
Federal election influence, federal law
        prohibitions, 144
Federal income tax, 33
    exemption qualification, 1
Federal Insurance Contributions Act (FICA)
    exemptions, absence, 3e, 4e
    taxes, 34
        election, exemption, 2e
Federal not-for-profit requirements,
        knowledge, 10
Federal requirements, research, 39
Federal Tax Deposit Coupon (Form 8109), 26
Federal Unemployment Tax Act (FUTA)

exemptions, absence, 3e, 4e
organizations, exemption, 2e
Federal unemployment taxes, 34
FICA. *See* Federal Insurance Contributions
    Act
Fidelity bond
    claim, 84
    reading, 82
Financial Accounting Standards Board
    (FASB)
    accounting standards, 171
    Interpretation #42 (*Accounting for Transfers
        of Assets in Which a Not-for-Profit
        Organization Is Granted Variance
        Power*), 240
Financial documents, components, 62
Financially interrelated organizations,
    244
Financial policies, 12–13
Financial position
    financial statements, presentation, 107
    statement, 253
Financial ratio, 249
Financial records, full audit (nonrequire-
    ment), 96
Financial reporting, 23
    fraud, 106
Financial statements, 23. *See also* Internal
    financial statement
    accuracy, full assurance, 88
    basics, 171
    comparison, 210
    contributions, classification, 221–232
    CPA opinion, 87
    fairness, front opinion, 121e
    footnotes, 88
    notes, 213–214
    opinions, expression, 106
    preparation, GAAP usage, 171
    presentation, 90, 161, 164, 221
    recognition of contributions, 219
    types, 172
    understanding. *See* Primary financial
        statements
Financial Statements of Not-for-Profit
    Organizations (SFAS #117), 19, 159
First Amendment rights, infringement, 147
Fixed-assets funds, 161
Flow-through funding, complexity, 113

Foreign corporation, domestic subsidiary (PAC nonestablishment), 144
Foreign nationals, PAC establishment, 144
Foreign parent corporation, PAC financing, 144
Forms. *See* Internal Revenue Service forms
Fraud
 allegations, 108
 detection (prevention/detection), programs/controls (design/implementation responsibility), 107–108
Fraud action plan, 249
 documentation, 69, 81–85
Fraud scheme, victimization, 81
Fraud triangle, 78–80
 illustration, 80e
Fringe benefits, risk, 69
Full audit, nonrequirement, 96
Functional accounting, 250
Functional basis, example, 196e
Functional classification, 249
Functional expenses, statement, 22
Functional matrix, 199, 201
 example, 200e
Functional method, 195
Functional reporting requirements, 192–193
Funded activities, eligibility, 118
Funds
 noncomingling, 13
 reduction, as needed basis, 118
FUTA. *See* Federal Unemployment Tax Act

GAAP. *See* Generally accepted accounting principles
GAAS. *See* Generally accepted accounting standards
Gains, reporting, 191–192, 235–237
General funds, 160, 249
 internal restriction, 160
Generally accepted accounting principles (GAAP), 87, 250
 conformity, 92, 106, 107
 requirement, 185
 usage, 171
Generally accepted accounting standards (GAAS), 87, 116, 250
 accordance, auditor report (usage), 120e–121e

Generally Accepted Government Auditing Standards (GAGAS), 116
 accordance, auditor report, 124e–125e
 usage, 121e
Ghost employee, presence, 74
Ghosts on the Payroll, spotting mechanism, 73
Gifts, offers/acceptance, 47
 form, 50e
Giving
 conditional promise, 247
 unconditional promise, 253
Government audit, compliance, 124e–125e
Government grants, provision, 113
Grants
 accounting/auditing, 111
 agreement, 112
  budget document, reference, 112
 audits, preparation, 117–119
 availability period, 119
 award, 111
 debarment, 119
 federal reporting, 113
 funds, 13
 nonprofit organization provision, 112
 procurement, 119
 program income, 119
 project, progression, 112
 provision, 113
 specifics, 111–112
 state reporting requirements, 113
 subrecipient monitoring, 119
 suspension, 119
 terminology, 114–116
 understanding, 111–114
Grants and Other Assistance to Organizations, Governments, and Individuals in the US (Schedule I), 23
Grassroots lobbying, 128, 250
Gross income (debt-financed property), equation, 29
Gross revenues, 250
 production, 29
 taxability, 29
Group returns, 41

Hard money, 250
 regulations, 145
 soft money, contrast, 136–137, 146–147

term, usage, 136, 146
Hatch Act, 3e
Health insurance benefits, damages, 37
High-speed scanners, 77–78
Holiday leave, damages, 37
Hospitals (Schedule H), 23

Imprest fund, 250
Income allocation, monitoring, 133
Income-producing property,
      acquisition/improvement, 29
Income Statement (Statement of Activity),
      10, 250
Independent auditor report
  adverse opinion, 93e
  compilation, 99e
  qualified opinion, 91e
  review, 97e
  unqualified opinion, 89
Independent-contractor status, IRS issues,
    33–34
Independent CPAs, internal audit commit-
    tees (relationship), 151
Indirect cost rate proposals (ICRPs), submis-
    sion, 116
Indirect costs, allowance, 115
Indirect method, 208
Individuals, intermediate sanctions (impact),
    168–169
Information
  accuracy/completeness, 107
  confidentiality, maintenance, 107
  organization assessment, 117
  returns review, 13
Information disclosure, 39–43, 248
  exemptions, 43
  expenses, reimbursement, 42
  group returns, 41
  issues, 40
  policies, 39–40
    sample, 43
  records, board of directors examination, 45
  records, disclosure, 43–44
  records, inspection, 40
    availability, 40–41
    exemption, 41
    IRS, impact, 42
    location, 41
  requests, 42–44

statement requirements, 42–43
In-house lobbying expenditures, level,
    136
Initial excise tax, process, 169
Insurance coverage, adequacy (review),
    12
Intangible asset, 250
Intellectual property, surrender, 49
  form, 51e
Interest, exclusion, 29
Intermediate sanctions
  basics, 167
  impact, 168–169
  legislation, impact, 169
Internal audit committees, 149, 250
  independent CPAs, relationship, 151
  members, 149
    education, 150
  organization office visit, 74
  outside assistance, 151
  reports, 150
  responsibilities, 150
  surprise visit, 151
  training, 149
  visits, 151
Internal controls, 250
  back report, 124e–125e
  establishment, responsibility, 107
  evaluation, 70–77
  maintenance, responsibility, 107
  policies
    adequacy, 12
    documentation, 74
  system, advantage, 69
Internal documents, development, 69
Internal financial statement, 250
  forwarding, 11
  monthly preparation, 11
  revenues/expenses, actual/budget
    contrast, 11
Internal Revenue Code (IRC)
  162(e), guidance, 133
  501(c)(3) public charities, 127–131
  527 organizations, legal entity separation,
    134
  6033(e) reporting/notice requirements,
    132–134
  6033(e) requirements, exceptions, 132
  6033 guidance, 133

Internal Revenue Service (IRS)
  field audit, location, 64
  issues, 33
  position papers, 129–130
Internal Revenue Service (IRS) audits, 59
  advice, 66–67
  audited financial statements, copy (usage),
    60
  audited records, separation, 65
  avoidance, 59–60
  board-approved accounting policies/
    procedures manual, usage, 66
  contractual documents, components,
    62–63
  CPA office, impact, 61
  delay, 60–61
  documents, signing (professional advice),
    65
  exposure, increase, 56
  filing, timeliness, 59
  financial documents, components, 62
  handling, 60–66
  informal handling, 61
  IRS attention, avoidance, 60
  IRS field agent, location, 64
  IRS fishing expedition, avoidance, 65
  letters, components, 60
  mock audit, conducting, 63
  offensive approach, 64
  organizational documents, components, 61
  preparedness, 61–63
  publications, components, 63
  staff preparedness, 63
  volunteer, avoidance, 65
  writing request, 64–65
Internal Revenue Service (IRS) classifica-
    tions, 1–6
  Section 501(a), 1
  Section 501(c), 15
  Section 501(c)(1), 5e
  Section 501(c)(2), 5e
  Section 501(c)(3) organizations, intermedi-
    ate sanctions legislation (impact), 169
  Section 501(c)(3) private foundations, 2e
    mailing lists, rental, 28
    organizations, contributions deductibil-
      ity, 37
    public disclosure, change, 45
    status, 17

Section 501(c)(3) public charities, 127–131
  list, 2e
Section 501(c)(4), 130, 132–136
  intermediate sanctions legislation,
    impact, 169
  list, 2e–3e
  social welfare organizations, 133
Section 501(c)(5), 3e, 132–136
  labor/agricultural/horticultural
    members, 132
Section 501(c)(6), 3e–4e, 132–136
  business leagues/boards of trades, 132
Section 501(c)(7), 4e
Section 501(c)(8), 5e
Section 501(c)(10), 5e
Section 501(c)(11), 5e
Section 501(c)(12), 5e
Section 501(c)(13), 5e
Section 501(c)(14), 5e
Section 501(c)(15), 5e
Section 501(c)(16), 5e
Section 501(c)(17), 5e
Section 501(c)(18), 5e
Section 501(c)(19), 4e
Section 501(c)(20), 5e
Section 501(c)(21), 5e
Section 501(c)(22), 5e
Section 501(c)(23), 5e
Section 501(c)(24), 5e
Section 501(c)(25), 5e
Section 501(d), 6e
Section 501(e), 6e
Section 501(h) election, 130–131
Section 501(k), 6e
Section 527, 6e, 130
  group, PAC election, 139, 143
  organizations, 134
Section 527S, 141
Section 528, 6e
Internal Revenue Service (IRS) forms
  990, 18–24, 136, 249, 251
    appendixes, 24
    balance sheet, 23
    basics, 15
    compensation, 21–22
    copies, availability, 42
    Disclosure, 21–22
    due date, 15
    effective date, 15

filing failure, penalties, 16
filing location, 15
financial statements/reporting, 23
governance/management/disclosure,
    20–21
impact, 15
inspection, availability, 40–41
items, 19–23
organization filing, 18
organization procurement, 16
public disclosure, change, 45
related schedules, 23–24
required schedules, checklist, 20
signature block, 19
Statement of Functional Expenses, 22
Statement of Program Service Accom-
    plishments, 20
Statement of Revenue, 22
tax accounting methods, 19
990, copies, 13
990-BL, inspection (availability), 40–41
990-EZ, 16–18, 249
    attachments, 17–18
    basics, 15
    copies, availability, 42
    disqualified person, definition, 18
    due date, 17
    extensions, allowance, 17
    filing date, 15
    filing failure, individual responsibility, 17
    filing failure, penalties, 17
    inspection, availability, 40–41
    mailing location, 17
    organization filing, 16
    organization procurement, 16
    public inspection, 18
    return, signing, 18
    schedules/attachments, requirement,
        17–18
990-N (e-Postcard), 249
    information, requirement, 16
    organization procurement, 16
990-PF, 249
    copies, availability, 42
    reporting requirements, 2e
990-T (Exempt Organization Income Tax
    Return), 41, 136
990-T (Unrelated Business Income Tax
    Return), 21, 249, 251

990-EZ, relationship, 17
advertising income, IRS consideration,
    29
business, consideration, 27
considerations, 30
controlled organizations, income, 29
copies, 13
debt-financed property, term (usage), 29
due date, 25
estimated taxes, computation, 26
estimated taxes, underpayment penalty,
    27
estimated tax payments, due date, 26
estimated tax payments, process, 26
estimated tax payments, requirement,
    26
extensions, granting, 25
filing failure, penalty, 27
filing form, identification, 25
gross revenues, taxability, 29
public inspection, 17
regularly carried on, term (usage), 28
returns, public inspection, 26
substantially related, term (usage), 27–28
tax, 25, 30
tax examples, 31–32
tax-exempt organizations filing, 25
tax rates, 26
trade, consideration, 27
Unrelated Business Income, definition,
    27
Unrelated Business Income, exclusion,
    28
Unrelated Business Income, inclusion,
    28–29
1023, 1, 21
    inspection, availability, 41
1024, 1, 21
    inspection, availability, 41
1065, inspection (availability), 40–41
1120-POL (U.S. Income Tax Return for
    Certain Political Organizations), 41
1120-W (Corporate Estimated Tax), 26
1128, 17
3115, 19
5768, 131
7004 (Application for Automatic Extension
    of Time to File Corporation Income
    Tax Return), 25

Internal Revenue Service (IRS) (*Continued*)
  8109 (Federal Tax Deposit Coupon), 26
  consideration, 15–16
  N, 15
Investment gains/losses, reporting, 235–236
Investment policies, 12
Involuntary terminations, 48–49
  discussion, 48
  form, 50e
Issue ads, 146

Lease. *See* Capital lease; Operating lease
Leasehold improvement, 251
Leaves of absence, 48–49
  discussion, 48
  form, 50e
Legal entities, separation, 134
Legislative caucuses, PACs (relationship),
    143–146
Liabilities, 251. *See also* Current liabilities
  assets, aggregation, 186
  isolation, 55
Life insurance benefits, damages, 37
Liquidation, Termination, Dissolution or
    Significant Disposition of Assets
    (Schedule N), 17, 23
Liquidity information, recordation, 186
Litigation, impact, 94
Lobby expenses, activity exclusion, 131
Lobbying, 251. *See also* Direct lobbying;
    Grassroots lobbying
  accounting calculation, 135
  activities, curtailment, 127
  expenditures, nondeductibility statement,
    135
  expenses, allowance (amount), 130–131
  limit, 131
  member communication, 135
  proxy tax, option, 136
  reporting requirements, 136
  safe harbor, 136
  total expenditures, calculation, 131
  types, 128
Lobbying Disclosure Act (1997), 133
Lobbying expenditures
  deductibility, IRS issues, 33
  implications, 127
  optional proxy tax, 30
Local income taxes, 33

Local taxes, exemptions (absence), 3e, 4e
Lock Box service, usage, 71
Long-lived assets, recognition, 219
Long-range plan, 251
Long-term liabilities, 175
Losses, reporting, 191–192, 235–237
Low-speed scanners, issue, 77
Loyalty, duty, 9, 246

Management day, 48
  form, 50e
Management letter, 12. *See also* Certified
    Public Accountants
  importance, 109
  issuance, 103, 109–110
Management representation, 98
Manual checks, organization preparation, 72
Matching, 118–119
Material misstatement, absence, 106
Matrix method, example, 212e
McCain, John, 145
McCain-Feingold Act, 146
  challenge, 147
McConnell, Mitch, 147
McConnell v. Federal Election Commission, 147
Medicare
  contributions, damages, 37
  employer share, 37
  taxes, 34
Membership forms, required statement, 33,
    37
Mock audit, conducting, 63
*Model Policies and Procedures for Not-for-Profit
    Organizations* (McMillan), 66, 154
Money. *See* Hard money; Soft money
Monitoring, organization element, 117
Multicandidate committees, PAC type, 141

Natural basis, 197
  example, 198e
Natural classification, 251
Natural matrix, 199, 201
  example, 200e
Natural reporting requirements, 192–193
Net assets, 175, 251. *See* Permanently
    restricted net assets; Temporarily
    restricted net assets; Unrestricted net
    assets
  changes

presentation, 107
  statement, 253
reporting changes, 191
section, change, 186–188
Net investment income tax, 180–181
Net operating losses, 30
Net revenues, 251
  tax computation, 30
Net worth, 251
Non-candidate capacity, 129–130
Non-Cash Contributions (Schedule M), 23
Nondeductibility
  rules, exemption, 136
  statement, 135
Non-multicandidate committees, PAC type,
  141
Nonoperating foundations, 182
Nonprivate foundation status, establishment, 179–180
Nonprofit, term (usage), 171
Nonprofit organizations
  features, 180
  personal views, 130
Nonreciprocal transfer, 251
Not-for-profit, term (usage), 171
Not-for-profit board members
  care, 10–13
  duties, 9–13
  financial responsibilities, 9
  loyalty, 9
  obedience, 9
Not-for-profit organizations, 251
  accounting issues, 103
  accounting manual, advantages, 153
  accounting statements, basics, 171
  accounting system, design, 153
  acronyms, usage, 71
  assets, receipt, 220
  balance sheet, 162e
  CPA, relationship, 87
  embezzlement, impact, 70
  events sequence, 103
  financial management, seriousness, 60
  financial policies/procedures manual,
    advantages, 153
  financial records, auditing, 100
  financial statements
    basics, 171
    disclosure, 221

recognition of contributions, 219
SFAS #117, 183
form 990-EZ filing, 16
functional matrix, 200e
governmental regulations, 106
grants, 113–114
information disclosure, 39
  issues, 40
internal audit committee, establishment,
  149
IRS issues, 103
IRS reporting requirements, 33
legislation, impact, 103
lobbying activities, 127
lobbying expenditures, 135
membership forms, 37
natural basis, example, 198e
natural matrix, 200e
political activity involvement, 143
protection, 83
risk areas, 69–78
specifics, 102
statement of activities, examples, 196e,
  198e, 200e, 203e, 205e
statement of cash flows
  direct method, 207e
  indirect method, 209e
statement of changes in net assets
  matrix method, 212e
  vertical method, 211e
statement of financial position, 165e
  example, 189e–190e, 194e, 202e
tax-exempt status, 40
tax returns, filing, 59
understanding, audit (usage), 107
violations, 106
Not-For-Profit Professional Accounting
  Standards, 19

Obama, Barack, 145
Obedience, duty, 9, 246
Office, immediate removal, 49
  form, 51e
Office of Management Budget (OMB), 114
  A-21, 114
  A-87, 114
  A-122, 114–115
  A-133 standards (Single Audit standards),
    116

Office of Management Budget (*Continued*)
    accordance, auditor report, 122e–123e
    circulars, 114, 251–252
    standardized forms, usage, 119
OMB. *See* Office of Management Budget
Omnibus Budget Reconciliation Act (1993),
    134–135
Operating costs, coverage, 133
Operating foundations, contributions, 182
Operating lease, 252
Operational policies, description, 155
Opinion, disclaimer, 94
    example, 95e
Opinion letter, 88
Optional proxy tax, 30, 252
Organizational documents, components,
    61–62
Organizations. *See* Not-for-profit organiza-
    tion; Tax-exempt organizations;
    Voluntary health and welfare
    organizations
    acronym, presence, 75–76
    budget, goals, 11
    CPA firm retention, 11
    Form 990 filing, 18
    FUTA exemption, 2e
    intellectual property, surrender, 49
        form, 51e
    intermediate sanctions legislation, impact,
        169
    minutes, budge review/action, 11
    property, surrender, 83
    punishment, 167
Out-of-state sales, 30

PACs. *See* Political action committees
Payroll ghosts, spotting mechanism, 73
Payroll preparation, involvement, 73
Payroll taxes, 175
    deficiencies, 33–34
    remitting, 73
    risk, 69
Pension contributions, damages, 37
Permanently restricted cash, 175
Permanently restricted funds, 13
Permanently restricted net assets, 164, 175,
    187, 252
Permanent restriction, 252
Perpetrator, office escort, 83

Personal leave, damages, 37
Personnel-related expenses, risk, 69
Physical checks, locking, 78
Plant, property, and equipment, 174
Plant fund, 252
Police report, collection, 84
Political action committees (PACs), 134, 141,
    252
    candidate party committees, relationship,
        143–146
    contributions, acceptance, 144
    corporate/union basis, 141
    donations, 134
    foreign parent corporation financing, 144
    legislative caucuses, relationship, 143–146
    nonestablishment, 144
    operation, 143
    types, 141
Political advertising, increase, 145
Political Campaign & Lobbying Activities
    (Schedule C), 17, 23
Positive Pay service, organizational usage,
    76
Postage, risk, 69
Prepaid expenses, 174, 252
Presidential campaign fund, contribution,
    145
Primary financial statements, understand-
    ing, 10
Printing, risk, 69
Private foundations, 501(c)(3), 7, 179
    definition, 179–180
    designation, 181
    IRS classification, 2e–3e
    taxation, relationship, 180–182
    types, 7
Private operating foundations, 180
Promise to give, 252
    disclosure, 221
    term, usage, 217
Property
    acquisition indebtedness, 29
    management, 118
    value, excess, 167–168
Prosecution, 49
    form, 51e
Proxy tax. *See* Optional proxy tax
    installation, 133
    option, 136

Publications, 63
Public charities (501(c)(3))
    IRS classification, 2e
    lobbying restrictions, 128
    substantiality issue, 127
Public Charity Status & Public Support
        (Schedule A), 17, 23
Public forums, permission, 129
Public office candidate, term (usage), 130

Qualified audit opinions, 87, 90, 245
    example, 91e
Quid pro quo contribution, 252

Real property, assistance, 119
Recipient organization, SFAS #136 require-
        ment, 240
Recognition of contributed services, 217–218
    examples, 218
Recognition of contributions. *See* Contribu-
        tions
Records, unavailability, 94
Regularly carried on, term (usage), 28
Related benefits, loss, 56
Relocation assistance, 119
Remote check scanners, usage, 78
Remote deposit scanners, organizational
        research, 77–78
Rents, exclusion, 29
Reporting at gross, 192
Requests for proposals (RFPs), 100–103, 252
    detail, 100
    example, 101e
Reserves policy, 13
Restricted funds. *See* Current restricted
        funds
    accounting treatment, 163–164
        financial statement, confusion, 159
    inclusion, 159–160
Restricted-fund transactions, 159
Restricted support, 253
Restrictive endorsement stamp, account
        number exclusion, 71–72
Retirement of assets, 253
Revenue Ruling 87–41, 253
    criteria, 35–36
Revenues, 177. *See also* Deferred revenue;
        Gross revenues; Net revenues
    reporting, 191–192, 234

statement, 22
Review, 96, 253
    example, 97e
RFPs. *See* Requests for proposals
Risk assessment, organization element, 117
Royalties, exclusion, 29

Safe harbor, 136
Salaries, risk, 69
Scanners
    types, 77
    usage, 78
Schedule A (Public Charity Status & Public
        Support), 17, 23
Schedule B (Schedule of Contributors), 17, 23
Schedule C (Political Campaign & Lobbying
        Activities), 17, 23
Schedule D (Supplemental Financial
        Statements), 23
Schedule E (Schools), 17, 23
Schedule F (Statement of Activities Outside
        the US), 23
Schedule G (Supplemental Information
        Regarding Fundraising or Gaming
        Activities), 17, 23
Schedule H (Hospitals), 23
Schedule I (Grants and Other Assistance to
        Organizations, Governments, and
        Individuals in the US), 23
Schedule J (Compensation Information), 23
Schedule K (Supplemental Information on
        Tax-Exempt Bonds), 23
Schedule L (Transactions with Interested
        Persons), 17, 23
Schedule M (Non-Cash Contributions), 23
Schedule N (Liquidation, Termination,
        Dissolution or Significant Disposition
        of Assets), 17, 23
Schedule of Contributors (Schedule B), 17, 23
Schedule O (Supplemental Information to
        Form 990), 23
    program listing, 20
Schools (Schedule E), 17, 23
*Seasongood v. Commissioner of Internal
        Revenue*, 127
Sections. *See* Internal Revenue Service classi-
        fications
Security. *See* Equity security
Self-dealing, excise taxes, 181

Services, value excess, 167–168
Sick days, 48
  form, 50e
Sick leave, damages, 37
Signature block, 19
Signatures, requirement, 70–71
Single Audit standards (OMB A-133
    standards), 116
Social Security, employer share, 37
Soft money, 253
  donations, ban, 146
  hard money, contrast, 136–137, 146–147
  term, usage, 136, 146
State income taxes, 33
Statement of Activities Outside the US
    (Schedule F), 23
Statement of Activity (Income Statement),
    10, 88, 175, 191–193, 253
  accounts/terminology, 176–177
  disclosure, 237
  example, 176, 203e
  net assets, reporting, 191–192
Statement of Cash Flows, 88, 210
  direct method, example, 207e
  indirect method, example, 209e
  preparation
    direct method, 206
    indirect method, 208
Statement of Changes in Net Assets, 88, 210,
    253
  matrix method, 212e
  vertical method, 211e
Statement of Financial Accounting Standards
    (SFAS) 115 (*Accounting for Certain
    Investments in Debt and Equity
    Securities*), 234
Statement of Financial Accounting Standards
    (SFAS) 116 (*Accounting for Contribu-
    tions Received and Contributions Made*),
    19, 159, 171, 215
  background, 215
  definitions, 216–217
  effective dates, 216
  highlights, 215
  inconsistencies, 216
  provisions, 216, 239
  scope, 216
Statement of Financial Accounting Standards
    (SFAS) 117 (*Financial Statements of

Not-for-Profit Organizations), 19, 159,
    171, 183
  background, 183
  effective dates, 184
  financial statements, 185
    notes, 213–214
  functional matrix, 199, 201
    example, 200e
  functional method, 195
  functional reporting requirements,
    192–193
  highlights, 183–184
  inconsistencies, 184
  natural basis, 197
  natural matrix, 199, 201
    example, 200e
  natural reporting requirements, 192–193
  program services, 193
  scope, 184
  supporting activities, 193
  terminology changes, 184
Statement of Financial Accounting Standards
    (SFAS) 124 (*Accounting for Certain
    Investments Held by Not-for-Profit
    Organizations*), 19, 171, 233
  background, 233
  disclosures, 236–237
  effective date, 234
  examples, 234–236
  highlights, 233
  inconsistencies, 234
  reporting revenues, 234
  scope, 234
Statement of Financial Accounting Standards
    (SFAS) 136 (*Transfer of Assets to a Not-
    for-Profit Organization Charitable
    Trust*), 19, 171, 239
  background, 239
  beneficiary, 240–241
  disclosure, 241–242
  discussion, 240
  effective dates, 239
  examples, 242–243
  highlights, 239
  inconsistencies, 240
  recipient, 240
  scope, 239
Statement of Financial Position (Balance
    Sheet), 88, 172, 186–188, 253

accounts/terminology, 174–175
definition, 174
disclosure, 237
example, 173–174, 189e-190e, 202e
presentation, 165
understanding, 10
Statement of Functional Expenses, 22
Statement of Program and Service
    Accomplishments, 20
Statement of Revenue, 22
State not-for-profit requirements,
    knowledge, 10
State requirements, research, 39
State taxes, exemptions (absence), 3e, 4e
State unemployment taxes, 34
Subrecipient monitoring, 119
Substantiality issue, 127
Substantially related, term (usage), 27–28
Supplemental Financial Statements
    (Schedule D), 23
Supplemental Information on Tax-Exempt
    Bonds (Schedule K), 23
Supplemental Information Regarding
    Fundraising or Gaming Activities
    (Schedule G), 17, 23
Supplemental Information to Form 990
    (Schedule O), 23
Supporting schedules, auditing, 104

Tax accounting methods (Form 990), 19
Taxation, private foundations (relationship),
    180–182
Tax-exempt, term (usage), 172
Tax-exempt organizations
    classification, 1
    correspondence, 41
    income-producing property
        acquisition/improvement, 29
    types, 2e–4e
Tax-exempt status, 56
    applications, public inspection, 1
Taxpayer Bill of Rights, 2, 167
Tax payments, estimation, 26
Tax Reform Act (1976), 130
Tax returns, review, 13, 59–60
Temporarily restricted cash, 175
Temporarily restricted funds, 13
Temporarily restricted net assets, 164, 175,
    253

restrictions, 187
Temporary restriction, 253
Term endowment, 160–161
Termination discussions, 48
Third-party service providers, usage, 107
Title-holding corporations, consideration, 30
Total current assets, 174
Total current liabilities, 175
Trade, consideration, 27
Transactions, documentary evidence (tests),
    106
Transactions with Interested Persons
    (Schedule L), 17
Transfer of Assets to a Not-for-Profit
    Organization Charitable Trust (SFAS
    #136), 19, 159
Travel reimbursements, risk, 69
Trusts, consideration, 30

Unallowable costs (Circular A-122), 115
Unconditional promise to give, 253
Unemployment benefits, damages, 37
Uninterrupted vacation, 48
    form, 50e
Unqualified audit opinions, 87, 88–89, 245
    example, 89e
Unrelated Business Income
    definition, 27
    revenue sources
        exclusion, 28
        inclusion, 28–29
    tax, examples, 31–32
Unrelated Business Income Tax (UBIT),
    253
    IRS uniqueness, 33
    Return (Form 990-T), 17, 249
    tax, 25
Unrestricted net assets, 163–164, 175, 187,
    254
    changes, 196e, 198e, 200e
    increase, 177
Unrestricted support, 254
U.S. Income Tax Return for Certain Political
    Organizations (Form 1120-POL), 41

Vacation leave
    damages, 37
    requirement, 72
Variance power, term (usage), 240

Vendors
files, organizational approval, 76–77
gift offers (form), 50e
Vertical method, example, 211e
Voluntary health and welfare organizations, 254
Voter education, 128, 129

Waivers, 136
Wholly owned taxable securities, 254
Wholly owned taxable subsidiaries, 55
activities, restraints, 55
administrative costs, increase, 55

advantages, 55
disadvantages, 55–56
dividends, 56–57
IRS audit exposure, increase, 56
liability, isolation, 55
related benefits, loss, 56
setup, 56
Witnesses, presence, 82

Yellow Book (GAGAS), 116
accordance, auditor report, 124e–125e
audit, 117
usage, 121e